PRAISE FOR
The Anaconda in the Chandelier

"This book is a manifestation of Perry Link's deep love for the Chinese people, their humor, struggles, and courage. *The Anaconda in the Chandelier* is packed with a deep understanding of China, astute observations of Chinese society, and unrelenting criticism of the Communist Party, all stemming from Link's devotion to one thing: truth. If you want to understand why the West got China wrong and how to get it right in the ongoing rivalry between democracy and autocracy, you need to read it."
—Li Yuan, *The New York Times*

"Incisive, wise, deeply humane, this collection is a true gem from a China scholar who is a rarity in his field. Distilled from a lifelong engagement with Chinese language and culture at an astonishingly high level, a wealth of compelling, compassionate observations and critical dissections, including some rather uncomfortable truths about China, is revealed here through fluid essays as well as Link's ironic personal transformation, to borrow CCP lingo, from 'a friend of China' to 'a hostile foreign element.'"
—Jianying Zha, author of *Tide Players and China Pop*

"Based in solid academic work and far-reaching historical vision, and steeped in the language and cultural psychology of the Chinese people, Professor Link, with a pen as sharp as a surgeon's scalpel, cuts to the core of issues that are hidden to most observers but profound in their implications. A fascinating book that you won't be able to put down!"
—Cai Xia, retired professor at the Central Party School
of the Communist Party of China in Beijing

"In contrast to Western apologists for the Chinese Communist Party, Perry Link actually does love China. His love is based on decades of friendship

with real Chinese people of all walks of life and on a thorough knowledge of Chinese society that he displays in this wonderfully written collection of essays. A must for anyone who wants to understand the world's other superpower."
—Jean-Philippe Béja, Research Professor Emeritus, National Center for Scientific Research and the Center for International Studies and Research at Sciences Po, Paris

"With a keen ear to the nuances of thought and speech in China, Perry Link opens an utterly fresh perspective upon the doings and misdoings of the Communist regime. This renowned scholar of literature has crafted a collection of graceful essays while being a first-hand witness to the complexities of US-China relations."
—Vera Schwarcz, Professor emerita of History, Wesleyan University

THE ANACONDA IN THE CHANDELIER

The Anaconda in the Chandelier

WRITINGS ON CHINA

Perry Link

pdb

PAUL DRY BOOKS
Philadelphia 2025

First Paul Dry Books Edition, 2025

Paul Dry Books, Inc.
Philadelphia, Pennsylvania
www.pauldrybooks.com

Printed in the United States of America

Library of Congress Control Number: 2024950347
ISBN: 978-1-58988-198-3

Contents

Day Job Joys

Preface

⬥⫶⬥

I WAS AN UNDERGRADUATE major in philosophy when I took beginning Chinese in the fall of 1963. I did it in part because I knew I liked
languages and wanted something that was "philosophically" more
challenging than the French that I had studied in high school. I did it in
part, too, because I came from a left-wing intellectual family. My father, a
history professor, had led study tours to the Soviet Union during America's
Great Depression. His devotion to high socialist ideals led him (feet off the
ground) to admire Stalin and Mao, to disparage Khrushchev, and to judge
that, in China, the Gang of Four pretty much had things right. His ideals
affected me, and when the late 1960s and early 1970s arrived on U.S. campuses, I was not only left-wing but an activist.

As I learned Chinese and went to live in China, I fell in love with it: its
language, poetry, fiction, food, humor—and, most of all, many of the people I met. From about 1967 on, more than half of my best friends in this
world have been Chinese. At the same time, through painful experience,
I came to see ever more clearly that the rosy socialism that had lived in
my father's imagination as well as my own was spectacularly wrong. The
Chinese people were not at all the happy subjects of a Communist Party
devoted to "serving the people" on rational, egalitarian principles. The
Party was a ruling elite whose highest principle was to remain a ruling elite
by any means, regardless of the costs to anyone else. The Chinese people
were its captives. In key respects they remain so today. In China, a distinction remains between the rules of Communist authoritarianism, which
have descended from above, and the garden-variety values of daily life and
of Chinese culture, which continue to live below. The distinction also lives
in many private minds, which simultaneously encompass the questions

"how can I get what want?" and "what should I pretend outwardly to want?," even as the two have very different answers.

The essays collected in this book illustrate the things I have come to learn about these matters during fifty years of study. Most of the pieces have been published before, although here I have revised them. I have arranged them in four categories: "Captive China" shows facets of what I have found; "Learning" explains some of the nudges from events in China that helped me understand; "Teachers" acknowledges people who guided me along the way; and "Day Job Joys" samples the related pleasures of being a professor in my field.

My college classmate Paul Dry (Harvard '66) has chosen the title *The Anaconda in the Chandelier* for this book. It is the title of an essay, included here, that I wrote in 2002 and that somehow became my best-known work—or at least my best-known essay title. I say "somehow" because I've never been sure why the phrase has, as the cliché puts it, "had legs." Legs, after all, are precisely the things that snakes have found they can do without.

CAPTIVE CHINA

The Chinese Communist Party's Culture of Fear

꒰⊱⋅⋅⊰꒱

(2021)

ROUGHLY TWO THOUSAND years ago, the arrival in China of Buddhism from India brought major changes not only to China's belief systems but to many aspects of its daily life. Buddhism's approach on the whole was gentle, and indigenous Chinese versions of it eventually flourished. Zen was a Chinese invention. Then, beginning about two hundred years ago, the only comparably large foreign cultural influence on China began with the arrival of British gunboats on the south China coast. This was more disturbing. To China the West seemed to say, "Catch up or perish." How to *modernize* became a Chinese obsession that led to many things, including the fevered contortions that the Chinese Communist Party (CCP) has put the country through over the past seventy years.

One way to measure China's urge to transform itself is to note how often the word *new* has been used by Chinese leaders. In 1902 the concept of the "new citizen" took hold in Liang Qichao's *New Citizen Journal*. Twenty years later the May Fourth Movement came to be known as the New Culture Movement. Its seminal magazine was called *New Youth*. In 1934 Chiang Kai-shek launched his New Life Movement. The Communist takeover in 1949 was the advent of New China, and the Cultural Revolution in the late 1960s touted a "new socialist man." After Mao Zedong died in 1976, the next few years were called "the new period." Today, Xi Jinping's watchword is "Socialism with Chinese Characteristics for a New Era." It is important to note that *new* in these cases never refers to the same thing; each is a new *new*.

The tragedy of CCP policies in China can be seen as arising from excessive zeal for shortcuts. More successful East Asian transitions to the modern world, such as those in Japan, South Korea, and Taiwan, have done better by going step-by-step. Impatient for global preeminence, the CCP has rushed ahead several times and crashed. The Great Leap Forward in the late 1950s, which followed Mao Zedong's plans for "surpassing Britain and catching up with America," ended in the starvation of thirty million or more people. Cultural Revolution demands such as "make revolution in the depths of your soul" and "love Chairman Mao more than your parents" were intended as magical paths to a new human nature that China would exemplify for the world, but in fact they were a body blow to Chinese culture whose consequences have lasted until today. Deng Xiaoping's one-child policy, intended in the late 1970s to jump-start a modern economy, led by the late 2010s to problems in labor supply and elder support sufficiently severe as to require abrupt reversals.

Xi Jinping's recent flights of fancy suggest the same pattern. Some of his claims resemble those of Mao in the late 1960s: the East is rising over the West; China is a new model for the world; the Great Leader is correct by definition; Chinese people everywhere can identify with the New China and feel proud. During the "scar" years after the Cultural Revolution, Chinese intellectuals and officials were virtually unanimous in saying that nothing like it could happen again. At the time, I believed them. Now, I'm afraid I don't. Cyber versions of Cultural Revolution "struggle sessions" have already appeared. A return of the Cultural Revolution, adapted for the new era, is certainly possible.

In appraising the history of the CCP, it is important to distinguish between members who joined out of idealism in its early years and those who joined out of self-interest after the mid-1950s. Eloquent memoirs by people like Li Shenzhi, Wei Junyi, Liu Binyan, Fang Lizhi, Zi Zhongyun, and others show how young people were drawn to the Party for its announced goals (including free speech and democracy) in the 1930s and 1940s and risked their careers and even their lives to join. In 1991 the journal *Yanhuang chunqiu* (China Through the Ages) began carrying reminiscences by these now-elderly people, detailing how the CCP had misled them in their early years. Since they were time-honored revolutionaries, the regime could not easily shut them up. But the journal was suppressed in 2016.

When the astrophysicist Fang Lizhi, who later became a well-known dissident, went to Peking University in the fall of 1952, his dormitory building was not yet ready. He and his classmates had to sleep and do their physics homework on a gymnasium floor. Still, Fang was rapturous. He "felt a glow inside" and competed with his girlfriend to see who could join the Communist Party first. The distinguished journalist Liu Binyan, similarly smitten in the early 1950s by the idea of a new society, was working hard to bring it about when, abruptly, the government labeled him a "rightist." Startled, his first reaction was to think: My goodness! I must be a rightist and not realize it. Chairman Mao cannot be wrong. I'll have to look inside myself, dig this problem out, and correct it.

Experiences like this eventually led ardent young CCP followers to see another distinction: that between the core of the Party and themselves. They began to realize that they had radically misperceived Mao. No modern socialist, indeed not a modern leader of any kind, Mao had more in common with the charismatic leaders of peasant rebellions in earlier Chinese dynasties. For those adventurers, as for Mao, the aim was to achieve unquestioned power in as broad an area as possible. The Red Turbans in the fourteenth century, the White Lotus at the end of the eighteenth, the Taipings in the mid-nineteenth, and the Communists in the twentieth shared these elements: an egalitarian ideology that in fact concealed a hierarchical, exploitative, and highly secretive ruling structure, which in turn featured a magical, semidivine leader at the top who possessed some kind of *tian shu* (heavenly text) that prescribed how to live and also offered promises of ideal worlds to come.

In the 1980s, when I first heard the term *liumang zhengfu* (gangster government) used to refer to the CCP regime, I thought I was hearing hyperbole from people who were suffering under it. But in later years, I often heard it from even-tempered veterans of the CCP movement who originally had been supporters. And the term fits. The CCP runs on hierarchical power, on personal loyalties that are outside the law, and on ruthless pursuit of private interests that employs pretense, manipulation, and, where "necessary," lethal force. It is more like the mafia than a modern government. I hesitate to use words like "mafia" or "gangster," because some readers will simply conclude that "Link is an extremist" and stop reading. Aware of that cost, I use them anyway. There are also costs, indeed greater ones, to sheltering readers from difficult truths.

It is worth noting that the "heavenly texts" of peasant rebel groups have often had foreign origins. The foreignness added to their mystical aura and to the charisma of the semimagical leader who promoted them, and it could lend credibility to their promise of a coming heaven on earth. The Red Turbans and White Lotus magic texts were about the Maitreya Buddha, a bodhisattva from distant India who had achieved complete enlightenment and could preach the pure dharma for all to hear. The Taipings' exotic religion was an odd form of Christianity according to which the magic leader, Hong Xiuquan, was the younger brother of Jesus Christ, and his followers could go to Heaven. For Mao, the Marxist classics similarly were foreign, a touch magical, and predicted a coming paradise on earth. Stalin gave Mao much practical support, too, which was vital; but the "heavenly texts" of Marxism were a useful bonus.

Mao duly placed himself in the Marxist pantheon: Marx, Engels, Lenin, Stalin, Mao. He was a "great Marxist thinker." He borrows some Marxist terms, to be sure, but how much Marx did he read? In the last few years I have been working on a detailed biography of Liu Xiaobo, the Nobel Peace Prize winner who died in 2017 while serving a lengthy prison sentence for "incitement of subversion of state power." To me it is obvious that Liu read Marx far more conscientiously than Mao ever did.

Mao's unstinting interest was in power. Before 1949 his CCP and its army escaped the Kuomintang government, evaded the brunt of a Japanese attack, and then defeated the Kuomintang in a civil war. Ends justified means throughout. Capture a city by starving 150,000? If it works, do it. After 1949, eliminate counterrevolutionaries—several million? Fine. Mao actually established quotas, by district, of people to be killed. Moreover, his goal, from beginning to end, was not power for the CCP but power for himself. Mao began outmaneuvering and purging rivals in the 1930s and continued doing so into the 1970s.

The Great Leap Forward, sometimes taken in the West to have been a utopian effort to bring communism to the Chinese countryside, was, for Mao, something very different. It was a (failed) strategy to overproduce in agriculture and to use the surplus harvests and freed-up labor to support heavy industry, which he desired in order to increase his might. While millions of Chinese farmers starved in the resulting famine, Mao shipped grain to the Soviet Union in exchange for know-how—not only in construction but, very likely, in atomic bomb technology.

A fine example of how the outside world has misperceived Mao's motives is the lore that has grown up around the phrase "women hold up half the sky." Mao has been seen as a feminist, an egalitarian, a leader in progressive thought. Nonsense. The evidence of his extreme disrespect for women could not be clearer. And in fact, Mao did not say, "Women hold up half the sky." He said, "Women *can* hold up half the sky." His implication was that they were not yet holding up half, but could: they could get out of the house, go into the fields, go into the factories, and work, alongside the men, to push the Mao project forward. (By the way, Mao's words became a set phrase and extremely common. In Chinese, no one doubts that the word "can" is there.)

One of the most devastating results of the campaigns of late Maoism, from 1957 to 1976, was the hollowing out of the idealistic language of the early 1950s. Phrases like "serve the people" turned into dead words, but one still had to mouth them and, moreover, had to do it "correctly." That made systematic pretending necessary. Manipulation of ideological language became an important life skill. At the extreme, during the Cultural Revolution, people were required to attend "study sessions" in which they took turns at *biaotai* (display of a viewpoint). Viewpoints were presented as one's own but scrutinized by others for hints of divergence from "correctness." Finding flaws in someone else's presentation could earn one credit.

Contemporaneously with this language shift came a dramatic shift in reasons why people joined the CCP. Chinese society now offered a single ladder of success; joining the party was the first step toward almost anything. Idealism was passé. It had been replaced by imitation idealism, which worked so long as the imitation was done "correctly."

During the decade after the death of Mao, an interesting countercurrent in this trend appeared. Some people who, despite everything, were still inspired by ideals decided to join (or rejoin) the Party, not because they saw it as a vehicle for their ideals but because it was the only gateway through which to try to make a difference. Fang Lizhi, who had been expelled from the Party in the late 1950s, rejoined in the late 1970s on this principle and urged his graduate students, most of whom were good-hearted young physics geeks, to do the same. His reasoning? The Communist Party runs our society whether we like it or not. We have no choice but to adjust to this fact—just as we have no choice but to adjust to the weather. What we *can* do is to get inside the Party and try to make it less awful than it otherwise would be.

During the 1980s Chinese intellectuals sought dialogue with the Party. Certain leaders—Hu Yaobang, Zhao Ziyang, Hu Qili, Tian Jiyun, and others—showed themselves to be relatively liberal-minded and would sometimes even listen to voices in society. But this pattern ended with the massacre of pro-democracy demonstrators on June 4, 1989. Not only were liberal intellectuals so disgusted that they no longer had an appetite for dialogue, there now was no one in the leadership with whom to have it. Hu Yaobang had died and the other reform-minded leaders were either imprisoned or frightened into silence.

In the late 1980s, popular complaints about *guandao* corruption—by which officials who have control of factories, mines, and other "work units" use their political power to divert public resources toward private ends and thereby gain enormous unearned profits—were circulating in society and became the grounds for many of the protests in the streets. In the post-massacre 1990s, as the top leaders dropped even the pretense of interacting with society, they turned to a pillaging of the Chinese economy that resembled *guandao* but dwarfed it. High-ranking officials lopped off great chunks of the economy—electricity, IT, banking, shipping—and placed control in the hands of their own families, who then raked in stupendous wealth. This pattern seeped downward as they essentially said to those under them, "We give you license to plunder as long as you prevent 'trouble' by keeping the lid on in your area."

It is important to understand why the CCP, having become as cynical and materialist as it is today, still needs ideology. The pretense of "socialism" remains highly conspicuous in Party rhetoric even though Marx, were he to return to earth, would find the claim baffling. Why do it? Certainly not for nostalgia. Broadly speaking there are two reasons—one for international purposes and the other for domestic ones.

To present the label "socialist" to foreigners—among many of whom the term resonates warmly, or at least neutrally—is effective. Foreigners are generally unaware of the mafia-like nature of the CCP and cannot see how it diverges utterly from the socialist claim to put group interests above individual interests. (By such a criterion, Taiwan society is much more "socialist.") The CCP can use the term "socialist" on the international scene to instill a sense of moral equivalence between itself and democratic governments. It can say: "'The two sides' have 'different systems,' so mutual respect is needed. You speak for your people through democracy and we represent ours through socialism." The huge fact in the background—so huge that people don't see it—is that the CCP does not represent the Chinese people.

It represents a group that seized power in 1949 and holds it still. To imply moral equivalence between "the two sides" is soft-spoken fraud.

This point was on display (although unnoted by many Westerners) in Anchorage, Alaska, in March 2021, when U.S. secretary of state Antony Blinken sat across a table from Yang Jiechi, officially presented as director of the Central Foreign Affairs Commission of China. There were "the two sides"—as symbolically clear as they could be. Each man had to guard his words—not only for what they meant in the room but for what they would sound like to audiences back home. But who were the audiences? Here the two cases diverged radically. Blinken had to have in mind the possible reactions of the U.S. media, of other U.S. politicians (including in the opposition party), and, ultimately, of American voters. In short, he had to look diffusely in several directions, including downward. Yang, by contrast, peered upward, and not diffusely in the least. His crucial audience was a single person, Xi Jinping. He was in Anchorage to say what Xi wanted to be said in Anchorage. People who know Yang personally have told me that he did not sound like his normal self at the meeting. He sounded rehearsed. I would be surprised if important passages in Yang's statements were not dictated directly by Xi.

The domestic function of socialist ideology in China is different, although in one respect it is akin to the international function. When Chinese people who live far from the corridors of power behold the shining ideology's ponderous claims of glory and correctness amid seas of red-and-gold pomp, they tend, as do foreigners who hear phrases like "Chinese socialism" and "the two sides," to accept the assertion that "we are legitimate." Inside the system, though, ideological language has another function. Mao's "Serve the People," Deng's "Four Principles," Jiang Zemin's "Three Represents," Hu Jintao's "Scientific Development Doctrine," Xi's "Socialism with Chinese Characteristics for a New Era"—as well as many less prominent examples too numerous to list here—are pieces one plays on a political chessboard in order to get what one wants. The meaning of the chess pieces is not nearly as important as the act of playing them correctly, and such acts are important because they proclaim one's loyalty to power.

Phrases that originate from present-day leaders are naturally more important than earlier phrases, but the linguistic pedigrees reach as far back as Mao—and it has to be that way, because the Party's claim to legitimacy also reaches back to Mao. The lineage of top-leader thought is an ideological third rail that must not be touched. It is hard to say whether the CCP regime actually would collapse if the line were broken, but it is easy to say that every ruler since Mao has feared that this would be the case.

In the CCP's system, advancement in an official career depends overwhelmingly on the views of one's superior. But when a superior wants to punish someone, he or she still needs formal reasons, which can be such things as "corruption" (even if arbitrarily defined), sexual misbehavior (even if invented), failure to meet quotas or to "maintain stability," or—and here is where ideology is vital—evidence that one's speech has been "incorrect." A correct performance in the language game is more important than what a person actually thinks, and everyone knows that missteps can bring punishment.

There is a spectrum of punishments that begins with police "visits" to discuss whether your future wouldn't be better if you didn't say or do certain things; then proceeds to subtle threats that, for example, your children might not get into the schools that you like; and then to the harsh end of the spectrum: 24-7 monitoring, house arrest, prison, torture, death. In the society at large, knowledge of this spectrum of punishment creates a generalized fear that induces self-censorship. By "fear" here, I do not mean a sharp pang of panic. Because the hazards are so constant and unchanging, people get used to them and just avoid them—rather as a hiker steps around boulders on a mountain path. We might speak of "fossilized fear." It does not need to be sharp in order to be effective in guiding behavior.

Western social scientists sometimes use survey research to try to uncover popular thought in China. On many topics this is possible, if done carefully. But on political topics, especially about support for the CCP, it is not. Fossilized fear plays too big a part—as does the twin problem of bad information about what the CCP actually does. We might recall Fang Lizhi's comparison of the presence of the CCP to the presence of the weather. "Do you support it?" comes as an odd question.

The years 2002 to 2008 saw the rise and fall of the most hopeful democracy movement in China since 1949. Informally known as the Rights Defense Movement or Citizens Movement, it was different in nature from the efforts in the 1980s to engage in dialogue with the CCP elite and to effect change from the top down. The 1980s had ended with rejection and a massacre. Now, the idea was to work from the bottom up. Activists went among the people and listened to their problems; then, using the internet, helped them to establish that other people shared their complaints; then often succeeded in exposing miscreant officials; and eventually were able, at least sometimes, to use the pressure of public opinion to change behavior and even to bring about new laws.

This approach owed something to precedents from Václav Havel in Czechoslovakia and Adam Michnik in Poland, but most of the strategy and tactics were homegrown. The Citizens Movement had no formal structure or appointed leaders. Its activists included Liu Xiaobo, Wen Kejian, Liu Junning, Ai Xiaoming, Teng Biao, Hu Jia, Cui Weiping, He Weifang, Liu Di, Yu Jie, Xu Zhiyong, Wang Yi, Zhang Zuhua, Pu Zhiqiang, Guo Yushan, Guo Feixiong, and many others. The movement ended in December 2008 when Liu Xiaobo, who was the titular sponsor of Charter 08, a blueprint for democratic society that the group had produced, was taken from his home by police and never returned. Signers of the charter were "invited to tea," and Charter 08 was expunged from the Chinese internet and all state media.

This happened under Hu Jintao, who headed the CCP from 2002 until 2012. Hu succeeded in keeping a lid on society, but problems arose during those years. A wealth gap, cronyism in business, and environmental problems all worsened, and popular protests (recorded by the police as "masses incidents") increased sharply in number. At the top, within the powerful Standing Committee of the Politburo, Hu reputedly was a leader by consensus, allowing the committee's eight other members to manage their own bailiwicks while Hu jockeyed at the center. A widespread view among Chinese intellectuals was that, near the end of Hu's term, he was "passing the flower to the beating of a drum." (The reference is to a game in which people sit in a circle and pass a flower from one to the next while a drum beats; whoever holds the flower when the drum stops beating "loses" and has to sing a song or accept some other punishment.) The image was a way to portray Hu's apparent longing to get out of the hot seat.

My impression of Xi as he came to power in 2012 was that, after elbowing his rival Bo Xilai aside, he had a strong sense that *something* had to be done to respond to the country's problems. Passing a flower was not it. But what could he do? A man of limited intellect, not well read, and with little knowledge of the outside world, Xi could imagine nothing beyond going back to Mao's model, which at least he knew. So he opted for the recentralization of power, the building of a personality cult, the stoking of a crude nationalism, harsh repression at home, and a chip on the shoulder abroad. Given the political culture that I have sketched in this essay, these steps could meet with initial success even if guided by a mediocre hand.

Will the Xi juggernaut succeed? The problems are that Xi is no Mao, in either intelligence or charisma, and the society that he rules is better informed and much more sophisticated than the one Mao ruled. When Xi's Ministry of Foreign Affairs announces a "Research Center for Xi Jinping Thought on Diplomacy" and another called "Research Center for Xi Jinping Economic Thought," do intelligent people really go rushing to study "thought" that lies inside Xi's mind, waiting to be appreciated? Of course not. People in the Mao era, whether in enthusiasm or in pain, took Mao's commands to heart; in Xi's case, the conformity is a mere shell.

In the short run, the most frightening possible outcomes for the Xi juggernaut are two: that it will fly or that it will crash. Successful flight would be bad news for the Chinese people and for the people of the world. No one needs a model of technofascism that, with its facial recognition software and DNA registration, goes beyond what even Orwell imagined. On the other hand, a crash would also be bad news, at least for a time. It would bring chaos and likely bloodshed. One of the major accomplishments of the decades-long CCP rule is that it has obliterated all structures in society that might replace it. Whatever happens, I see no grounds for optimism in the short run.

Chinese civilization has survived paroxysms of tyranny before, however, and in the long run it will likely do so again. Mao admired the first emperor of Qin (ruled 221–206 BCE) and the second emperor of Sui (ruled 604–618 CE). Like Mao, these two unified the realm, ruled by "legalism," drafted corvée workers and soldiers (Mao did this in the 1930s and 1940s), assembled large armies, and eventually earned reputations for "burning books and killing scholars." Qin, Sui, and the CCP all built Great Walls (be they stone ones or a Great Firewall in cyberspace), and all launched campaigns against Central Asian peoples (Xiongnu, Uyghurs). There are other parallels, some better than others, but neither Qin nor Sui, despite their scorching violence, killed Chinese humanism. One might fear that Xi has technology to help him, while Qin and Sui did not. But I agree with the China scholar Minxin Pei, who has argued that, with or without high tech, the crux of tyrannical behavior still lies within the human mind, not in machines. Notions of "proper behavior"—for example, that people in superior social positions have duties to be fair to people in lower ones and are subject to moral criticism from bystanders if they are abusive—are deeply embedded in Chinese culture. Such values have, despite everything, survived Mao, and will outlast Xi Jinping.

Originally published in *The New York Review of Books,*
October 21, 2021

Popular Chinese Views of Official Corruption

֍

(2007)

H OW IS IT possible to know what Chinese people think and feel about their government? Western naiveté shows its colors most vibrantly in the belief that one can just go over to China and ask. People will say what they think and then you can compile the answers. Groups like World Values Survey, AsiaBarometer, and the Pew Survey on Global Attitudes have been using this method and getting some startling results. They find that large majorities of Chinese support their political system and that virtually everyone finds it "legitimate." When Pew asked people around the world "Are you satisfied with the state of your nation?," eighty-one percent of Chinese said "yes." This put China at number one in the world in positive answers to this question. Fewer than thirty percent of Americans said "yes."

The problems with using the "do ask, do tell" method in China are as layered as an onion. The first problem is that Chinese culture values giving "the right" answer (rather than a candid answer) whenever one is asked a formal question in public. I first learned this is 1979 while doing a survey on reading preferences among students at Sun Yat-sen University in Guangzhou. Nearly every student said *Dream of the Red Chamber* was his or her favorite work of Chinese fiction. Later in the survey it emerged that few had read the novel. They just knew that it was best and the "right answer" to the question "Which is your favorite?" Such problems are compounded when the question is asked by a foreigner, because now national "face" becomes involved. Beyond that, when topics are politically sensitive, the factor of fear enters and indeed dominates: Would I dare say that I oppose the Communist Party, even if I felt that way? Would my family (who would join me in suffering the consequences of a wrong answer) ever forgive me for being so stupid? And in addition to all of these psychological impediments to survey research, government rules add practical barriers: no foreigner can do surveys in China without an approved Chinese partner, and all results must be reviewed and approved by Party officials before publication.

If we interpret the word "legitimacy" rigorously—to mean not just "Do I like what my government is doing?" but "Do I recognize the right of my government to be my government?"—then I feel quite certain that the average Chinese citizen has never asked herself or himself the question and might even have trouble understanding it. In daily life the Communist Party is like the weather: you deal with it, but you don't, you can't, entertain alternatives.

But do people have feelings? Opinions? Complaints? And how! And there are a number of ways that one can discover and study them.

Ways to Study Popular Political Thought in China

We will look below at three kinds of sources—"anti-corruption fiction," blogs on the internet, and popular ditties called *shunkouliu* that are passed around orally. We know that these materials are very popular. Simply by asking the question, "What kind of ideas and values would a person need to have in order to find these materials attractive?" we can infer a considerable amount about popular thinking. The method is not perfect, to be sure, but is far superior to distributing a questionnaire written by foreigners that asks, "Do you think your government is legitimate?"

A few months ago, a distinguished Chinese writer named Sha Yexin wrote an essay and posted it on the internet. In it, he records an incident that occurred on a public street in the Wanzhou district of Chongqing City, at 1:00 p.m. in the afternoon of October 18, 2004. A worker named Yu Jikui accidentally bumped a woman named Zeng Qingrong with his carrying pole. The woman's husband, Hu Jieao, became incensed, seized the pole, and began beating Yu Jikui's legs in what appeared to bystanders to be an attempt not only to hurt the man but to break his legs, depriving him of his future livelihood as a coolie. When a few among the onlookers tried to intervene, the irate husband yelled, "I am the Chief of the Housing Bureau! Even if I kill him, to me it's only a 200,000 *yuan* fine!" The brazen comment further incensed the crowd. A mob surrounded Zeng and Hu, trapping them until a passing policeman helped them into his police car and drove away. The spectacle of "officials helping officials" only angered the onlookers more. Word of the incident spread, by mouth and on the internet, and in the following days more than 30,000 people arrived at the government building in Wanzhou to shout protests and demand that the offending Hu Jieao be punished. Authorities assigned a column of policemen to protect the office building. Protesters overturned some cars and burned them. The Communist Party Committee of Chongqing City went into emergency session and produced a three-part plan to "quell the riot": 1) Send an official out to the protesters to promise a full investigation of the carrying-pole incident and a heavy punishment for the offender; 2) Wait until late night to send 1000 armed police to deal with any lingering protesters, and 3) Run a story in the press saying that protesters "did not understand the true facts" and were being manipulated by people with "ulterior motives." The protests ended.

In his essay, Sha Yexin records the government's cynical tactics but then asks an astute question about popular psychology:

> The bumping of one person by another with a carrying pole is a tiny event, about as weighty as a chicken feather or a garlic skin, and it happens every moment of every day across our land. So what exactly caused this particular incident in Wanzhou to flare up? The trigger was Hu Jieao's announcement that he was "Chief of the Housing Bureau." Hah! An "official"! For the people on the street this changed everything. It led to a surge of pent-up anger against officialdom. When the police intervened to protect Hu, and when Hu took refuge in government offices, it only confirmed the whole issue as one of people-versus-officials. There is no way a bump with a carrying pole, or even beating someone on the legs, was the cause that brought 30,000 people to the streets ready to burn cars.

Sha quotes government statistics to show that such flare-ups are not unusual. There has been a steady rise in recent years, all across China, in the number of "masses incidents" that police have had to repress: in 1993 there were 10,000 such incidents involving 730,000 people, and by 2003 the numbers had risen to 60,000 incidents involving 3,070,000 people. In July 2005 the Minister of Public Security acknowledged a six-fold increase of such incidents over the past decade and noted that they were larger, more frequent, more violent, and "reached more realms" (i.e., involved more different kinds of people in society) than before.

Why do ordinary Chinese resent their officials, and, in the absence of effective polling, what means do we have of uncovering their thoughts and feelings? The issues that bring people to the streets in China have included such things as confiscation of land, forced relocations, firings from state enterprises, and arbitrary fees and taxes. Officials are blamed not only because they are the ones who order such actions but because they are seen as profiting personally: when land is confiscated, it is because officials and their cronies are "developing" their own projects; when workers are laid off, it might be because an official has turned a state factory into his private enterprise; when arbitrary taxes are levied, it could be because officials want to squeeze more money from citizens. What grates on ordinary people is not "development" per se, or even the large income disparities that it creates, but the perception of *unfairness* in the processes. Sha Yexin calls his essay "The Culture of Corruption." This word *corruption* is probably the best umbrella term for the objects of popular Chinese complaint.

There is plenty of evidence beyond participant-observation to confirm this conclusion. After the shock of the 1989 June Fourth massacre, dozens of *fanfu xiaoshuo* 'anticorruption novels' appeared, especially between 1995 and 2002. China has a long tradition, dating from the eighteenth century, of fiction that satirizes officialdom, and now the tradition returned as a way to express complaint vicariously. There were *romans à clef* that told true stories in thin disguise. Others were imaginary but used detail that rang true—and often *was* true, but just stitched together as fiction. The most popular titles, such as Zhang Ping's *Choice*, reached as many as a million in sales. Total readership, if one accounts for book sharing and book pirating, was much more than that.

All books in China must be published at presses that are licensed, and technically owned, by the state. Authors who write about corruption therefore need to think of ways to side-step censorship. One method is to publish in province X the story of corruption in province Y. Another is to make it clear that the misbehavior is by bad apples that hide within a healthy pile. Another is to put the "incorrect" assertions into the mouth of an "incorrect" person: you can write that the Communist Party is a private membership group and that the People's Armed Police is its band of hired thugs—and can describe in detail how the whole mafia-like web hangs together—so long as the person making the analysis is a hoodlum or confessed criminal. Your novel can still pass muster if you write that an official from the Central Discipline and Inspection Commission appears, *deus ex machina*, to set things right in the end. In 2002 the government clamped down on anticorruption fiction, but it could not stop popular complaint, which had other outlets.

In the mid-1990s a large number of what were called *shunkouliu*—popular quips, rhymes, and rhymical ditties—appeared on oral grapevines in China. Their most common topic, by far, was official corruption. Here is an example:

> Officials are addicted to money
> While the people labor and sweat
> If something else counts, then it's funny
> That no one's run into it yet.

(In my translations of such things I try to preserve rhythm and rhyme. This sometimes requires corner-cutting in literal meaning, but that loss is more than compensated for by fidelity to the art of the whole.) Here is another:

> For fifty long years, ever more perspiration
> And we just circle back to before Liberation
> And speaking again of that big revolution
> Who, after all, was it for?

Like jokes in the West, *shunkouliu* were authorless—a fact that made it hard for anyone to be held politically responsible for them. That fact, in turn, allowed their inventors to be wonderfully frank. The government itself saw value there. In the 1990s the State Administration of Radio, Film, and Television compiled and circulated classified reports on what *shunkouliu* were revealing about popular opinion. This resembled the way emperors in earlier times set scribes among the people to collect what they were saying.

The rise of the internet in the early 2000s made citizen-to-citizen transmission of *shunkouliu* and much, much else far easier than it had been before. Until then, all published media—books, magazines, radio, film, television—sent messages downward and outward from an approved authority at the top. With the internet, anyone, at top or bottom, could initiate a message. To be sure, the internet came to be monitored by countless thousands of police, who were aided by filters that could scour cyberspace for politically "sensitive" content. They could then remove the content and punish the people who wrote it. But still, a lot got through. Bloggers could play cat and mouse and sometimes win. They put out messages that, even if scaled back a bit, left no doubt in readers' minds about what was being said.

Corruption in the Popular View: Hypocrisy, Dissolution, Plunder

Chinese cultural tradition has some deeply embedded assumptions, for example that literary learning brings improvement in personal character, and that improved character in turn qualifies a person to lead a family and to help govern society wisely and fairly. When the scholar-gentleman-ruler adheres to morality and learning, things will be well around him. If, however, he fails in his role by falling into idleness (teahouses, story-telling, wine, song, and the like) or into more serious vices (gluttony, inebriation, brotheling, gambling), then society will suffer. If he descends even further, into downright dishonesty (bribery, embezzlement, fraud, cheating on exams), then his role becomes pernicious. The health of society depends, in short, on whether officials are clean or corrupt.

Despite the tremendous impact of the modern West on China, and despite the Communist revolution, these fundamental attitudes about the importance of official rectitude have persisted. At the same time China's tradition of satiric fiction, which we briefly noted above, has remained hard-hitting in its exposure of corruption. Wu Jingzi's eighteenth-century novel *The Scholars,* a landmark in the genre, is whimsical in approach when compared to today's anticorruption novels. The major vices in Wu's novel are stupidity and hypocrisy; one official advises another, for example, on how to be a sycophant: "…even kowtowing when it is not strictly necessary will do no harm." At the turn of the twentieth century a series of "castigatory novels" by Li Boyuan, Wu Woyao and others were less gentle. Here corrupt officials, "with the trickery of wolves," stole the country's wealth and sapped its strength. *Chi he piao du* "eating, drinking, whoring, gambling" dominated their thinking.

Today, anticorruption novels and *shunkouliu* are even more pungent. A *shunkouliu* describes the "princeling" generation of new leaders this way:

> Dance all night until the dawn,
> Throw back booze and don't feel gone,
> Bed eight girls and still feel brawn,
> Never touch what they're working on.

Sexual misbehavior in particular is denounced more sharply now than it was two centuries ago. In traditional Confucian culture, the main reason for frowning on sexual indulgence was that it was a dalliance, an improper diversion of one's attention and energies. Now, after the arrival of Western attitudes and, in particular, Communist puritanism, the notion has crept in that sexual excess is definitive depravity, not just a waste of time. When Mao Zedong's physician Li Zhisui published his memoirs, which exposed many details of betrayal, blackmail, and cruel indifference to death and suffering in the Great Helmsman's thinking, it was nevertheless the detail of Mao's escorting of dancing girls into his bedroom that seemed to grab the most attention on China's rumor mill. *That* was the detail that showed his iniquity! The connection of sex and power draws popular denunciation of a special intensity, as shown in this *shunkouliu*, which takes the viewpoint of an honest prostitute:

> First, I don't pilfer,
> Second, I don't rob,
> I just embrace Communists;
> That's my job!

A novel packed with sexual innuendo and sarcastically entitled *Serve the People*, by Yan Lianke, was published in Guangzhou in 2005. It was promptly banned but still gained wide circulation and enthusiastic comment on the internet. Set in the later years of the Cultural Revolution, it tells of the bored young wife of a general in the People's Liberation Army. The wife craves sex that her older (and apparently impotent) husband does not provide. A strong young soldier-attendant obliges her. Whenever she is ready for action, she hangs a sign reading "Serve the People" outside her door and the young man arrives to put Mao's slogan into practice. The couple achieves special ecstasy when they copulate after smashing plaster busts of Mao and ripping up his photos and his Little Red Book. The high-ranking husband, meanwhile, is attending a meeting in Beijing on how to prepare for nuclear war with the Soviet revisionists and how to smash the separatists on Taiwan. The relevance of his impotence to his bravado is left for readers to ponder.

In general, though, the top item in popular views of official corruption has not been sex. It has been money. Officials grab money illicitly, hoard it jealously, and use it selfishly. A *shunkouliu* sketches a money-baron this way:

> He's got the finance system on his left,
> And the banking network to his right.
> He taxes all of industry
> With all his beastly might
> He's the king of electric current
> And prince of the water pipe,
> But what's he care for kids at school?
> Not a piece of tripe!

Many kinds of evidence show that—in fact as well as in rumor—corruption in China's urban economy grew dramatically beginning in the mid-1990s. A main reason for the pro-democracy protests in 1987 and 1989 was the popular perception that, while the agricultural economy had become much freer in the 1980s, the urban economy was still held back by the iron framework of Soviet-style "work units." After the June Fourth massacre Deng Xiaoping took the radical gamble of opening the urban economy to private enterprise, but this move also opened the way for people who held political power to use that power in order to convert state-owned resources to private use. The pattern was a whole new—vast and breathtaking—kind of corruption. It was so brazen that it made garden varieties of corruption (bribery, gift-giving, graft) seem minor by comparison and thus, in a sense, acceptable. He Qinglian's 1998 book, *China's Pitfall*, documents this great plunge into new corruption in considerable detail.

In popular opinion, the new corruption was especially galling because it seemed like robbery. When officials grab public property, it is wealth that rightfully should be *ours*. A *shunkouliu* says:

> I worked my whole life for the Party
> And had nothing at the time I retired
> Now they tell me to live off my kids
> But my kids one by one have been fired

As if expanding on this ditty, a laid-off worker named Chen Hong, in the city of Changsha, Hunan Province, began in July 2006 to post some incisive views on his blog. In less than four months the blog had more than a million hits. "To us workers," Chen wrote, "economic 'reform' has meant lay-off and unemployment; it has meant that the wealth and benefits born of our labors of yesterday have been plundered by the privileged elite.... [Back] in the era of the planned economy, the entire production and profit of our factory went to the state, while we workers got only nominal monthly sustenance." We were supposed to be "masters of the state," he said, and the surplus value we produced was supposed to be saved for our pensions. Now our pensions are practically zero. The managers lay us off to make the work units more efficient, they say. That might be fair if you had been capitalists in the first place. But you weren't and you aren't. You are managers of state enterprises owned by us workers. You don't own the factories—so where do you get the power to fire us? Chen concludes: "This [rip-off of labor] is a classic *political* process, not a market mechanism, and maybe it is only this unbridled force that has created the economic miracle in our country."

In another essay, Chen addresses the Communist Party. You "won" in the 1950s when you converted private wealth into public property; now you win again when you turn public wealth into private. The flip and the flop are opposites except that the same group of people win.

Another blogger, writing as Liu Yide (presumably a pseudonym for anonymity), cites a report from the Chinese Academy of Social Sciences that showed that, in March 2006, there were 3,220 people in China who had assets of at least 100 million yuan; of these, 2,932, or 91 percent, were family members of senior officials.

If anything has been as widespread as corruption it has been cover-up of corruption. Cover-up techniques are themselves covert and sometimes subtle. Fiction and blogs offer interesting examples of how bribery is disguised. Gift-giving—of food, liquor, appliances, cars, vacations, and so on—happens without either side acknowledging the *quid pro quo* that both sides are aware of. Another device is to invite the person whom one is bribing to a game of mah-jongg and "lose" large sums by playing badly on purpose. Who can fault that? Where is the evidence of a bribe? To the world one says, "Look, I lost!"; to the "winner" one is saying "Nice doing business with you." One needs, of course, to trust one's partner in the bribery, but trust can result from each side knowing that it is vulnerable to exposure by the other side.

Once corrupt, officials want those around them to be corrupt, too. An internet story from Sichuan in 2006 told of a factory manager who was offered a bribe and reported the matter to his superior, the Party secretary. The higher official urged acceptance of the bribe. Why? Not because he would get part of it, and not because he had the best interests of his subordinate's pocketbook in mind, but because he himself was already corrupt and *wanted* his underling to be corrupt so that the underling would not be in a position to expose anything. "If you know that I know that you took a bribe, then you will keep quiet if you learn that I also take them." Hence people in subordinate positions face a dilemma: if you take bribes and your boss does not, you are vulnerable; if you refuse bribes and your boss does not, you again are vulnerable. What to do? It's safest to follow the boss. Moreover: if the boss pulls in large amounts, illicit or not, some of it will trickle down to the rest in the factory, no?

In short, corruption became a pervasive, even necessary, part of daily life. One needed to bribe in order to get things done. You want to get your child into a good school? (The principal will receive your sealed envelope.) You want water to flow to your field? (The irrigation officer awaits your visit.) You want a competent surgeon for your mother's appendectomy? (The nurse will be your go-between—and quickly, if the price is right.) A sense grew that ordinary people should not be blamed for corruption that had become standard. Morally speaking, moreover, when the higher-ups are so rapacious, why should we little people have scruples? A *shunkouliu* offers a primer for the ordinary citizen:

A cigarette gets you in the door,
And with the wine you hear the deal;
But if you want the problem solved,
It's gotta be a great big meal.

The tone here is still satiric. Bribery is wrong. But the briber is understandable; the problem lies in the system. It is worth looking in a bit more detail at what kinds of attitudes and values seem to be implied by the satire in fiction, blogs, and *shunkouliu*.

WHAT DOES COMPLAINT ABOUT CORRUPTION MEAN?

It would be a mistake, in my view, to see the flood of complaint about corruption in today's China as adding up to nihilism. The corruption is real and egregious, to be sure. But *complaint* about it is a sign of hope. It has long been the case in China—as elsewhere, I presume—that muckraking cuts two ways: the bad news is what it digs up; the good news is that we readers, writers, and bystanders are indignant, and our indignation shows that we have better values in mind. Wrongdoing interests us precisely because we reject it. We oppose it because we know better standards. The most depressing situation would be one in which an ugly reality marches forward and everyone applauds it. The numerous and spirited ways in which Chinese people are expressing objection to corruption—despite repression, risks, and sometimes their own involvement in the problems—show that popular notions of morality remain alive and well. When Yan Lianke, author of *Serve the People*, was asked why he would opt for a title that so obviously derides a Mao slogan, he answered that "my intention was to satirize not the phrase, but those who fail to serve the people." This answer, given inside China, may have been offered in part to defend the author from political attack. But it is also true that the thrust of Yan's satire is to uphold value, not to tear it down.

A good way to understand how complaint can imply value in China is to refer again to habits of mind that are deep in Chinese tradition. Confucius taught that harmony results when people play their social roles properly. The father must be a proper father, the son a proper son, the husband a husband, the wife a wife, and so on. The values that made a Confucian system work were private values in the sense that every person needed to internalize them; but they were public values in the sense that they applied to everyone, everyone knew what they were, and anyone was subject to criticism if he or she did not play his or her role properly. Equality was not a Confucian value; in all the basic human relationships, one pole in any dyad was superior to the other (father was superior to son, husband to wife, sovereign to minister, and so on). But—and this point is crucial— each side in a dyad had its duties to the other, and each was subject to criticism, including public criticism, if the duties were not performed correctly.

Pre-modern Chinese fiction and storytelling offer many examples of how the "weak" side in a Confucian relationship could issue complaint about misbehavior of the "strong" side. A peasant dies from overwork trying to pay rent and taxes; his widow resorts to begging in order to feed her small children; the children die; the landlord still comes to demand rent; the woman gives up and commits suicide. She—who is poor, humble, illiterate and female—is on the "weak" side of the relationship with the landlord on every count. He—wealthy, elite, educated, and male—has every advantage. But now comes a telling detail: she decides to commit suicide *at the landlord's door*. That little fact says a great deal. It says that she feels she has a right to protest: you are strong, I am weak, you are rich, I am poor, you are educated, I am not—but I still have the right to tell you that you are wrong. Moreover, I do it publicly, at your doorstep. This shows that I know—indeed we both know—that the values you have violated are public values. Others will notice your violation and will judge you. Finally, that same little fact shows that the woman believes her values to be higher than any individual human life. My husband is dead, my children are dead, now I am leaving, too—but watch me stand up for principle on my way out! I die, but rightness lives.

During the years of high Maoism in the mid-twentieth century, public truth-telling in China took on an added layer of significance because of repression. By the time Mao died, a number of facts about society, although obvious to everyone, could not be said in public: that millions had starved during the Great Leap Forward, that the Cultural Revolution had been cruel and violent, that corruption and special privilege had pervaded ruling circles, and that a prescribed falsity pervaded official language. In the "scar literature" years that followed Mao's death in 1976, a number of writers skyrocketed to popularity when they dared to put forbidden truths onto paper. Readers loved their stories not because they learned anything new from them but for almost the opposite reason: they could finally see in print, in public, things that they had known for years but had never dared to say. The experience was called *jiehen*, "releasing resentment." In the relative relaxation of the post-Mao decades *jiehen* has become less important than it once was, but the sting of a good *shunkouliu* still comes more from "getting it just right" than from telling the listener anything he or she does not know.

In sum, the values crisis in China today comes not from any demise of the moral impulse in the Chinese people or their culture. The plethora of their complaints shows that the impulses themselves are still healthy. There is, moreover, abundant evidence that people are groping to re-establish some kind of value system that might do for China today what "Confucianism" used to do—that is, provide a set of values that are private in the sense that one can adopt them as one's own moral compass and public in the sense that one can rely upon others making similar adoptions and being similarly guided. I do not mean, of course, that any set of moral values was universally observed at any time in pre-modern China. I mean only that the framework—the standard—was accepted

The major obstacle to the present quest for a moral framework is the Communist Party, whose leaders fear and therefore repress any "thought"—political, moral, or religious—that they believe could possibly give rise to a rival organization. This is why the Party crushes groups like the China Democratic Party, unauthorized Christian churches, popular Chinese religions like Yiguandao or Falun Gong, or any autonomous Uyghur or Tibetan groups. The Party's own moral "teachings," such as Deng Xiaoping's "Five Pay-Attentions, Four Attractivenesses, and Three Adores" (*wujiang simei sanreai*) or Hu Jintao's "Eight Prides and Eight Shames" (*barong bachi*), have a fatal flaw: in the public ear, they have the same artificial ring that official language in China has had since Mao began to insist, in the late 1950s, that the Chinese people mouth official phrases even if their meanings departed radically from the evidence of daily experience. Today, schoolchildren memorize certain lilting official phrases, and everyone pays them lip service, but they have almost no traction at all in the ethics of daily life.

The only widespread public values today are money-making and a relatively superficial version of nationalism that emphasizes such things as Han pride, Olympics glory, and economic "miracle." But these things cannot solve the values crisis. They are too thin to carry the weight of China's longstanding cultural habit of relying on a shared ethical system. Notions of moral right and wrong, and the idea that one can learn to "be a good person" (*zuo ren*), are too deep in Chinese culture for even a Maoist conflagration to have annihilated them, and some day, when today's narrow and repressive rulers get out of the way, something better is sure to grow.

Originally published for the Tocqueville on China program on
the website of the American Enterprise Institute, 2007

The next three pieces concern the June Fourth massacre in 1989, when Chinese government troops in the heart of Beijing used tanks and machine guns to kill hundreds of young people who were peacefully protesting for democracy. The massacre became a major turning point in the cultural and political life of twentieth-century Chinese history.

June Fourth: Massacre and the Morality of Memory

(1999)

HUMAN MEMORY is a complex topic. University departments of psychology offer entire courses in the area, and yet the mysteries of how memory works—and how well—remain largely unsolved. Philosophers have asked a range of questions about memory—including whether, independently of memory, "the past" can even exist. Questions like this, although beyond our scope here, are worth pondering.

From ordinary life, we know that memory deteriorates with age, and that it does so in two ways: impressions usually grow weaker as they recede further into the past, and memory as a whole weakens after middle age. A further distortion of memory is caused when events—such as the June Fourth Massacre—are recalled and then retold for others. To tell an experience to others requires a person to convert memories into words, and such conversion necessarily involves simplification. Moreover, the teller of a story, whether consciously or not, tends to some degree to tailor his or her words to suit his or her own interests and values as well as the perceived needs and expectations of listeners. After such processing, the "story" of an event emerges as something distinct from the original loose pattern of memory impressions. Then, when a person returns to the warehouse of memory in order to recount events the second time around, he or she finds the once-told story standing there, alongside the jumble of original memory impressions. For the purposes of re-telling, the once-told story has clear advantages over the jumble. It is more orderly and ready-to-go. One turns to it first, and upon third, fourth, and fifth tellings, it can settle in and dominate the original memory impressions.

Hence we should try to be aware of what goes into a "remembered story" other than original data. In 1988 the Chinese writer Shi Tiesheng wrote a brilliant essay called "Wenge jikui" on "remembering my guilt" from the Cultural Revolution. In it, Shi recalls the late 1960s, when he hand-copied a piece of "counterrevolutionary" underground fiction that someone else had given him. He further recalls how the version in his handwriting was discovered by Public Security and how he faced the terrible dilemma of whether to divulge the name of the person who had given him the original. He remembers with regret that he did eventually confess his source, but on one crucial point memory fails him: he cannot remember whether his confession came before or after he knew that the police had already discovered the essential facts from another witness. He concludes his written account of memory with two alternate endings—one that exculpates himself and one that does not. He says that, if relying on memory alone, there is no way he can decide which account is true. Then he writes:

> I hope it was the former, but this very hope is strong evidence that it was probably the latter, because the sieve that is memory not only allows inconvenient details to leak out, but also lets self-protecting details seep in.

Shi's suggestion that memory can actually be creative, that it can invent details that its owner needs, recalls Mark Twain's whimsical observation that his own memory seemed to have grown more powerful with age, that he could now "remember things that didn't even happen."

An event like the June Fourth Massacre, searing in its own moment and politically controversial for years to follow, is especially vulnerable to distortion by human memory. The original scenes were, first of all, of the kind that any web of words can only suggest, never adequately represent. Eyewitnesses have had to simplify from the outset, and many of their accounts, under the wear of repetition, have been reduced to boilerplate. Inadvertent self-protection of the kind Shi Tiesheng describes has crept in, yet this tendency has been mild compared to a number of deliberate attempts to manipulate memory, the most spectacular of which has been the Chinese government's effort to repress authentic impressions and replace them with a package of sheer lies.

A useful way of to approach the problem of remembering massacres, genocides, and other disasters in which one group of people victimizes another is to divide the issue by three: the memories of perpetrators, victims, and bystanders. The division is not fundamental: all three must deal with the foibles of human memory and all three must come to terms with what were originally the same happenings, but the three different standpoints tend to produce separately generalizable patterns. Let's consider first the perpetrators.

The direct perpetrators of the June Fourth Massacre were the 27th and 38th Divisions of the People's Liberation Army of the Communist Party of China. (I did not write "...of the People's Republic of China" because the PLA—still—belongs to the Party in China, not the government.) The ultimate perpetrators were Deng Xiaoping, who gave the order for the attack, and Li Peng, the highest-ranking advocate for this course of action. In a related sense, all in the leadership who favored the massacre, including those who later fashioned and advertised falsified accounts of "rampage" by "hooligans" engaging in a "counterrevolutionary riot," can also be viewed among the perpetrators.

It is often observed that the perpetrators of the June Fourth Massacre have wanted the world to forget what happened that day. But the truth is more complicated. Inside China, at the time of the massacre and for several years to follow, the perpetrators wanted precisely the opposite. They wanted their political rivals and the Chinese people as a whole to note the bloodshed and to heed it well. Their purpose depended on memory.

The decision on the night of June third to clear Tiananmen Square by using tanks and machine guns—instead of billy clubs, tear gas, or water hoses—was not made because the more benign equipment was unavailable. (Li Peng's claim, made to foreign reporters a few days after the massacre, that bullets were used because Beijing lacked water hoses is a useful datum only in the study of official mendacity.) Billy clubs had been quite sufficient to clear Tiananmen Square of tens of thousands of protesters at a similar demonstration on April 5, 1976. Some of the billy clubs that year bore nails that were designed to tear flesh, but there was little if any loss of life. The regime's goal on that occasion was to clear the square by arresting protesters or driving them to go home. On June 3 and 4, 1989, the goal was not just to clear the square. It was to shock and intimidate the rival wing within the leadership as well as the demonstrators who were on the streets not only in Beijing but in Shanghai, Nanjing, Chengdu, and more than a hundred other cities across China. The purpose of the shock and intimidation was to bring a definitive end to all challenges to the ruling authority.

The plan worked. For three years following 1989, China's general mood was sullen. It turned better in 1992 with Deng Xiaoping's "Southern Tour" and its leavening message of "get rich quick"—but even then the populace bore in mind that only economic freedoms, not political ones, were permissible. For many years since then, memory of the massacre has continued to be an important tool in the leadership's maintenance of social control. The brutal message, which lurks unspoken but systemically beneath any religion, philosophy, or thinking that is not officially approved, is *watch out.* Loving parents have passed the warning to their offspring—with or without burdening the young ones with descriptions of exactly what happened.

But there is also truth in the observation that the perpetrators of the June Fourth massacre have wanted people to forget and to "look forward." They are aware that some of the images associated with them ("bloody hands," "butchers of Beijing," and so on) have political costs to them. So we need to ask: When do they want remembering, and when forgetting? Most of the answer, I think, depends on the audiences they have in mind. The June Fourth protesters, their families, their sympathizers, and any other Chinese groups who might harbor political criticisms of them are the people in whom they would like the frightening images to remain alive. But those (including foreigners) who were essentially bystanders to the events, who pose no threat of domestic protest, and who hence do not need to be intimidated had best forget or never see the horrid images. It is for the eyes and ears of these bystanders that the regime—like murderous or repressive regimes elsewhere—resorts to euphemism: the massacre of June Fourth was merely "events," or an "incident." The purpose of such softening is to lull people into forgetfulness.

The distinction between remembering and commemorating can also shed light on how perpetrators wish memory to behave. Commemoration is a special kind of remembering; it is a deliberate effort to establish public memory of something one regards as praiseworthy. People do not commemorate without forethought, generally do not do it alone, and do not do it for things of which they disapprove. Accordingly, the perpetrators of a massacre, although they may or may not want it to be remembered, are never eager that it be commemorated. This is why the rulers in Beijing do what they can to thwart commemoration of June Fourth, by banning the very possibility of a museum and by blocking off Tiananmen Square for several days each year around the anniversary. They know that commemoration of the events implies sympathy for the victims. If they truly believed their own lies about what happened—that "a tiny minority" of "hooligans" had "opposed the interests of the masses," and so on—then they would open Tiananmen Square and permit popular commemoration of the soldiers, machine guns and tanks.

It is worth trying to imagine what the perpetrators of the massacre themselves, in the privacy of their own minds, remember about June Fourth. What images do they recall? My own guess is that some day, if and when the "verdict is reversed" on June Fourth, we will see an outpouring of accounts by soldiers who say they regret what they did, were misled into doing it, suffer nightmares about it, and so on. (To what extent these accounts will be sincere and to what extent self-serving accommodations to a new line is a question that we will need to judge if and when the time comes.) But what about the ultimate perpetrators? What did Deng Xiaoping and Li Peng recall? Here my guess is that their memories were likely dominated by impressions of inner-Party struggle. I would bet that Li Peng recalled images such as Zhao Ziyang—with outrageous temerity, in Li's view—going to the square to meet personally with protesting students at dawn on May 19, the day before martial law was declared. Much else that Li recalled, I would guess, is likely to be about urgent phone calls, small late-night meetings, and other private and secret contacts among top leaders. Images of dead bodies or burning buses lurked only in the periphery of his memory, I would guess.

Let us turn to remembering by victims. The vantage point is obviously different from that of perpetrators, but is similar in not being as simple as it may initially seem. We need, first, to recognize that some victims are dead and (presumably) have no memories; any talk of "victims' memory" must hence be limited to the victims who survived. From other historical cases we can observe, moreover, that survivors do not always leap to their feet crying "never again!"; some prefer to remember quietly, or only privately, or sometimes not at all. Primo Levi, a survivor of the Holocaust and one of the most eloquent analysts of its victims' suffering, reports a sense of "shame" that victims, unfairly but quite commonly, carry with them for years. Before examining and publicizing their memories, he writes in *The Drowned and the Saved*, many sought the practical reassurances of returning to normal life. Victims of the Nanjing Massacre in 1937 and of the dropping of the atomic bombs on Japan in 1945 were similarly slow to produce publicized accounts of their memories. In several ways there appear to be questions, for victims, of whether the examination of memory brings a "coming to terms" and thus a healing, or only keeps wounds open and pain alive. When Ōe Kenzaburō visited Hiroshima twenty years after the disaster there, he found some of the victims resentful of his prodding them for memories. One of them wrote him a letter saying:

> People in Hiroshima prefer to remain silent...they do not like to display their misery for use as "data" in the movement against atomic bombs or in other political struggles. ...I detest those who fail to appreciate our feelings about silence.

Ōe came to respect the "dignity" of victims and arrived at a new appreciation of the distinction between victim and bystander. Voices from several angles—perpetrators, victims, and bystanders alike—sometimes say "let's put this behind us" and get on with life. Ōe concludes that if anyone is to take the lead in such matters, "victims can lay first claim to that right." We honor Ding Zilin for choosing to remember and to act; we cannot give less respect to parents who try to absorb their losses privately.

This brings us to the bystander's viewpoint, which may be, morally speaking, the most complex of all. The party who is not involved as either perpetrator or victim has the opportunity—or, many say, the responsibility—to "bear witness," by which we usually mean a bringing to the side of the victim the moral authority of a disinterested voice. Bystanders to crime—be it a mugging in the Bronx or a massacre in Beijing—can and often do opt against involvement. For Chinese writers in the twentieth century, beginning most notably with Lu Xun, this kind of apathetic bystander has drawn special scorn. The crowd at a beheading that only stares blankly—or, worse, "enjoys the spectacle"—is for Lu Xun almost as deplorable as the enemy itself. We can imagine, if Lu Xun were still with us, his revulsion—but lack of surprise—that ten years after the June Fourth massacre the apathetic bystander remains alive and well. Shoppers at Beijing's new malls often seem quite content to have exchanged their new walkways for memories of the blood that lies beneath them. In the Western democracies, some business interests and their allied politicians argue that it is time to "get over" memories of how a repressive government, still in power, used tanks in a massacre.

Sympathetic bystanders are much to be preferred, but they present ethical questions of other kinds. In Prague in the 1970s, Václav Havel occasionally received Western tourists who were eager to meet, and to offer support to, a "dissident." While naturally feeling grateful for the good intentions of such visitors, Havel also felt frustration when they asked, "What can we do for you?" The question seemed to imply that only the dissident's fate, and not the questioner's, was at stake. But, writes Havel in "Politics and Conscience":

> Was not my arrest an attack on him? ...the deceptions [by the regime] to which he is subjected an attack on me? Is not the destruction of humans in Prague a destruction of all humans?

Any sympathetic bystander (I include myself here) is susceptible to blind spots like those of Havel's tourists. Indeed, it seems to me that Havel's decency may have stayed him from expanding on this topic. I believe he could have presented a taxonomy of the ways in which the failure to appreciate the fundamental commonality between the situations of bystander and victim can lead the bystander into morally dubious attitudes toward victims. Let me sketch a few of those ways.

Lu Xun's distaste for viewing a victim as a "spectacle" applies not only when the victim is seen as wretched (Lu Xun worried about why human beings find psychological reinforcement in watching disaster fall upon others) but also when the victim is held up as a hero or saint. "We outsiders," writes Ōe Kenzaburō, "often want to find a sacrificial saint on every corner." The bystander's tendency to view victims this way stems in part, I believe, from the fact that some victims die. At the moment of death, a victim passes in our memories into an ethereal realm, where she or he stands in silent dignity, shrouded in an aura that suggests sainthood. We need to remember that the victims who do not die are still human beings, and we are mistaken, indeed quite unfair, to hold them up to the yardstick of sainthood. We should not need to be told that trauma and degradation tend, if anything, to make people less saintlike, not more. If we do need to be told, then accounts from texts as various as those of Primo Levi writing of Auschwitz, Bloke Modisane writing of a South African township under apartheid in *Blame Me on History* and Zhang Xianliang writing of a Chinese labor camp in *My Bodhi Tree* all converge to make it quite clear.

A spectator's desire to watch a hero win a contest is even more dangerous. When we watch a football game it is quite all right to root for a hero without asking why we ourselves are not out on the field helping him. But in contests over human rights in the real world it can be perplexing, indeed disgusting, for a bystander who lives in safety and comfort to ask someone else to be a hero and then to issue criticisms when the heroism is not stout enough. Fang Lizhi, for example, was a victim of the June Fourth crackdown. He and his wife quite unfairly had to spend thirteen months confined to a tiny, windowless room in an American diplomatic building. Fang made this choice in preference to surrendering himself to the Chinese government, in whose hands his fate would certainly have been worse, and perhaps far worse. It is legitimate to ask what the consequences of his decision were, and what the consequences of other choices might have been. But who—other than Wei Jingsheng, Xu Wenli, Zheng Yi, and others who have put their own safety and comfort on the line—has the right to chide Fang for lack of heroism? Moreover, and even less defensibly, some criticisms of Fang's decision have been based not on judgments of how China might have developed differently if he had chosen differently, but on essentially aesthetic judgments about Fang's image: a true hero, like Tan Sitong, would have chosen martyrdom. This would have shown true class; we could have applauded this. But to put the aesthetic satisfaction of bystanders who have chosen to risk nothing ahead of the personal safety of someone who has already taken major risks is to move from the dubious toward the truly odious.

Most readers of this essay may, like its author, not yet recognize very much of themselves in the problems of the bystander as thus far described. But I want to end with a bystander problem that I think applies to me and perhaps to you as well. Because we sympathize with victims, and over time get rather good at it, we can come to depend on the existence of victims in order, as it were, to maintain our skills in peak form. When we hear about yet another crackdown in China, the news can strike us at one level almost as good news, because it gives us more material to work with and more proof that our striving all along has been needed. Of course, this response is not right. We need to step back from our roles far enough to see that this kind of response, like some of the other ways in which bystanders can view victims, is self-serving. When we predict—perhaps with very good reason—that China's human rights problems are likely to continue or to worsen, we need to remind ourselves to hope that these predictions will be wrong.

How can we monitor ourselves to "stay honest" in this regard? To me, Václav Havel's insight, noted above, may help the most. As long as we can see the truth that ultimately there is no border between us and victims, that affronts to humanity do not happen in some separate sphere from which we are shielded but that, indeed, the "destruction of humans in Prague [or Beijing, or Capetown, or wherever] is a destruction of all humans," then I think we may be able to continue safely with our remembering, our commemorating, and our work.

Originally published in *China Rights Forum*, Special June Fourth
Ten-Year Anniversary Issue, Summer 1999

What the Tiananmen Mothers Offer China

⟨⟩

(2004)

T HE NIGHT of June 5, 1989, shortly after the June Fourth massacre, when the blood on the streets of Beijing had already dried, but before the dutiful scrubbing of it had begun, Professor Fang Lizhi and his wife, Professor Li Shuxian, received "the personal invitation of President George [H.P.] Bush" to stay in the U.S. embassy in Beijing. This stay turned out to last more than a year, during which the couple's specific location, living conditions, feelings, and thoughts were all shrouded in mystery. The diplomatic buzz over them was intense and acrimonious; by contrast their own silence and unknown condition lent them an air of transcendence. As any sage knows, to remain silent when others are hoping to hear one's words can create an aura of special wisdom. This aura fell upon Fang and Li even though they were not seeking it.

The only way a friend like me could reach them was to write to a post office box number in Washington, D.C., from which U.S. State Department couriers could pick up mail and see that it got delivered. This worked. Moreover, it was cheap. Only 25 cents, the domestic first-class rate at the time, got the letter all the way into Fang's and Li's hands in the bowels of an embassy building in Beijing. This little fact in itself was exciting. It felt almost like getting a message to Mars.

Sharing this excitement, Robert Silvers, splendid editor at *The New York Review of Books,* asked me if he could invite Fang to write an essay from Neverland, as it were. I went through the channel to ask, and Fang sent us a piece called "Communist Techniques of Amnesia" (*gongchandang de yiwangshu*), which I translated and the *Review* published.[1] All this went

1. Fang Lizhi, Perry Link trans., *The Chinese Amnesia,* 37 *The New York Review of Books* (September 27, 1990).

smoothly. But I must admit that I found Fang's choice of topic a bit odd. His theme was that the Communist Party of China crushes one generation after another of Chinese free-thinkers, and that each crushing is easy because one generation never remembers what happened to the last. The students at Tiananmen did not know much about the "Democracy Wall" activists of ten years earlier (or their eventual fates); those activists, in turn, were not very aware of the "1957 rightists." The recurrent amnesia arose from no particular problem with Chinese brains or Chinese culture, Fang argued; it was the result of deliberate techniques of the regime.

"All probably true," I thought. But why did Fang find this issue salient at a time when world opinion was ablaze in revulsion at the massacre? If one counts the television audience, the June Fourth massacre was without doubt the most-witnessed atrocity in world history. How could "forgetfulness" become a problem?

Now many years have passed. "The waters have receded and the rocks protrude," as the Chinese saying puts it. Fang was right, indeed prescient. The world has largely forgotten the massacre. More importantly, it overlooks the continuing violent nature of the political regime that caused it, that still applies violence behind the scenes, and that would no doubt risk another spectacular massacre if it concluded that its grip on power required one.

Not just the outside world, but the young in China, too, have fallen into amnesia. College students have heard vague reports of the massacre but tend not to care. They prefer fashions, video games, stock prices, and e-chats. To the extent that they have views on larger public issues at all, they tend to coast on a thin fuel of adolescent nationalism—a motivation that usually suits their rulers just fine. They are largely unattuned to the plight of the poor and oppressed in their society. Eerily, they also show little sign of realizing that if—for whatever reason—they themselves were ever to seriously cross purposes with their rulers, those rulers would certainly squash them as earlier generations have been squashed.

The regime's tactics of amnesia began right after the massacre with language manipulation. The first step was truth-inversion: army units using tanks and machine guns to slaughter unarmed citizens were officially described the next day as "heroes of the people" controlling "rioters" and pacifying "dregs of society." The next step was diminution: over the course of a decade the massacre became a mere "incident" (*shijian*), then shrank to a "fuss" (*fengbo*), then petered into a wisp of practically nothing. A friend from Hong Kong wrote to me recently that she had visited an internet café in Guangzhou and was happy to find articles about the Tiananmen Mothers accessible there online. Accessible, she said, but little noticed: youthful Chinese netizens were busy with computer games and money schemes. When she asked them about Tiananmen they looked at her blankly. A massacre? What?

Some very unsubtle methods of censorship have contributed to this forgetting. Textbooks, museums, and the media simply omit the massacre. Web sites on the topic are blocked; foreign broadcasts that discuss it are jammed. A recent general ruling (aimed not only at potential discussion of the massacre) has required all call-in shows in China to use equipment that allows a twenty-second delay before any expression from "the masses" can reach the airwaves, in order to "ensure the [regime's] guidance of public opinion." Radio stations that lack the requisite equipment are not allowed to do call-in shows. Somehow the remembering public, if it wants to speak out, must struggle past all these barriers.

But who are the rememberers, and how can they even try to speak? To be fair, any full survey should begin (in imagination only, of course) with the dead themselves. It is tautological that the dead cannot speak, but useful to imagine what they might say if they could see the pinging video arcades that now cover the sites where they lost their lives. Next are the many people who are alive but intimidated. The rights lawyer Pu Zhiqiang reminds us that the least audible voices on the massacre today are those of the ordinary workers and common folk of Beijing ("social dregs," to speak officially) who supported the students, whose names we do not know and who still mourn, in silence, their dead and wounded. They and many others remember the massacre and discuss it in private. But private talk on sensitive topics in China is covered in public by a stifling blanket of self-censorship. This rule is based in a fear that has become so customary that it seems almost a natural part of daily life. To defy it can seem counterintuitive, even stupid. Dissidents report that family members often upbraid them for speaking out—not because of any disagreement with the truth or moral principle of what they say, but because the act risks punishment for the family.

This context of self-censorship is what makes the Tiananmen Mothers movement so extraordinary. It is a lonely thread of truth across a fetid swamp of suppression and lies. There are several reasons why these remarkable people (who include some men as well as women) have been able to poke through the web of lies and "live in truth," as Václav Havel puts it. First, they own an irrefutable moral authority from having personally lost children or other relatives in the massacre. Second, the regime finds it hard to attack them directly because most were not "dissidents" to begin with; they had been dutiful members of the system, indeed sometimes leaders, before murder jolted them free. Third, of course, is simple courage, which is especially clear in the cases of Ding Zilin, Zhang Xianling, Huang Jinping and others who have taken leadership roles. Chinese people well know that "the first bird to stick its neck out gets its head blown off" and that it is always easier to follow a lead than to take one.

What benefits have the Tiananmen Mothers brought to China? The most concrete has been comfort—and sometimes modest aid—to dozens, and eventually hundreds, of family members of massacre victims. In order to comfort them, one first needs to find them, and that task has not been easy. The government naturally opposes such searches, and victims' families are often reluctant to come forward. They need to weigh the value of comfort against the danger of standing out—and thereby inviting further punishment. (Communist Chinese culture is one of the few in the world in which A can slap B in the face and B is expected to apologize.) Many families opt to lie low. But for those who do accept support, the against-all-odds quality of the experience only enhances it. The Tiananmen Mothers "carry charcoal through a blizzard."[2]

That aid, though, is only a small sliver of what the Tiananmen Mothers movement can offer China. Far more important, potentially, is the use that society as a whole can make of the basic values of the movement. This point needs some explanation.

For more than three decades, China has experienced an obvious decline in what might be called "public ethics." In the 1950s and 1960s, Mao Zedong launched conscious attacks on traditional Chinese social morality, and these took their toll. By the late 1960s many young Chinese had concluded that "the Four Olds" truly did "stink." But much more devastating—truly a body blow to Chinese ethics—was something that Mao did

2. A literal translation of a Chinese idiom that means "bringing vital aid to people in a dire situation."

inadvertently. He put out new, super-idealistic verbiage of public morality that repeatedly collapsed and exposed its fraudulence, leaving the Chinese people in profound cynicism. "Serve the People!" sounded wonderful, and many Chinese in the early 1950s not only applauded the ideal but sacrificed for it. But then, in the 1957 Anti-Rightist Movement, Mao decided to kick some of China's most sincere idealists in the teeth. His next present to the Chinese people was the Great Leap Forward and the famine that it created during 1959–62. Easily the largest man-made famine in world history, this cataclysm was caused almost entirely by the forcible application of crack-pot science in the form of inspirational slogans. For the Chinese people a gap opened, in Liu Binyan's memorable phrase, between "two kinds of truth"—the kind that filters down through the newspapers and the kind that arises out of daily life.

In the mid-1960s, Mao again exploited Chinese idealism for his own purposes. The bureaucrats in his governing system had already given rise to considerable popular resentment. Mao decided to corral this resentment and use it to attack his political rivals. He induced naïve young Red Guards to quit school, head for factories and farms, "serve the people," "smash the dog-headed enemy," "create a new Socialist Man," and so on. All this felt highly moral to the youngsters at the time. But soon they, too, discovered a huge rift between ideal and reality: poverty and oppression in the villages, dirt and blood in "class struggle," and lies—and then more lies about the first lies. They felt cheated and angry. Disillusionment in the Red Guard generation was even sharper than in its predecessor. In the long run that disillusionment had a bright side, though, because the Red Guard genera-tion became the first in Communist China to reject received wisdom and begin to think independently. But it groped for a new ethical framework to replace the false one that had crashed.

After Mao's death a toned-down version of idealistic socialist language held on for another decade or so, but it had turned into a shell game. People in the 1980s manipulated words to try to get what they wanted out of offi-cials (who were still obliged to pretend that the words meant something), but no one took verbalized ideals at face value.

During the same years, and with the blessings of top leaders Deng Xiaoping and then Jiang Zemin after him, "make money" emerged as the overwhelming public value in China. A "wild West" form of unbridled competition made corruption, fraud, breach of contract, and private appropriation of public funds the order of the day. The urban economy boomed and millionaires proliferated, while the poor remained as badly off as ever. Connections, lies, and violence kept the engine of growth humming along.

And where did this leave "public ethics"? The ruling elite has made corruption and rip-off acceptable; an oral grapevine of rumor and anecdote spreads their example nationwide; people at lower levels have concluded that ethics are stupid in a world where the big rollers are foul, so they, too, trick, cheat, and steal.

Yet moral devastation has still not completely won the day. Ethical ideas lie deep in Chinese culture. Notions of "being a good person" and "behaving properly" remain embedded in the grammar of everyday Chinese language, where they subsist even if unnoticed and survive even if baked for decades under the scorching sun of harsh government. What's more, the Chinese impulse to do good, although deeply "Chinese," is not just Chinese but a fundament of human nature that philosophers as various as Aristotle, Mencius, Wang Yangming, Hume, Kant and many others have observed. It is hard to imagine that descriptions of "moral intuition" could be as coincident as are Wang Yangming's and David Hume's without there being something in human nature—not just Chinese or British nature—that both philosophers were noticing.

In any case, in the midst of China's ethical collapse, many Chinese people have also been groping—from off the mat, as it were—to try to re-build an ethical world. The Falun Gong spiritual movement calls for "truth, goodness, and forbearance." Buddhism, Daoism, and popular religion have all made comebacks. In the last quarter-century, Christianity in China has gained at least twenty times as many followers as were produced in the hundred years between 1850 and 1950 by ten thousand American Protestant missionaries. (Mao might squirm in his sepulcher; might he himself have done more to spread Christianity than the missionaries did?) But all of these "values" enterprises are kept politically weak. Any relatively organized group—like Falun Gong or the "non-patriotic" churches—is crushed because of the Communist Party's intolerance of any organization it does not control. And there are deeper questions, as well, about what kinds of values might be best suited to become the new "public ethics" of China today. Are the traditional Chinese religions the answer, or are they seen as too un-modern? Is Christianity too foreign-flavored? Chinese people aren't sure about these questions, and as they are not allowed to discuss them in public, a "values vacuum" persists.

And this is why I believe the Tiananmen Mothers have the potential to make a very large contribution to China. Their movement promotes and exemplifies two profound values—truth and love—that could do much to re-anchor a Chinese nation that has gone morally adrift. The Tiananmen Mothers' commitment to truth has been fired in the hottest crucible of all— explicit public contradiction of the lies of a violent government that holds decisive power over them. The love that they highlight is the kind called "mother's love," a love so deep and so universal that it is clearly observable not only in all cultures and historical periods but even in animals—in a doe protecting a fawn across a roadway. For the Tiananmen Mothers, parental love takes on an even greater penetrating power because the children in their case were killed. Can anyone, after all, imagine anything more painful than to watch the violent death of one's own child? (Any parent, in any culture, will know the answer. Non-parents will not have trouble guessing.) Is there any more deep, solid, and unambiguous value around which a confused Chinese nation might rally?

China's great modern writer Lu Xun raised this question nearly a century ago. His classic story "Medicine" tells of a sick boy who dies of an indeterminate disease despite his parents' superstitious belief that feeding him human blood might cure him. The blood, it turns out, is fresh from an execution ground where another young man, an idealistic reformer, has had his head severed because he opposed the dynasty. Both boys have surnames that suggest "China," and they symbolize two visions of China in balanced, almost yin-yang, opposition: one old, the other new; one superstitious, the other enlightened; one eating blood, the other with blood eaten; and so on. The parallel extends to many levels that can only be appreciated by reading the whole story. In the end, though, a different, somewhat surprising, over-arching value emerges. It is broad enough to span the story's opposite poles. It is mother's love.

Both boys have living mothers; both mothers are in grief; the two mothers meet on a footpath that separates two graveyards—one for paupers, where one boy lies, and the other for executed criminals, where the other rests. Several symbolic differences between the two boys are still visible in this graveyard scene, but in essential respects the two mothers are the same. Their love is of the same kind. Their loss is of the same kind. So is their pain. The mother's love that they stand for is bigger than all of the mayhem in the world that brought them together onto that sad path.

I doubt that the leaders of the Communist Party of China will ever be able to perceive that some values far outweigh their own petty grip on power. But the Tiananmen Mothers clearly see this, and so can the good people of China.

Originally published in *China Rights Forum*, no. 2, 2004

Why We Remember June Fourth

⊰)|(⊱

(2019)

Some people recently asked, "Why must you remember June Fourth?" Thirty years have passed. It is history. Get over it. Move on.

A simple question, but there are many answers. No single answer is adequate, and all of the answers together still leave the question hanging in mid-air, asking for more.

WE REMEMBER June Fourth because Jiang Jielian was seventeen at the time. He is still seventeen. He will always be seventeen. People who die do not age.

We remember June Fourth because the lost souls that haunted Liu Xiaobo until he died will haunt us, too, until we die.

We remember June Fourth because the glint of bonfires on bayonets is something one does not forget, even if one did not see it personally.

We remember June Fourth because it taught us the essential nature of the Communist Party of China when all of the clothes, every shred, fell away. No book, film, or museum could be clearer.

We remember June Fourth because of the ordinary workers who died then. We cannot remember most of their names because we do not know most of their names. We never did. But we remember them as people, and we remember that we never knew their names.

We remember June Fourth because the worst of China is there—but the best of China is there, too.

We remember June Fourth because it was a *massacre*—not just a crackdown, or an "incident," an event, a *shijian*, a *fengbo*; not a counterrevolutionary riot, not a faint memory, and not, as a child in China might think today, a blank. It was a *massacre*.

We remember June Fourth because, as Fang Lizhi noted with his characteristic wit, it is the only case he has heard of in which a nation invaded itself.

We remember June Fourth because Xi Jinping's fat smile is a mask.

We remember June Fourth because we want to know what the soldiers who did the killing remember. They were brainwashed on the outskirts of the city before they carried out their deadly orders. So they were victims, too. We do not know what their thoughts were. But we remember that we want to know.

We remember June Fourth because Ding Zilin is still alive. She is eighty-four years old. When she goes out, plainclothes police follow to provide security. Security for her? No, security for the state. That's right, a regime with 100 trillion yuan in GDP and two million soldiers needs protection from an eighty-four-year-old lady. Protection from her *ideas*. This is worth remembering.

We remember June Fourth because remembering it makes us better people. Remembering is in our personal interests. When politicians talk about "interests" they mean material interests. But moral interests are just as important—no, they are *more* important. More important than owning a yacht.

We remember June Fourth because it was a historic turning point for one-fifth of the world. A turn in a frightening direction. We hope it won't be such a sharp turn as to throw the whole world into a ditch. But we don't know. We'll have to see.

We remember June Fourth because, if we didn't *remember* it, it could not have gotten into our minds any other way. Could we possibly have *imagined* it? No.

We remember June Fourth because there are people who dearly *want* us to remember. It comforts them to know that we remember.

We remember June Fourth because there are also people who desperately want us *not* to remember. They want us to forget because forgetting helps to preserve their political power. How foul! We would oppose that power even if remembering massacres were the only way to do it.

We remember June Fourth in order to remind ourselves of the way the Chinese Communist Party lies to itself and to others. It says the Chinese people have long since made their "correct judgment on the 1989 counterrevolutionary riot at Tiananmen Square." But each year, at June Fourth, plainclothes police block people from entering the Square. Why? If the Chinese people all believe what the government says they believe, then why not let them into the square to denounce the counterrevolutionaries? The presence of the police shows that the regime does not believe its own lies.

We remember June Fourth because shocks to the human brain last a long time. We would not be able to forget even if we tried.

How to Deal with the Chinese Police

(2013)

A review of *In the Shadow of the Rising Dragon: Stories of Repression in the New China*, edited by Xu Youyu and Hua Ze, translated by Stacy Mosher

A CASUAL VISITOR to China today does not get the impression of a police state. Life bustles along as people pursue work, fashion, sports, romance, amusement, and so on, without any sign of being under coercion. But the government spends tens of billions of dollars annually (more than on national defense) on domestic *weiwen*, or "stability maintenance." This category includes the regular police, courts, and prisons, but also censors and "opinion guides" for the internet, plainclothes police, telephone snoops, and thugs for hire—all of whose work is to keep citizens in line. The targets are people who tend to get out of line—petitioners, aggrieved workers, certain professors and religious believers, and others. The stability maintainers are especially attentive to any sign that an unauthorized group might form. The goal is to stop "trouble" before it starts.

Weiwen does blanket coverage, but the blanket, most of the time, is soft. This is because citizens are well accustomed to monitoring themselves. They are aware of what kinds of public speech and behavior are to be avoided and they know that kicking the police blanket is not only dangerous but nearly always futile. People who do it, they feel, are odd, perhaps even stupid.

Those who do choose to stand out from the crowd, risking the label of "troublemaker," immediately come into focus for the *weiwen* brigades. Police arrive for "visits." They warn. They cajole. Failing that, they threaten and harass. Beyond that, they detain and charge with crimes. At each step they check with "superiors."

It takes unusual character to stand up to this. People who do it are strong, stubborn, and, as their families and friends sometimes see it, high-minded to the point of obtuseness. The passions of some have been kindled by personal loss—an imprisoned brother, a murdered son, a razed home—while others are indignant primarily at the injustices they see around them. Many are idealists, oddly willing to risk personal safety because China falls short of what they want it to be. Some are lured by the image of heroism, even knowing that its price could be martyrdom. For many, there is a mix of these motives. *In the Shadow of the Rising Dragon*, a translation of essays from a book published last year in Hong Kong called *Encounters with the Police*, introduces fourteen such people.

A first question is why they are important. They are a small minority, nonviolent, not wealthy, and not high-ranking. Many are women. Why are they not just marginal irritants—like "lice on a lion," as the regime says (if indeed it says anything about them at all)? It is quite clear that they are much more than that, and that their audacity poses a genuine threat to the regime. The best evidence for this comes from the regime itself—not in how it speaks of them but in how it handles them. It regularly "invites" them to tea and asks that they "coordinate" with police by sharing their plans; it monitors and, if necessary, confiscates their telephones and computers; it stations police at their doors (where, during "sensitive" times like anniversaries of the Tiananmen massacre of 1989, they remain around the clock).

Among its many anecdotes, *In the Shadow of the Rising Dragon* tells how, on a cold day in 2010, Ding Zilin, a seventy-three-year-old retired professor of philosophy, leaves her house with her husband, Jiang Peikun, to travel from Wuxi to Beijing. Jiang is ill. Two plainclothes policemen intercept the couple, tell them to get out of their car and into a police car, escort them to the Wuxi rail station, and then board the train to "share a compartment" with them. In Beijing, another car from State Security awaits them. Why all the attention, time, and expense? What does an elderly professor have that calls for such solicitude from a government that owns the world's largest reserves of foreign currency and commands the world's largest standing army?

Ding Zilin has—and it is all she has—the power to tell unapproved truths. Her son Jiang Jielian was killed when the army invaded Tiananmen in June 1989, and she later organized and led the Tiananmen Mothers, a support group for families of other victims of that massacre. She also became a mentor to Liu Xiaobo, who, just four days before her train ride to Beijing with the police, had been awarded the Nobel Peace Prize in Oslo. The prize was given in absentia because Liu was inside a Chinese prison, convicted of "incitement of subversion of state power." These facts, at this "sensitive time," were more than enough to assign police escorts to her. Their appearance was a symptom of a real fear that she plants in the minds of the men who rule China. What if her ideas get out and begin to spread?

Václav Havel, observing the response of the Soviet government to Alexander Solzhenitsyn in the 1970s, described

> a desperate attempt to plug up the wellspring of truth, a truth which might cause incalculable transformations in social consciousness, which in turn might one day produce political debacles unpredictable in their consequences.

The mentalities of the Kremlin in the 1970s and today's Zhongnanhai (the headquarters of the Chinese Communist Party and state) differ in important respects, but this fear of truth-from-below, so well described by Havel, is something that the two share. It arises from awareness that public acquiescence to their rule is often performance more than conviction.

Official language, obligatorily true at one level, at another level is hollow. The rulers themselves need to deal with this language bifurcation. On the topic of the 1989 massacre, for example, they can announce that "the Chinese people have made their correct historical judgment" on the "counterrevolutionary riot." But do they themselves believe this? If they did, would they not open Tiananmen Square every year on June 4 to allow the masses to come in and denounce the rioters? What they actually do, each year, is the opposite: they send plainclothes police to prevent any sign of commemoration of any kind. They plug that "wellspring of truth," as Havel calls it. Ding Zilin and everyone else in *In the Shadow of the Rising Dragon* are plug-pullers.

The "superiors" who order the repression do not appear in the book. They operate behind the scenes. The people we see face-to-face with the plug-pullers are several kinds of underlings. They are normally young and more often male than female. They receive assignments and are paid to carry them out. They sometimes show respect for the people they are watching and speak frankly of "just doing my job." They make it clear that they are not very well paid, and sometimes talk about their work schedules. Overtime work can be welcome if it entails following someone to a restaurant where state-issued coupons can be used to order fancy meals.

They are sometimes not even state employees but ordinary people, including migrant workers, who are willing to work as temporary hirelings. These street-level police workers do not answer any questions about policy; they refer all such to their superiors. Sometimes they don't even use the word "superiors" but just point a finger upward to explain why they are doing what they are doing. At the level directly above them are the police who work in local stations or detention centers. These personnel are generally older, more experienced, and better trained in methods of interrogation. We see some of them in *In the Shadow of the Rising Dragon*. They have a certain latitude to make tactical decisions, but on weighty questions (like how to handle the travel of a truth-telling seventy-three-year-old professor) they, too, turn to their superiors.

What fills the pages of the book, therefore, is mostly the verbal stand-offs between two very different kinds of people: on one side, obdurate truth-tellers insisting on principle; on the other, people trying to do their jobs in order to earn salaries. The two sides do have one thing in common: an incentive to keep talking to the other side. For the truth-tellers, truthful talk is a passion; for the police, it is a tool in control work. The symbiosis generates a language game that seems unusual by standards of other cases in the world to which it might be compared. Police in Soviet-dominated Eastern Europe were not nearly so talkative. They were brusque; business was business. In South Africa under apartheid, black citizens dissimulated in their use of language in order to get by, and in that sense also played a language game, but there was nothing like the extensive give-and-take of the game that has evolved in recent decades in China. The matching of wits, the thrusting and parrying, and the posing (even while pretending not to pose, and even though both sides see through the pretending) are innovations of Chinese political culture.

For example, a young woman named Huang Yaling, two days after Liu Xiaobo's Nobel Peace Prize was announced in Oslo in October 2010, went to the Norway Pavilion at the Shanghai World Expo to present a bouquet of flowers and a note that said "I love Norway." The police noticed and invited her to tea. Here are excerpts of her exchange with a male policeman.

"Did you go to the World Expo?"

"Yes."

"To which pavilions?"

"Norway and Denmark. The others had too many people and I didn't want to wait in line...."

"Was there anything you found especially memorable?"

"Oh, I met the director of the Norway Pavilion! He was as handsome as a movie star!"

"You're married and you notice the good looks of a foreigner?"

"Why can't I admire somebody's good looks? My husband can enjoy the beauty of a foreign woman, and I bet you do, too!"

"I'm not married, so of course I can look at pretty girls. What about that director? You know what we're asking about, so just cooperate!"

"I gave the director a bouquet."

"And what did he do?"

"Accepted it."

"What was the director's name?"

"Aiya, what a pity! I forgot to ask the name. Do you know his name?"

"How would I know his name?!... What did you say when you presented the bouquet?"

"I love Norway and I'm offering these flowers to Norway."

"Why give flowers to Norway?"

"I like Norway.... What else can I do?"

"Why do you like Norway?"

A few minutes later:

"All right, enough chit-chat, I'll cooperate. You want to know why I brought a bouquet to the Norway Pavilion? I'll tell you, but first you have to show me your ID...."

"Why do you care about our IDs? You're still not cooperating. Do we need to get a subpoena?"

"Who asked you to be so rude? Come on, let's shake hands and then I'll give you all the details."

"We came to do our jobs, not to shake hands. Our job is to understand the situation. Why did you bring flowers to the Norway Pavilion?"

"OK, it was because of the Nobel Peace Prize."

"What about it?"

"I was happy about it. Aren't you? Aren't you happy that a Chinese won the Nobel Peace Prize?"

"It's not our job to talk about being happy."

For police at this level, "our job" means primarily the extraction of information. In training sessions that are basically the same all across China, they are taught the methods to use. It is a priority to uncover a person's contacts. Twenty years ago, this meant examining address books; today it means confiscating computers and cell phones. The police note email addresses and read email. They sometimes imitate a person's style in order to send out bogus email, hoping to lure unwitting responses. In interrogation, many questions are about a person's associates: Who told you to do this? Who was with you? and so on. For their part, detainees often announce in advance that "I will talk to you, but in principle will say nothing one way or another about anyone else."

Some of the CCP's methods for putting psychological pressure on detainees are used throughout the world. The interrogated can be surrounded by questioners, placed under bright lamps, made to sit uncomfortably, deprived of sleep. They can be separated from colleagues and manipulated. (So-and-so has already told us everything; our reason for asking you what happened is not to learn what happened, because we know it, but to measure your sincerity, which will affect your punishment.) An abrupt change of topic is sometimes an attempt to catch a detainee off guard. A sentence that begins, "In Marx's socialist theory, regarding democracy..." can be cut off with, "When did you arrive in Nanjing?"

Threats are useful, and they come in many kinds: *We can lock you up for years, you know. Would you like three, or four? How are your children? Going to school? Would you like them to stay at the same school? You are a lawyer; would you like to keep your license?* Travel permissions—passports, visas, exit permits—are useful as levers. For "troublemakers," China's border has become a political toll booth. Whichever direction you want to cross it in—into the country? out of the country?—you will need political approval, and permission to cross can be leverage that makes you cooperate. Some police threats are aimed at keeping the threats themselves secret. Detainees are asked to sign statements in which they agree not to "sully the image of the motherland" by talking about what has happened to them.

Police the world over are familiar with the "good cop, bad cop" technique, and Chinese interrogators use it often. One moment an interrogator is saying, "We've looked at the material in your computer and all your online postings, and we sympathize with you"; the next, someone "poked my head, kicked the tiger seat [made of welded metal bands] and yanked my shoulders back and forth, ensuring that in my extreme exhaustion I couldn't fall asleep."

If extraction of information is a goal of police work everywhere, in China there is a twin goal—not found in most other repressive societies, past or present—and that is to change a detainee's political attitude. This goal does much to explain why Chinese police want detainees to talk. Talking draws people out, engages them, and might be the road to changing their views— or at least their calculation of their own best interests. Hence much time is spent on questions like: Why do you bother writing articles like this? Isn't China much better off than it was twenty years ago? Can't you see that your friends have BMWs and you still have only a Toyota? Why go to prison? Don't you want your children to have a father at home?

Teng Biao, a well-known human rights lawyer, had the question put to him bluntly. There were "two roads" for him to choose between: "detention, arrest, trial, and prison" or "lenience for a good attitude, and... release." Which would it be? "Just say a few words admitting error, even if you don't believe it," his interrogator advised, then added, "just as a favor to me." Those last words were not merely an attempt to manipulate Teng Biao. They were in part sincere. If the official record showed that Teng Biao had achieved no "ideological transformation," the interrogator himself could be faulted. Here we see one way in which detainees can gain leverage in arguments with police and sometimes even put them on the defensive.

There are others. One, for example, is to argue from law. China's laws give rights to citizens, detained or not, and the police, although they violate these rights flagrantly and often, are obliged to pretend that they do not. At the rhetorical level China's constitution is sacrosanct, and the distance between that level and what actually happens in interrogations gives detainees grounds for attack. During the verbal games that ensue, the police hold the trump card of knowing that overwhelming state power will always be on their side. But except for that, detainees almost always have the stronger position in argument because they know the law better than the less-well-educated police do. Xiao Qiao, a regime critic who traveled to Sweden and then was barred from reentering China through Hong Kong in 2009, asks the Chinese border police, "Which part of the Regulations stipulates that a Chinese citizen can be prevented from entering her own country?" Receiving no answer, she presses further, demanding the return of books the police have just confiscated. What rule allows them to confiscate those books? Apparently beaten, but still bound to obey orders from superiors, the unfortunate border guard can only retreat to informal language: "Let it go, those few books aren't worth anything, just buy some more when you get back to Hong Kong."

The strong reluctance of low-level police to give their names or show their IDs—depicted repeatedly in *In the Shadow of the Rising Dragon*—is explained by their vulnerability to legal argument from the people they detain. They feel trapped. On the one hand, they have been trained to detain people and extract information. On the other, they are not supposed to violate the law. In essence they have been given contradictory guidelines, but if they err, it is they, not the authors of the guidelines, who will take the blame. Some clever detainees come along, citing all the rules in the book and asking for their names and IDs. What can they do?

Yet an appeal to the laws can go only so far if the police are the only ones hearing it. Hence a related tactic has emerged among detainees: expanding the audience to include bystanders. Xiao Qiao, arguing with border police over her right to reenter China, raises her voice sufficiently that others can overhear, and the police, perceiving her tactic, urge her to lower it. In courtrooms, an accused can sometimes turn a gallery into a sort of informal jury, drawing titters from it, even applause, by speaking common sense.

Xu Youyu, one of the editors of *In the Shadow of the Rising Dragon*, tells how police, after knocking on his door one night, tried to use the bystander effect themselves. As Xu stood in his doorway, talking to them but not inviting them in, they said, "Let's not argue outside. It won't look good to the neighbors." They knew that ordinary Chinese fear the police and (whatever their private sympathies) tend to shun neighbors like Xu who often get police visits. The message to Xu, as he stood in his doorway, was clear: Do you want to be tainted by our presence here or will you let us in? Xu was already tainted enough that adding more would hardly make a difference, and in any case he knew that his neighbors largely respected him, so he turned the tables. He raised his voice and shouted that he hoped everyone in the building would know he was arguing with the police.

The internet has greatly enhanced the bystander effect. Anecdotes about police misbehavior travel quickly online in China and become the focus of group discussion. After any report of confrontation between police and citizens, popular sympathy heads almost reflexively to the side of citizens. Smart phones, which have made photography much easier than before, have become important tools for activists and a new headache for police. Anything the police do might be on the internet within minutes and visible to uncountable numbers of virtual bystanders—at least until internet censors have a chance to take the photos down.

Having accounts of repression published abroad can be viewed as looking for bystander sympathy overseas. (The book under review is an example.) Police in China seek to deter such activity with the threat that "patriots" do not cooperate with "hostile foreign forces." Westerners sometimes shy away from contact with Chinese protesters out of fear that they might get them into trouble, but this is almost always a mistake. Usually, detainees and prisoners in China are treated better, not worse, when the police know that the outside world is watching. The best course for outsiders is to let people inside China make the judgments about risks. If they reach out to you, or do things that invite international attention, to shy away is to second-guess them about what they know best.

Chinese protesters rely on the bystander effect because of an assumption that human beings, on average, share a basic civility that will naturally bring the sympathy of bystanders to the side of the aggrieved. This assumption of a common ethical bedrock is visible even in their face-to-face encounters with police. The verbal jousting of both sides observes some basic civilities, even if only for show. For example, a few days after a police raid, Ding Zilin, the seventy-three-year-old professor, was so shaken that she fainted and was sent to the hospital. The police then returned to ask her to sign a statement that said, "The patient fainted due to a dispute among family members."

The police—not just the individual police but the system they work for—do not want it on record that they were the cause of the fainting. The statement they offer her is a lie, to be sure, but the lie itself is evidence of a need to honor a common value: it is uncivil to cause old ladies to faint. (One could imagine them saying, "We are right, you are wrong, and fainting serves you right," but they do not say this.) Ding Zilin objects to the statement they proffer. It is not true. But the police persist and ask her to consider their personal situations. A more factual record of the fainting episode would "cause problems" for them. Ding sees their point, and in the end assents, albeit grudgingly. She, too, takes bedrock civility into consideration.

In the Shadow of the Rising Dragon shows many examples of such accommodation. The two sides are always adversarial, and sometimes hostile, yet share a tacit understanding that there are certain values of decency that a person does not violate. Both sides use the assumption to gain advantages. Even a tough-minded lawyer like Teng Biao shows respect (or pretended respect) for police interrogators' anxiety over losing face and concedes that "some of the sentences and phrases in my essays were somewhat inappropriate" before he gets to his "but" clause and says what he really wants to say.

Nearly everything is on the side of the police, but argument from decency, in the end, works better for activists than for their interrogators. Beyond its utility in face-to-face debate, decency is the basis on which they appeal to bystanders. (No bystander in any country needs to be told that raiding police should not shock seventy-three-year-old professors into fainting.) Moreover, it undergirds their advocacy of democracy, the rule of law, and human rights, all of which are assumed to be bedrock values that decent people do not oppose. When human rights lawyers call for the rule of law, the police, at least at the rhetorical level, have to agree. When activists call for democracy, the regime has no real grounds on which to differ; it can only grope for a distinction between "Western" and "Chinese" democracy. In short, the jousting takes place on a slanted field. One side can say what it thinks while the other is obliged to pretend.

Chinese activists publish books like *In the Shadow of the Rising Dragon* outside China because they sense that the slanted playing field extends worldwide. They note that the world's dictatorships feel obliged to call themselves democracies—the Democratic People's Republic of Korea, the Democratic Republic of the Congo, the Democratic Republic of Vietnam, among others. By contrast, people who live in democracies (even if they sometimes admire the efficiency of dictatorships) never feel a need to pretend to the mantle of the other side—by calling themselves, for example, the Glorious Monarchy of India or the Authoritarian State of Canada. To Chinese activists, this rhetorical imbalance is a telling fact: for all the repression in China, including the many thousands in prison for speaking the truth, it implies that the fundamental assumptions of the world's people, as embedded in ordinary language, are on their side.

Originally published in *The New York Review of Books*,
November 7, 2013

Your Brain Needs Washing? Hong Kong Can Help

⊰╫╠⊱

(2022)

A S THE POLITICAL system of the People's Republic of China continues its takeover in Hong Kong, local officials in the city sometimes seem only too eager to please their Beijing masters. An official in Hong Kong's Correctional Services Department has recently, and with evident pride, explained how the department uses brainwashing techniques that have long been standard on the mainland.

In the past three decades, the Chinese Communist Party has spent immense sums on "stability maintenance," a budget item for funding not only police and prisons but also a legion of "thought workers" who blanket the country to nip in the bud any possible threat to CCP authority.

Mainland dissidents, accustomed to "chats" and "invitations to tea" can become adept at sparring with thought workers. But they need to learn the rules of the game as they go; the regime does not publish them. In Hong Kong, the Correctional Services Department does.

In a budgeting document for the fiscal year ending in 2023, the department describes how prison authorities work on "persons in custody" (abbreviated as "PICs"), who are not famous dissidents but ordinary protesters, most of them young, who have been charged with political offenses. At the end of 2021, Hong Kong prisons held 1,787 PICs between the ages of eighteen and thirty and nearly 200 more under eighteen. The standard CCP thought-work techniques to which they have been subjected include these:

We are pinning a negative but unclear label on you. During huge street demonstrations in Hong Kong in 2019, some young protesters began wearing black outfits; this led the Correctional Services Department to inaugurate the term "black-clad violence." The color black has a storied history on the China mainland. During the Cultural Revolution in the late 1960s and early 1970s, the most politically despised people were classified into "Five Black Categories." In 1989, leaders of the Tiananmen Square pro-democracy demonstrations were labeled "black hands." There are many other examples. And what exactly are "black" characteristics? You needn't ask. All you need to know is that *black = wrong* and that you are on the defensive.

If you oppose us, you are by definition a minority. PICs are described in the Correctional Services document as "radical" lawbreakers who are "extreme" in their "anti-social" mind-set. Never mind that they marched in demonstrations that brought more than a quarter of the city's entire population into the streets. In police rhetoric, they were at the fringes. During the equally immense demonstrations in Beijing in spring 1989, CCP media stalwartly held that "a tiny minority" was causing all the trouble.

The regime occupies the moral center. The question for "extremists" is always whether they will choose to return to the mainstream. It is the *right* thing to do. Just as the words *black* and *wrong* have no specifiable empirical content, the word *right* has none, either. The Correctional Services Department wishes that young Hong Kongers will take the "right" path and set the "right" goals, but what does *right* mean? The government knows.

Your family is in the mainstream, not with you. In one sense, there is sometimes truth in this claim. Families, even while privately sympathizing with their PICs, often play it safe. Dissidents in mainland China have often observed that relatives are the first to criticize them, since a brash dissident can endanger an entire family. Accordingly, in Hong Kong, the Correctional Services Department touts special family programs that are aimed to help PICs "form stronger determination to turn over a new leaf through family support."

You must be clear on history. It is both essential to Marxism-Leninism and deep in Chinese cultural tradition that the legitimacy of a ruler depends upon a *correct* view of recent history—as determined by officials. The department provides "Virtual Reality history learning activities" for those who need it because a "sense of national identity" helps "build positive values" and will steer PICs "back on the right track."

Your government is here to help. It knows that PICs have "special rehabilitation needs." Case managers "adjust [prisoners'] rehabilitation programmes as and when necessary" to account for changing "psychological and emotional disturbances, difficulties in controlling impulsiveness, etc." Special programs include an Information Literacy Group to teach prisoners "to judge the authenticity of online information"; and a Zen Photography Workshop to "help them think over their problems from a different perspective."

Government care follows a PIC out of prison. It begins with "Project Landing," which has a mission to help them "de-radicalise, cultivate multi-perspective thinking, develop empathy skills and rebuild family relationships." Next comes a police-sponsored "Walk with YOUth Programme" that helps PICs to "re-establish correct values...with a view to reducing... recidivism." A psychological service center called "Change Lab" aims to build up "psychological resilience" and help "resist temptations."

In mainland China, it is well known that punishments are reduced for people who show gratitude for psychological help. Similarly, in Hong Kong, according to the Correctional Services Department, "de-radicalisation rehabilitation programmes have received positive and favourable response from participants."

Originally published in *The Washington Post* as
"How jailed Hong Kong protesters are subjected to 'thought work,'"
July 20, 2022

Capitulate or Things Will Get Worse

〜❦〜

(2013)

A review of *For a Song and a Hundred Songs: A Poet's Journey Through a Chinese Prison* by Liao Yiwu, translated by Wenguang Huang; *This Generation: Dispatches from China's Most Popular Literary Star (and Race Car Driver)* by Han Han, translated by Allan H. Barr; and of *Ai Weiwei's Blog: Writings, Interviews, and Digital Rants, 2006–2009*, edited and translated by Lee Ambrozy

THE MASSACRE of protesters in Beijing on June 4, 1989, and the harsh repression during the months immediately following put China in a foul mood. Among ordinary Chinese, the prestige of the Communist Party, whose leaders had ordered the assault, fell to a new low. Western governments applied sanctions and (at least in public) distanced themselves from "the butchers of Beijing," to borrow Bill Clinton's phrase. Some China-watchers wondered how long the regime could hold on.

Then, it did hold on. Moreover, it grew stronger. Today, China-watchers are writing about the regime's "resilience" and "adaptability." Sebastian Heilmann and Elizabeth Perry have published a conference volume called *Mao's Invisible Hand*, in which they describe in detail this surprising resilience. They trace its origins to Mao Zedong, whose "guerrilla policy style" permitted flexibility in all things but one: that Mao stay on top. The approach, they write,

> is fundamentally dictatorial, opportunistic, and merciless. Unchecked by institutions of accountability, guerrilla leaders pursue their objectives with little concern for those who stand in their way.

In the years since 1989, the ways in which Deng Xiaoping and Mao's other successors have continued the tradition have included (this list is mine, not Heilmann and Perry's): (1) "political education" in textbooks that omit much of modern Chinese history and distort much of what remains; (2) stoking nationalism by staging events like the Olympics and a World's Fair, using publicity that presents "China" and "the Party" as synonyms; (3) distracting attention from problems in people's lives by magnifying rivalries with foreign countries and domestic "splittists" like Tibetans or Uyghurs; (4) use of hundreds of thousands of cyberpolice to delete "unhealthful" posts from the internet and to "guide opinion" by inserting pro-regime posts; (5) pouring a fortune (more than is spent on health, education, and social welfare programs combined) into "stability maintenance," which includes, in addition to ordinary police work, monitoring people to stop "trouble" before it starts. Troublemakers are counseled to concentrate on moneymaking instead of wandering into such dangerous topics as fairness, justice, or clean air.

The methods work. It is possible, whatever one thinks of the regime's goals, to admire its savvy. Western commentators sometimes laud the obvious efficiency. Things do get done. The economy booms.

A great virtue of Liao Yiwu's new book, *For a Song and a Hundred Songs*, is that it suggests the things we must consider before crediting the regime with efficiency. It shows that not only cleverness but a beastly ruthlessness undergirds the resilience of the Party. Liao, who is well known for his essays on life from the bottom up in China, spent 1990–1994 in prison for a long poem called "Massacre" about Beijing in 1989 and a plan to turn the poem into a film called *Requiem*. The film was never made, but in 1997 Liao completed a prison memoir called *Testimony*, from which *For a Song and a Hundred Songs* is adapted.

The book shows what happens to people who ignore the regime's gentler advice against causing trouble. Penalties increase as resistance increases. First permits of all kinds—business or law licenses, passports, and the like—are canceled. Next come loss of employment and placement under surveillance. Dare you persist? Next comes house arrest (which Liu Xia, wife of China's Nobel Peace laureate Liu Xiaobo, currently endures). If that fails, then detention, then prison. At each stage the choice is clear: "Capitulate or things will get worse." Inside prisons, the gradations continue. There are fairly comfortable prisons, middling ones, and awful ones. Within each there are social hierarchies: the wardens rule the inmates, but among inmates there are chiefs who help the wardens and "enforcers" who help the chiefs. Even the people at the very bottom are ranked by those who must, and those who need not, for example, sleep next to the toilets or have last chance at the food.

Liu Xiaobo read Liao's *Testimony* in 1999. Liu had already been imprisoned three times (his current incarceration, for which he is serving an eleven-year sentence, is his fourth) but the first three had been in relatively comfortable prisons, and the contrast between those and what he read about in Liao's account brought mild embarrassment to Liu. He wrote to his friend that "I probably shouldn't even say mine were imprisonments, compared to yours." Liao shows us prison life in color and three dimensions: inmates being cursed, spit at, and kicked in the head; rivalries and snitching; endless and boring forced labor (gluing packets of painkillers, in Liao's case); solitary confinement for special offenders that lasts for weeks, and sometimes as long as a year, in cells seven feet long but only three feet high, so that the prisoner cannot—ever—stand up inside; disease, and the faking of disease in quest of respite. Much else is faked as well, including language. Forced drudgery is called "socialist labor." Wardens file the "appeals" of prisoners with not the slightest intention of making a genuine appeal but only to get it onto the record that they have filed appeals. Cynical language is so entrenched as to seem ordinary.

The extremes of both cynicism and ruthlessness are illustrated in the nicknames that prison authorities give to forms of torture. They liken them to cuisine. At the Song Mountain Detention Center in Chongqing, "the menu," which Liao annotates for his readers, includes:

> *Tofu Fried on Both Sides*: Two enforcers punch the inmate on the chest and back. The sustained blows sometimes cause the inmate to go into shock....
>
> *Stewed Ox Nose*: The enforcer rams two fingers up the inmate's nose until it bleeds....
>
> *Sichuan-style Smoked Duck*: The enforcer burns the inmate's pubic hair, pulls back his foreskin and blackens the head of the penis with fire....

Noodles in a Clear Broth: Strings of toilet papers are soaked in a bowl of urine, and the inmate is forced to eat the toilet paper and drink the urine.

Liao lists thirty-four other dishes and comments on which of them could end in permanent injury or death for the inmate.

Elsewhere, he notes how death-row prisoners live with the awareness that their organs will be harvested and sold after their executions. Somehow, though, Liao's square look at painful and degrading treatment does not cloud his poet's eye. Riding in a police car, he observes "the shops on both sides of the street blurring into a colorful sliding stage"; famished inmates "crammed chunks of rice into their mouths, stretching their necks like crowing roosters to help swallow." The translator, Wenguang Huang, deserves much credit for keeping Liao's art alive.

Released in 1994, Liao finds that China outside of prison "remains a prison of the mind: prosperity without liberty." His book ends on that unexplored note.

As if to take up that challenge, Han Han's *This Generation* shows, with wit and in remarkable depth, how Chinese citizens, especially the young, chafe under restraints. Han Han is careful (as Liao is not) to steer clear of explicit "dissidence"; the reward for this caution in China is that he can have hundreds of times more readers than Liao. Yet it is easy to see, with just a bit of reflection, that Han shares much with the explicit dissidents. Sometimes he penetrates even more deeply than they do. His writing lacks Liao Yiwu's colorful metaphors, but it is delightful for its terse, droll irony, reminiscent of the great essayist Lu Xun (1881–1936). The translator, Allan Barr, apologizes that he cannot get every facet of Han Han's wit into English, but his results are still wonderful.

Born in 1982, Han Han failed high school examinations repeatedly and eventually dropped out, but not before he wrote a searing indictment of the Chinese education system in a novel called *San chong men* (*Triple Door*). Published in China in 2000, it was an immediate hit and eventually sold more than two million copies. Han also became a prize-winning race car driver and, in part because of his good looks, began to appear on magazine covers as well. He started blogging in 2005, and as of today (October, 2013) his website has received more than 600 million hits. The blog essays collected in *This Generation* appeared between 2006 and 2012.

Han's total internet hits would be even higher if his more provocative posts were not deleted by cyberpolice shortly after they appear. Seeking to minimize the deletions, Han watches his words and frankly admits to his readers that "every essay has undergone self-censorship." Foreign journalists sometimes frustrate him, he says, because they do not understand that he cannot—"at least, not now"—be as candid as he would like to be. He actually is "more expansive when responding to questions from Chinese reporters" because he knows he can trust them to do the requisite self-censorship for him. Yet he still gets his points across, and censorship sometimes even magnifies their force. The day after Liu Xiaobo's Nobel Peace Prize was announced in Oslo, for example, Han posted a blog entry that consisted only of a pair of quotation marks: "". A flood of comment followed. His readers had figured out that this was an open invitation to comment on something that was officially unspeakable.

Many of Han Han's views, although artfully put, are unsurprising versions of what other critics of the regime have been saying for years. He writes, for example, that Mao Zedong regarded "the masses" as nothing more than "gambling chips in his effort to achieve power and prestige"; and that China's current economic "miracle," which allows "our politicians... to pump up their chests on the world political stage," is hardly a miracle of leadership but simply "because of you, China's cheap labor." Are you injured or aggrieved? The only real function of China's system of administrative appeal, Han observes, as many others have, is to induce troublemakers to report themselves to the authorities. Nor is Han the first to observe that Chinese law is a tool that lies on the shelf for on-demand use by people in power, not ordinary Chinese; that "our leaders" write "fake, pretentious, empty-headed essays"; or that educators have to inculcate "political allegiance" in their students or be fired.

But Han Han does more than just put well-known complaints into clever form. On some topics he is uniquely astute. For example, he defends China's young people who are not always vocal about justice from the charge, which their elders sometimes level, that they are materialistic and do not "care about politics." Han answers that the older generation has a horrific record of being knocked around by politics, but

being [that kind of] victim is no decent topic of conversation, any more than being raped has a place in a proper range of sexual experiences. The era when one can care about politics has yet to arrive.

Elsewhere, Han brings deep insight to the question of cultural insecurity. Several essays satirize what he sees as Chinese hypersensitivity to insult:

> The virtues that we celebrate here in China—modesty, sincerity, diligence, simplicity, helpfulness, warmth, unity—are, in fact, the qualities that we most lack. We're actually quite hopeless at these things…[but] of course, we Chinese always rate the Chinese people very highly. We should be content with that. After all, a full one-fifth of the world's population thinks we're wonderful.

He goes on to cite examples of a very low tolerance for any publicly expressed view that China is not wonderful and, analyzing the problem a level or two more deeply than most people do, concludes that "the reason why we Chinese so often feel insulted is that we have so little self-respect." He finds this malady extending into the government, which for many is the public face of China's pride. "The government often lies," he writes, yet sometimes, on the other hand, it does not lie. But whether lying or not, it "always handles issues as though struggling with a guilty conscience." One could write a book about that insight.

Han is especially perceptive on how language is used in Chinese politics. The word "correct" (*zhengque*) is a central concept in Communist jargon, but what exactly, he asks, does it mean? The sarcasm of his answer is a cover for a very serious and accurate point:

> Everything that bolsters their interests and their power is, of course, correct, and everything not conducive to promoting their interests and enhancing their power is naturally incorrect. As soon as you have grasped that principle, you'll never have to tie yourself in knots wondering what is right and what is wrong.

Han observes that, in officialese, statements about the people supporting the government are not empirical claims but true by definition. This is because anyone who withholds support automatically is not one of the "people" but some other category—"reactionary," "bad element," or whatever.

He argues that, to ordinary Chinese, the "news" in the official media, even if it is true, always seems phony after its official packaging, *because* of its official packaging. But—and here his remarkable perspicacity appears again—that doesn't matter, because the regime does not ask credence from its citizens, only the *pretense* of credence. As long as your outward behavior respects our power, we don't care what you believe. (Here Han echoes Václav Havel's famous line in "The Power of the Powerless" about a regime that pretends much but "pretends to pretend nothing." I do not think Han has borrowed from Havel; this is a case of two sharp intellects perceiving the same thing.)

Han goes on to argue that the Party actually prefers that people not be too sincere about loving the Party. After all, where might that lead? To cleaning up corruption? To telling the truth? To the other things the Party says it wants? A person should not do such things, Han advises, "because among a bunch of people who don't believe any of this stuff and just want to use their position to get some benefits, [you are] going to stick out like a sore thumb"—and eventually come to no good end.

Some of Han's readers have wondered how such a young man—a high school dropout—could have written such penetrating observations on Chinese society and history. In 2012 some bloggers claimed that Han's writing—or at least some of it—was ghostwritten by his father, and a firestorm of controversy ensued. The accusations against Han are far-fetched, in my view. But there is an important sense in which the answer doesn't matter. The insight and wisdom of the Han Han essays are the same, regardless of who wrote them, and the immense popular response to them still says something of great importance about popular thinking in China today, regardless of where the thoughts originated. In one essay, Han Han addresses the relation between his writing and Chinese popular thought. "I don't think it's the case that my essays have influenced readers' tastes," he writes. "Rather, they have simply been consumed by readers who share the same tastes." I think Han Han is right about that, and, if he is, this is a portentous fact for the Communist Party's struggles to maintain "resilient authoritarianism." Han Han's large readership is the best evidence we have of a broad survival of common sense in China.

Liao Yiwu and Han Han both grew up in families of modest social standing, and neither had been abroad until Liao made a visit in 2010 to Germany (where he returned the next year as a political refugee). Ai

Weiwei—a sculptor, architect, installation artist, filmmaker, artistic photographer, and what might be called an "artistic activist" ("Everything is art. Everything is politics," he says)—has a different background. His father, Ai Qing, was a distinguished poet who joined the Communist Party at its revolutionary base at Yan'an in 1942. In 1957, the year Ai Weiwei was born, the Mao regime began a persecution of Ai Qing as a "Rightist" that lasted two decades. But long-standing Red pedigrees such as the Ai family's could survive Mao, and by the time the young Weiwei began his career as an artist in the late 1970s (Mao died in 1976), he could draw upon an inner confidence that derived from his family's Red legacy.

Then, between 1981 and 1993, he lived in the U.S., mostly in New York, where he attended Parson's School of Design, lived in the East Village, and was fascinated by the art of Marcel Duchamp and Andy Warhol, among others. Three decades later, Ai's own exhibitions have appeared in New York, Tokyo, Munich, Venice, Sydney, and many other places around the world. His international reputation protects him when he voices political criticism and broadens the range of what he knows he can get away with. He is the best example in China today of an explicit dissident who can avoid both jail (although he did suffer two months of detention in 2011) and exile.[3]

Ai's following inside China is smaller than Han Han's but still numbers in the millions and is stoutly loyal. Hundreds of people hand-painted 100 million bits of porcelain for a 2010 installation that Ai called *Sunflower Seeds*. When the government accused him of tax evasion in 2011, tens of thousands of people sent him the equivalent of more than one million U.S. dollars to help out. His fans pardon him even when he chooses, à la Warhol, to paint "Coca-Cola" in red across a Neolithic (5000–3000 BCE) Chinese vase.

Ai began writing blog entries in 2005 and by 2008 had crossed into explicit dissidence. He satirized the government's political exploitation of the 2008 Summer Olympics even though he had been one of the art consultants who designed the Olympic stadium called the Bird's Nest. The themes of his blog posts overlap with the thinking of Han Han and Liao

---

3. Although, beginning in 2015, Ai began a life in exile in Germany, England, and Portugal.

Yiwu. On cheap labor as the "secret" of China's economic miracle, Ai asks, "Who doesn't see the inevitable relationship between the dirt, the chaos and [the poor] to the superwide highways and the luxury shopping plazas?" On harvesting organs from executed prisoners, he remarks that the practice shows that it really is true that "everyone is born equal" in China— not during life, to be sure, but at the moment of death, when every kidney and liver becomes salable. Disgusted by a plethora of taxes, Ai makes satiric suggestions about what other taxes could be considered: these include a "sobriety tax" (in addition to the alcohol tax) on people who discover that their alcohol was fake; a noncompliance fee "for cadavers unable to discharge waste"; a "Chanting Fee" for Buddhist pilgrims, "levied for occupying intangible space"; and a "First-Time Fee" on the purchase of sex with virgin women, to be "used for the retirement pensions of women and for research on mental illness in men."

Ai's creativity seems to come in bursts. He lacks the reflective mood that allows Han Han to achieve analytic depth, and his essays are not as carefully written as Han Han's. But his intuitive eruptions sometimes yield stark, profound perceptions. On the inner malaise of China's population today, he writes:

> Years of abuse, crudeness, and wantonness have caused the people in [China's] cities to walk with a quickened pace, and to see with lifeless eyes. They have nowhere to go, and nowhere to hide.... They aren't attached to their homes, villages, or cities, and they become strangers in permanent exile.

And:

> Invisible and immeasurable psychic disasters [have taken] place deep within our psychology.... What happened? What caused the hurt? Where is the source of the shock? These questions are always avoided....

Ai's strongest work is performance art, and he is peerless at fusing art with political resistance. He films his confrontations with the police, berating them in ways no American cop would tolerate, and filming everything that happens, including, camera to camera, their filming of him. He will expose all of it on the internet. The police seem to know what he is up to and that they are bound to lose; one almost feels sorry for them. When the regime ordered that Ai's studio be bulldozed, Ai responded by calmly videotaping the bulldozing. Everything is art.

The combination of Ai's fame, his cleverness, and the internet seems too much for the police. They can—and certainly do—continue to abuse less famous dissidents, but even there Ai's example helps. Drawing on his experience, workshops for "rights defenders" include drills on how to use cell phones to transfer images to the internet as a tactic in forestalling police abuse.

Perhaps the pinnacle of Ai's politics-as-art is a photograph of himself leaping into the air, stark naked except for a stuffed animal that he holds over his genitals. The animal, famous on the Chinese internet, is a "grass mud horse"—in Chinese the word for it is *caonima*, a near homonym for "fuck your mother." The placement of the *caonima* is crucial. It "blocks the center," in Chinese *dang zhongyang*, a homonym for "Party Central." The image thus invites Ai's viewers to imagine the full sentence "Fuck your mother, Party Central." The elegance of the art is that Ai can produce this thought in viewers' minds without uttering a single syllable. To the police he can say, "You said it, not me."

"A Spring with Caonima" Credit: "Courtesy of Ai Weiwei Studio"

Will China's one-party rule, however "resilient," hold? The power of an artist like Ai Weiwei, the broad appeal of an essayist like Han Han, and the continuing growth of the internet raise important questions about the spread of dissent. But we need to remember that Han Han's readers, although they are likely the largest blog readership in the world, are still not a majority of the Chinese populace. Many young people in China today, reading state-approved textbooks and watching state-approved media, do not know the history of CCP-led disasters in China and do not understand the underlying mechanics of today's "miracle."

Older Chinese, many of whom do understand these things, have learned long ago that it is wiser to pretend that they don't. Party leaders, for their part, often argue that "you cannot do without us"—if we were to exit, chaos would follow. This disgusting argument is enough to nauseate a stone Buddha, but in an important sense it is true. After six decades of Communist Party rule, potential rivals of the Party have been so thoroughly devastated, the ground of society so thoroughly scorched, that the question "transition to what?" indeed is frightening. There may be good ideas, like those in Charter 08 that appeared a few years ago, but no institutions to implement them.

In an essay called "Speaking of Revolution," Han Han warns of the possibility that, in a post-Communist era,

> a Chinese-style leader is going to be nothing like the kind and humane person that you imagine when you sit there in front of your computer. A Chinese-style leader most likely will be arbitrary and imperious, selfish and crazy, vicious but also an effective demagogue.

For examples of "Chinese-style leaders," Han points to the White Lotus uprising (1794–1804) and the Taiping Rebellion (1850–1864), in which millenarian and egalitarian ideologies attracted followers to regimes that turned out to be hierarchical, secretive, and brutal. Han Han adds the wily line, "Hmm, yes, that does sound a bit familiar, doesn't it?" to invite readers to think of Mao as well. Han wrote this essay as the Communist "princeling" Bo Xilai, "singing Red songs" in Chongqing, was exploiting the same time-tested techniques that combine crude populist appeal with authoritarianism. The pattern has deep cultural roots, and the success of the Communists in blocking the growth of modern institutions in education, media, and law leaves the nation still highly vulnerable to what grows from those roots.

In a 2006 essay, Liu Xiaobo wonders whether "the Communists [will]

succeed in once again leading China down a disastrously mistaken historical road." No one—certainly not Liu—wishes this. But it is far more possible than most people in the West assume.

Originally published in *The New York Review of Books*,
October 24, 2013

Seeing the CCP Clearly

(2021)

IN A SPEECH at the Republican National Convention in August, 2020, Chen Guangcheng, a blind, iron-willed human rights lawyer and dissident from China whom the Obama administration brought to the United States in 2012, said:

> Standing up to tyranny is not easy. I know. When I spoke out against China's One Child Policy and other injustices, I was persecuted, beaten, sent to prison, and put under house arrest....
>
> The CCP is an enemy of humanity. It is terrorizing its own people and it is threatening the well-being of the world.... The United States must use its values of freedom, democracy, and the rule of law to gather a coalition of other democracies to stop the CCP's aggression. President Trump has led on this, and we need the other countries to join him in this fight—a fight for our future.

Within hours, Teng Biao, an old friend of Chen's who is also a Chinese human rights lawyer based in the U.S., tweeted, "I completely oppose what he is doing." Teng, too, is a veteran of persecution, beating, and imprisonment at the hands of the CCP, and he would not disagree with what Chen said about the CCP. What he opposed was Chen's bow to Donald Trump. "For Chinese human rights defenders, there is zero logical consistency to supporting Trump," Teng tweeted.

The split between the two friends is a small example of a wider disagreement between "Trump boosters" and "Trump critics" in the Chinese dissident community. The rift is plainly visible both inside and outside China and is likely to persist in one form or another into the Biden years.

Its causes have little to do with basic value judgments. Neither side approves of putting Uyghurs into concentration camps in Xinjiang, of crushing democracy in Hong Kong, of installing hundreds of millions of surveillance cameras across China, or of any of the many other symptoms of the CCP's obsession with power. And neither side sees much to distinguish in the political instincts of Trump and Xi Jinping. Xi controls the press in his country and Trump would do so if he could; each labels his critics "enemies of the people"; both imagine (and Xi succeeds in) locking up opponents; each contemplates (and Xi achieves) abolishing term limits for himself; both demand loyalty from subordinates; and both surround themselves with yes-men. One online wit in China, using indirection that is common on the Chinese internet, noted that Trump had, however barely, been voted into office in the U.S. while Xi, in China, had not, and then offered the arch observation that the most crucial similarity between the two men is that neither is the elected representative of China.

Trump critics in China include the distinguished legal scholars He Weifang and Zhang Qianfan, who have a sophisticated grasp of why much of his behavior is intrinsically antidemocratic and how it damages both U.S. democracy and prospects for democracy elsewhere in the world. But among dissidents generally, both inside and outside China, Trump supporters outnumber Trump critics, and it is important to understand why. It is not because they are a far-right fringe. In ideological terms, they are closer to classic liberals on a U.S. political spectrum.

They are "pro-Trump" because they feel that for decades U.S. administrations have been naïve about the CCP, and they see Trump as the first U.S. president to stand up to it. His tariffs on Chinese goods, imposed in mid-2018 in retaliation for what he saw as unfair trade practices, appear to have sprung from a blunt "America first" impulse, not from an intention to weaken the CCP domestically, as dissidents would have preferred. Still, he imposed them, which marks a clear contrast to George H.W. Bush's tolerance of the Tiananmen massacre of June 4, 1989, for the sake of "the relationship"; Bill Clinton's about-face in separating trade from human rights; George W. Bush's ushering China into the World Trade Organization; Barack Obama's launch of his China policy with the assurance that human rights would not "interfere" with trade, climate change, or security; and other examples of U.S. government indulgence of the CCP. Standing up to the Chinese government for any reason seemed to dissidents a long-awaited turn of events, and enough to outweigh all the drawbacks of Trump's character and other policies.

In late October Yu Jie, a well-known Chinese dissident who now lives in the U.S., published the names of ninety-seven critics of the CCP from China, Hong Kong, Taiwan, and overseas whom he judged, by what they had said publicly, to be either critics or boosters of Trump. In supplementing Yu's list with some inquiries of my own, I was surprised to find how many Chinese freethinkers were pro-Trump.

In addition to Chen Guangcheng and Yu Jie himself, they include some remarkable figures. Cai Xia is a retired professor of CCP ideology at the Central Party School in Beijing who, because of her criticisms of Xi Jinping, left the upper levels of the CCP and now lives in exile in the U.S. She told an online chat group that she found ordinary Americans ingenuously truthful, and "that, of course, is a good thing. But it also has its negative side: Americans are simple and just don't grasp the evil of the CCP regime." Wang Dan, a prominent student leader of the 1989 Tiananmen demonstrations, has noted that the recent imprisonment of the dissident publishing magnate Jimmy Lai and other CCP resisters in Hong Kong is likely a test of the Biden administration: a lack of response will be a sign of a return to pre-Trump appeasement policies.

He Qinglian, whose book *China's Pitfall* was the first to reveal how China's economic boom was funneling huge sums of ill-gotten money into the pockets of the political elite in the 1990s, and Liao Yiwu, who has also been reviewed, published, and interviewed here, are both Trump supporters. So are Li Jianglin, author of the splendid book *Tibet in Agony*; Liu Junning, a major figure in the Charter 08 movement; Liu Suli, manager of All Saints Book Grove, Beijing's beloved (and precariously surviving) bookstore; Hu Ping and Su Xiaokang, distinguished critics who have lived in U.S. exile for decades; and Shi Tao, a poet from Hunan who in 2004 had forwarded to friends in New York a government order to make no public mention of the fifteenth anniversary of the Tiananmen massacre. He was charged with "revealing state secrets" and sent to prison for eight and a half years after Yahoo revealed his identity to the CCP.

In short, it would be a mistake to write off dissident Chinese Trump boosters as poorly educated or ill informed. They are not, and their views on the reluctance of Western democracies to stand up to dictatorships have roots that go much deeper than the Trump presidency.

Fifteen years ago Liu Xiaobo, the winner of the 2010 Nobel Peace Prize, wrote a set of articles that he called "The Four Big Mistakes of the Free Countries in the Twentieth Century." How, asked Liu, who died a political prisoner in 2017, could Western intellectuals in the 1930s have been enamored of Stalin? Why did Britain and France compromise so easily with dictators in Germany and Italy? After World War II, why did America and Britain concede so much to the Soviet Union? In the 1960s and 1970s, how could leading European intellectuals have caught "Mao Zedong fever," and how could that fever have lasted so long?

Especially galling to Liu was the claim of Western intellectuals to be speaking, through Mao, for ordinary people—the downtrodden, the underdogs, "the masses." In fact, they were doing the very opposite: they were siding with the oppressors. In 1989, when the Soviet empire collapsed, the West heaved a sigh that "the Cold War is over." Over? What about China, North Korea, Vietnam, Cuba? Why does the West not see some parts of the world?

U.S. policy has not just overlooked dictatorship in China; it has aided the growth of CCP power. Within days of the Tiananmen massacre, despite international sanctions on Beijing, President Bush secretly sent emissaries to assure CCP leaders that he wanted to maintain good relations. While Congress was extracting its annual human rights concessions from Beijing in return for "most favored nation" trade terms in the early 1990s, President Clinton, under pressure from Wall Street, abruptly "de-linked" trade and human rights in 1994. U.S. capital and technology (some of it purloined) began to drive a boom in Chinese manufacturing for export.

With U.S. support, China joined the World Trade Organization in 2001 and secured billions in World Bank loans, helping its economy to take another leap. In 2005 Robert Zoellick, a U.S. Deputy Secretary of State, gave a widely reported speech in which he said that the CCP might become a "responsible stakeholder" in the world system. To Chinese dissidents, the speech revealed more about American naiveté than about what could be expected of the CCP.

Unfortunately, Zoellick was not unusual among westerners. In capitals on both sides of the Atlantic, a faith grew that "they will come to be like us." At the spectacular Beijing Olympics in 2008, Joshua Ramo of the consulting firm Kissinger Associates, which was long a proponent of "engagement" with the CCP, predicted that China was "a nation about to put a match to the fuse of a rocket." He made no mention of the hundreds of thousands of ordinary people who had been forced from their homes to assure that the great Olympic salute to the CCP looked as perfect as possible. Barack Obama, whose image among Chinese dissidents was generally good, said publicly in 2015 that the CCP's antipoverty program was "one of the most remarkable achievements in human history." He did not acknowledge that the Great Leap agricultural disaster of 1959–1962, which thrust hundreds of millions of people into dire poverty (and killed at least 30 million), was a direct result of CCP policies as well as the most direct cause of the poverty that later needed to be alleviated.

For decades the work of managing the U.S. relationship with China fell, on the U.S. side, to a small group of specialists in government and academia, whose approach was remarkably consistent across both Democratic and Republican administrations. Their first principle was that "the relationship" must survive, and "the other side" in the relationship was limited to their formal interlocutors, who were duty-bound representatives of the CCP. These experts gave speeches in which terms like "China" or "the Chinese view" referred exclusively to a very few people at the top of the regime. The Americans were indeed expert in the study of that elite but not well versed in Chinese language, culture, and society more broadly. Beijing knew how to use these Americans to impose its view that the U.S. must respect the "core interests of China" (that is, interests that directly or indirectly affected the CCP's power), failing which, the relationship would be in jeopardy. Only the U.S., not the CCP, could endanger it, in this framing.

Trump's demotion of this China policy elite is one reason why Chinese dissidents have come to favor him. Under Trump, with China advisers like Miles Yu at the State Department and Matthew Pottinger at the White House, it seemed that people in the U.S. government were finally beginning to understand the CCP. Pottinger, who is from Boston, learned Chinese unusually well in the mid-1990s and, as a China correspondent for Reuters and *The Wall Street Journal* from 1998 to 2005, was a quick study in how the CCP goes about things. In 2005 he joined the marines for five years and was deployed to Iraq and Afghanistan; in 2017 he joined the National Security staff at the White House, where his intelligence showed not only in China policy but in his ability to get things done without getting fired (he resigned on January 7, in response to the attack on the Capitol).

Yu left China in 1985 at age twenty-three to study at Swarthmore and then got a Ph.D. in history at Berkeley. After the 1989 massacre, he began editing a newsletter called *China Forum* that exposed the methods of the CCP as trenchantly as any publication I have seen before or since. He is a professor of history at the Naval Academy, from which he took leave to serve in the State Department.

In an interview with Voice of America on November 16, 2020, Yu pointed out three departures in China policy that the Trump State Department had launched. One was to stop using "CCP" and "China" as synonyms. The point was not to stick fingers in Beijing's eyes at a linguistic level; it was to wean Americans from the bad habit of thinking of China and the CCP as the same thing. Only when the distinction is clear can one begin to understand the damage that the CCP has done to China. A second change concerned "engagement," the name of a strategy that the China-expert group had long promoted. According to the engagement theory, exchange in commerce, education, tourism, and other areas would induce the CCP to adopt international norms, but the result was that considerable influence began flowing in the opposite direction. The CCP has made inroads in Western media, industry, finance, research, education, personal data collection, and other areas, and that sort of engagement had to be opposed.

Third, agreements with the CCP needed to be "results oriented." For many years, the CCP had been using the negotiating tactic of shelving urgent questions, like North Korean denuclearization or Iran sanctions, by saying they needed more study, more consultation, and more time—until the U.S. finally grew tired of waiting and just accepted the result that there would be no result. We don't do that anymore, Yu said.

Puzzled Chinese democrats have wondered why U.S. policymakers have indulged the CCP to the extent that they have over the years. For the business community, the reasons are not hard to understand. A large, inexpensive, and captive labor force was naturally attractive to American manufacturers, as was the lure of potentially huge markets. Cross the CCP and these prizes might disappear. But why, Chinese democrats ask, is it so easy to set political ideals aside? Is there something that prevents Westerners from seeing that the CCP resembles their own mafias more than it does their governments? Why should Western liberals show respect for a thuggish regime? Do the pretty labels "socialist" and "People's" fool them?

About a decade ago the word *baizuo* appeared on the Chinese internet. Highly derogatory, it means literally "white people on the left" who unwittingly betray the ideals of Western civilization. Jean-Paul Sartre, who visited China in the 1950s, was an early example. Sartre excoriated Western imperialism and wrote about the beauty he perceived in Mao's China even as Mao was tyrannizing millions. Does *baizuo* thinking, some have wondered, help to explain why Westerners still can't see the CCP for what it is? Why do Americans, who are eloquent when they denounce human rights abuses in their own country, apply different standards when abuses happen in countries that call themselves "socialist"?

Chinese critics of *baizuo* are not uniformly harsh. Louisa Chiang, an American from Taiwan who has worked closely with mainland dissidents for decades, wrote to me:

> A lot [of *baizuo* thinking] is well-intentioned, and liberals are just as entitled to the kind interpretation and allowances that all should receive. But this is to remind them that their power can do even more good, and that they could gain even more insights, if they were to truly heed third-world voices. Open their hearts and listen hard. It might advance their domestic agenda and make unexpected international accomplishments in their fight against any and all imperialism.

Chiang and others are annoyed when they see Western liberals condescend to Chinese victims, whom they assume are less qualified to make political judgments than they themselves are.

Chen Guangcheng came to the U.S. in 2012 with the help of both the law program at New York University and a Christian group in Texas called ChinaAid. He brought with him a formidable record of making his own political decisions, and yet somehow people in both his host groups expected him to accept their tutelage in how to behave politically in the U.S. Later, when Chen turned out to be a Trump booster, some observers became even more confident that what he most needed was political guidance: Chinese people have grown up in a repressive society, after all, where awareness of rights is weak, so it is understandable that they are easy prey for charlatans like Trump. But in viewing matters this way, Americans in effect attribute greater powers of judgment to CCP leaders than to CCP critics. While the critics apparently need advice in choosing between Democrats and Republicans, CCP bosses like Hu Jintao and Xi Jinping, when given the choice to join the world as "responsible stakeholders," can be trusted to make the right decision (until, it turns out, they do not).

Up to a point, dissidents can accept this sort of criticism from Western liberals; struggles with the toxin of authoritarian thinking have often been part of their own experience. Liu Xiaobo wrote in 2003 that "it may take me a lifetime to rid myself of the poison." After they survive the ordeal, however, they emerge with an understanding that is deeper than that of the leisured bystanders who mean them well. They need no pity. They find it strange that veteran dissidents like Liu Binyan, Fang Lizhi, Hu Ping, and Su Xiaokang, who could have been of immense help to Washington in understanding the CCP, lived in the U.S. for decades without ever being consulted.

Many have told me they find it hard to understand how the price their nation has paid, and continues to pay, goes largely unnoticed in the West. Why are the lessons that the West has learned in opposing dictators like Hitler, Mussolini, and Stalin so difficult to apply to China? Will things be different now that the CCP is shifting its power grabs outward? Will the West be ready? Or is the West already trending in an authoritarian direction? A friend inside China asked me—jokingly, but with a serious point— if the censors working for Twitter were Chinese immigrants. "They have the expertise," she quipped, and added, "When a person in the U.S. says something not politically correct, the response to him seems to be not only to reject it automatically but to begin examining his motive. How Maoist!"

Freedom of expression has been a major issue between supporters and critics of Trump. Xiao Shu, a journalist who has long struggled, mostly in vain, for media freedom in China, cringes to hear a U.S. president refer to the press as the "enemy of the people." Does he know how those words have been used elsewhere in the world—or care? Wang Tiancheng, the author of a book on how China can transition to democracy, writes that China's Trump boosters present "a huge problem: they put passing policy advantages ahead of principles of democratic constitutionalism."

Pro-Trumpers can concede some of these points and still say that things must be kept in perspective. New, perhaps short-lived, improvements in

Washington's China policy are better than no improvements at all, which is what we have been living with for decades, and a U.S.-style democracy, even if damaged, is immeasurably better than what China has. Take the question of lying. Does Trump lie? Yes. Does the CCP's Department of Propaganda (later renamed the Department of Publicity) lie? Su Xiaokang gently told me that the question is naive. The CCP system, he explained, has an entirely different way of measuring the value of statements. Truth and falsity are incidental. A statement is valuable if its "social effects" are "good," and the effects count as good if they support the power interests of the CCP. (For politically innocuous matters like weather reports or basketball scores, support of the Party does not apply, but avoidance of harm to the Party still does.) Hence a "good" statement might be true, half-true, or untrue—and it is beside the point.

A tendency toward including truth does become relevant when someone judges that a statement will influence people more effectively if a bit of verisimilitude is supplied. But truth is never the first criterion, and in that sense neither is lying. American democracy's headache over a president who lies is a fundamentally different problem from that of China living under the CCP's propaganda apparatus, whose roots date from the 1940s and whose experts by now are very good at what they do.

Readers of the Western press, whether aware of it or not, have seen examples of that expertise. In the run-up to the 2008 Beijing Olympics, the international wing of the Xinhua News Agency instituted frequent use of the phrase "lifted from poverty." This was what "China" (meaning the CCP) had done for hundreds of millions of Chinese people. The world's media—*The New York Times*, *The Wall Street Journal*, Reuters, Al Jazeera, Kyodo News, the BBC, and many others—picked up the phrase, as did Western politicians on both the left and the right. The World Bank used it in official reports. Those words were, in short, highly successful in achieving the intended effect: the world came to believe that the CCP was doing great good.

A more transparent account of what it had done, beginning in the 1980s and 1990s, is that it released its controls on the Chinese people so that, for the first time in decades, they could make money for themselves; hundreds of millions responded by working long hours at low wages without the protection of labor unions, workers' compensation insurance, a free press, or independent courts; and, yes, they made great amounts of money, escaping poverty for themselves and simultaneously catapulting the CCP elite, who still rode high above them, to truly spectacular wealth.

In short, the word "lifted" begs analysis of who lifted whom. That question did not normally occur to people around the world who read the words "China lifted." The grammar of such sentences, combined with the formula China = CCP, left no need for a question. Was this word-engineering deliberate? Anyone who doubts that it was should note that CCP media used the "China lifted" phrase in publications in English, French, German, and other foreign languages but not in Chinese-language media at home. That made good sense. What would happen if the CCP started telling the Chinese people "We lifted you"? The people would know better. Both sides know better. To make such an assertion might generate unfortunate "social effects," such as a greater number of demonstrations, strikes, sit-ins, roadblocks, and other examples of what the Ministry of Public Security labels "masses incidents" and counts in the tens of thousands per year.

When debate between Chinese Trump critics and Trump boosters heats up, attention sometimes shifts (although not really more than in political debates elsewhere) away from issues and toward personal attacks. The boosters say the critics are too close to Western liberals, from whom they have learned their anti-Trump talking points, and that this shows an inappropriate subordination of China's struggles to the political battles in America. They further claim that the Trump critics exert a gentle form of moral blackmail that says, essentially, "If you people don't denounce Trump you must be racist, fascist, and misogynist." That pressure, they say, again conjures the Mao era, when people were asked to search their souls and examine their thoughts until they arrived at public expression of "correct" views.

As Trump leaves the scene and Biden forms his foreign policy team, how realistic will its grasp of the CCP be? It would be not just a gesture of bipartisanship but a brilliant inoculation against backsliding into naiveté if Biden were to recall Yu or Pottinger or both to service in his administration. Yet it's hard to see that happening. At stake is not just the question of U.S. policy toward China but the logically prior question of whether the CCP is accurately seen for what it is.

Originally published in *The New York Review of Books*,
February 11, 2021

Sixty Years of China-Watching

(2023)

A s XI JINPING seeks a partial return to Mao, Western journalists and scholars have sometimes wondered whether we are returning full circle to the 1960s, when China was closed and we had to study it from a distance. There is much to fear in China's current trajectory, to be sure, but a return to square one in China-watching should not be a major worry. Both the watchers and China itself have changed too much for that.

We tend to forget that during the 1960s the U.S. officially sent more people to the moon than it did to China. In that era, the "People's Republic" under Mao Zedong seemed not only other-worldly but quasi-metaphysical, something constructed in the mind based only on whiskers of evidence. China seemed like Shangri-la. My own first in-person glimpse came in fall 1966, when friends in Hong Kong brought me to peer over the colony's northern border at Shenzhen (then a farming village, now the fourth largest city in China). I counted myself lucky to spot a water buffalo.

Among Westerners, only a few privileged travelers were allowed to enter. Han Suyin, a Chinese-Belgian who wrote fiction and memoirs, and Felix Greene, a British journalist (and cousin of Graham Greene) were among them, and to those of us on the outside, thirsting from afar, the words of such writers glowed—not only because of their scarcity but because they were uplifting. They attested that Shangri-la was real. In retrospect, one can blame the authors for not mentioning the rain of executions during land reform in the early 1950s or the immense, mind-boggling famine of 1959–62—but that would be unfair. Traveling with government guides, they were sealed off from such facts. They took rosy façades at face value in the same way that I, on the outside, took their rosy words at face value. Our mistakes were similar.

China opened wider during the four years after Mao's death in 1976. Western journalists who worked mostly from Hong Kong could now move to Beijing. Fox Butterfield opened a bureau for *The New York Times* in Beijing, Richard Bernstein went there for *Time*, Melinda Liu for *Newsweek*, and Jay and Linda Mathews for *The Washington Post* and *The Los Angeles Times*, respectively. These and other writers produced books that not only went deeper than the China journalism of the Mao era but were much more expansive in scope. For readers, the effect was like moving from street stalls to supermarkets.

In the 1980s, Western graduate students and scholars could stay in China for months or full years, using libraries and archives and sometimes even conducting surveys or doing field work. It made an important difference to be able to sink into life. I spent the academic year 1979–80 in Beijing and Guangzhou studying contemporary Chinese literature and noticed that I learned much more in the second half of the year than in the first. In that, I was not unusual. Sinking in paid compound interest.

The early 1980s were when I learned that "dissident" writers (like Liu Binyan, author of the earth-shaking exposé "People or Monsters?"), although in one sense at the fringes of society, were actually the ones telling the most truth about its core. It was precisely because they dared to address the core that they were pushed to the fringes. Writers who flourished in the mainstream did so by not looking at it.

The shock of the June Fourth massacre in 1989 put a temporary stop to Western scholarly exchange with China and made working conditions for international journalists considerably more difficult. During the next two decades, though, under the regimes of Jiang Zemin and Hu Jintao, foreign scholars and journalists returned to China and conditions became more regularized. Journalists grew accustomed to the rules that they had to work under as well as to the ways and the risks of circumventing them. Scholarly exchange moved away from centralized national programs toward ties between individual scholars and their laboratories.

In the Xi Jinping era, which began in 2012, the CCP continued its quest to harvest technical know-how from the West, but intellectual exchange in all other areas declined. Xi, a "second-generation red," came to power well-schooled in the skullduggery one needs in order to rise within the CCP system but otherwise narrow of vision, wanting in charisma, and educated only to the junior-high level. He felt that the China he inherited from Hu Jintao was sufficiently precarious that he needed to *do something*. But what? Unable to envision other alternatives, he turned to the only model he knew, which was the Mao model. (His only significant departure from Mao was to offer himself as an avatar of the great and ancient Chinese civilization, which Mao derided, in his later years, as "the four olds.")

And so it happened that the trappings of a Great Leader fell again upon the Chinese people. Power was re-concentrated into the hands of a single man while panoply and verbiage that idolized the great leader returned: Xi Jinping Thought, Collected Works, a New Era, "Core" leadership, and so on. In 2023, the National People's Congress elected Xi to a third term by a margin of 2952 to 0. Even the rhythms of slogans from the Mao era have been resuscitated. (Lin Biao's famous 1967 instruction to Red Guards, "Read Chairman Mao's Works, Obey Chairman Mao's Words, Carry Out Chairman Mao's Directives" returned verbatim—only with "Xi" now replacing "Mao".) For Western China-watchers the turn back toward Mao was magnified by how they themselves were treated: visas denied, travel constrained, informants intimidated. Hence the sense of circling back.

But China-writing and China are both quite different now. A few Western writers (Daniel Bell and Martin Jacques come to mind) still do consistently figure out how to defend Beijing, despite the intellectual contortion that the exercise requires. But even they do not gaze toward Xi Jinping with the sense of wonder and awe that Mao Zedong inspired fifty years ago. Today, a Westerner might feel frustrated to be denied a visa; back then, the very thought of one glowed in the dark like the tail of a firefly. In those days information arrived from China in drips; now information and online commentary are a roiling river.

More important, China itself is different. In Mao's day, information in all public media (blackboards, loudspeakers, meetings, radio, magazines, school curricula, books) flowed unidirectionally from the top down. An individual's "platform" was limited to the reach of his or her unamplified voice, and, in the worst of times, it was dangerous to say what one thought even within family. Today, there are internet and messaging platforms galore, and you can mock Xi Jinping at will so long as you do it privately and without an organization. But at the same time, the CCP has invested immensely to monitor and intimidate people electronically, and the result might eventually become (who knows?) an asphyxiating technofascism that exceeds even what George Orwell imagined. I am not arguing that things are rosier now, only that they are different.

Consider this example: on March 5, 1970, teachers in Beijing were instructed to bring schoolchildren to the Workers' Stadium in Beijing's Chaoyang District to witness the execution, by bullet to the back of the head, of Yu Luoke, a twenty-seven-year-old writer who had dared to criticize the Communist Party. On June 15, 2023, in that same stadium, an eighteen-year-old Chinese soccer fan ran onto the playing field to embrace the Argentinian star Lionel Messi. Pursued by security, the youngster circled the field, outrunning the less fit agents. The crowd cheered him on, chanting "*niubi! niubi!*" (roughly, in English, "fricking awesome!"). In no dream could a crowd in the Mao era have done that.

Xi and Mao both sought uniformity of thought, but they achieved very different results. Under Mao, people usually believed what they were shouting; under Xi, they are often protecting their interests through outward performance. In 2002, Liu Xiaobo wrote a pungent essay called "A Nation that Lies to Its Conscience" in which he observes how Jiang Zemin drew on Maoist language to enforce society-wide "unity" against Falun Gong. Jiang achieved the unity only in appearance, but that was all he needed. From the ruler's perspective, a populace afraid to say that it does not hate Falun Gong is just as good as one that does hate Falun Gong. Liu ends his essay asking which is more frightening—a regime that imposes uniform thought or one that demands uniform lies?

Is Xi Jinping aware that his popular support is, in Liu Xiaobo's sense, hollow? There can be no doubt that he is. Why else would his government spend enormous sums of money on "stability maintenance" that includes fine-grained monitoring of people, even an elderly matriarch like Ding Zilin? Xi's insecurity is as visible at the top of his power pyramid as at the bottom. Does a leader who has confidence need to stand at the center of resplendent panoply and declaim "I am confident!"?

Still, there are some constants between 1949 and now. For both Mao and Xi, the Party's grip on power, and their own grips on personal power, have been the highest priorities. Ideology, the economy, Taiwan, historical legacy, and other issues are secondary. This priority will not change; it is an axiom of the system.

Constant, too, is a condition of the society that foreign observers seldom notice even though it is huge and has always been present. It is that people's lives are filled with quotidian concerns—food, family, health, the weather, and so on—not Xi Jinping Thought, the wicked Falun Gong, or the like. When an ordinary citizen does have a political thought, it is more likely to be about how to handle bullying by a local official. The seam that separates the bottom-up lives of people and the top-down interests of the state was present in Mao's China and has remained present ever since.

The seam also exists in individual minds, from those of ordinary people to those of the highest officials. The two questions "How do I perform properly within the system?" and "How do I get what I want?" seldom have the same answer. The two modes of calculation exist in parallel, and with time and custom, their co-existence comes to seem utterly normal.

Far too often, Western writers on contemporary China have passed along the official language of the CCP as what "China" wants or thinks. In Henry Kissinger's 630-page book *On China*, it is hard to get a sense that the author even knows that indigenous thought in China exists, let alone what it contains. The covers of other recent books by Westerners often advertise that their authors have lived in China for years or have made dozens of trips there—and yet, usually, the writing inside looks only at one side of the seam. As the Chinese cliché puts it, the authors "scratch the itch from outside the boot." Of course, it is better for a China analyst to travel to China than not to, but the frequent failure to get inside the boot suggests that more than visa denials are barring the way.

Language is a major barrier. Books on China are often written by analysts—Kissinger is not alone here—who read only in English translation and do interviews through interpreters or with English-speaking Chinese officials. It is hard to describe in brief what a world of difference is made for the China-watchers who can listen, read, speak, and think in Chinese. We might ask who gets closer—the writer in Beijing interviewing in English or the one in New Zealand reading in Chinese? Since the 1950s, the Western China-watchers who have been best at "crossing the seam," so to speak, have been good at Chinese language. Father Laszlo Ladany—whose *China News Analysis* appeared between 1953 and 1982—scoured the official CCP press and, as the Chinese writer Wu Zuxiang put it, could read it "upside-down." If Ladany read that heroic PLA soldiers rescued thirteen miners near Hefei, he knew there had likely been a catastrophic mine collapse near Hefei. Later, Simon Leys, followed by Geremie Barmé and Michael

Schoenhals, showed how entering the world of Chinese language could make very large differences.

Since the late 1980s, China-watching in the West has underused the native-Chinese talent that has resided abroad. Miles Yu, who recently served as principal China policy and planning adviser at the U.S. Department of State, was the first and so far only exception within the U.S. government. Before him, PRC exiles like Liu Binyan, Hu Ping, Su Xiaokang, and Yan Jiaqi were almost entirely overlooked by American government and journalism. Part of the problem was that their English was limited; but the other part was that the China-watching field, whose culture has been dominated by English-speaking scratchers-of-the-boot, did not welcome them.

The growing attention paid to Xiao Qiang's *China Digital Times* and to such fluid writers of English as Zha Jianying, Fan Jiayang, Cheng Yang-yang, and others give us hope that this bias may be on the way out. The English-language fiction of Ha Jin, although imaginative in part, gets us deep into the region on the other side of the seam—as do translations of the autobiographies of Ai Weiwei and Fang Lizhi. Writers who come out of Chinese culture pick up on things that Westerners miss. The Song poet Su Shi had a point when he wrote, "When the river turns warm in spring, the ducks are first to know."

I doubt that the Chinese people I have mentioned in the previous paragraph would feel very comfortable with the label "China watcher." The term suggests a view from a distance and one that concentrates on government policies, and it is precisely transcendence of that viewpoint that makes culturally-imbued Chinese views so valuable. The terms "China expert" and "China analyst" have similar problems, to say nothing of "old China hand" (which was still alive when I first went to Hong Kong in 1966). In Chinese, when Chinese people refer to a Westerner as a *Zhongguotong* 中国通 "one who knows China through and through," the point is almost always ironic. It is either a gentle put-down or a joke. Everybody knows that it is impossible for a Westerner to get to the bottom of knowing China.

While reviewing six decades of writing on China by Westerners, we might also note how Chinese views of the West have shifted. In 1950, with the Korean War, Mao launched a "Resist America and Aid Korea" campaign, and in the years that followed he continued to denounce American imperialism. Yet it is unclear how deeply that attitude sank into ordinary

Chinese life. Beginning about a hundred years before then, America had already been *Meiguo* "the beautiful country." The term originated not from the idea of beauty but because of the second syllable in the word A*meri*ca, but homonyms carry weight in Chinese culture, so the sound itself was a fortuitous start for the American image. Moreover, by the late 1970s, the U.S. had become the go-to example in China of what "modernization" looked like. In the 1980s I had to work hard to persuade young Chinese that the U.S. had flaws.

But in recent years a tide of anti-Americanism has appeared. Some of it is state-sponsored. Two decades ago, the CCP began paying people fifty cents a post to publish anti-American comments on the internet. Prisoners could earn perks and even early release for such work. But other anti-Western vitriol, based in a feeling of national pride and of rivalry with (not hatred of) the West, is heartfelt. An example was the nationwide uproar in April 2023 after BMW, at a car show in Shanghai, was caught on videotape apparently giving free ice cream to foreigners but not to Chinese.

At a deeper level, some Chinese intellectuals who had long seen the U.S. as a model for democracy have felt some disillusionment. The insurrection at the U.S. capitol on January 6, 2020 made the foundations of American democracy seem less iron-clad than before, and the insistence on political correctness pressed by an elite reminded others of the Cultural Revolution. The idea of an external pressure that says "you have to believe X and if you don't you need to look inside yourself to find the reason why and then confess and then correct yourself" was chilling.

In short, Chinese discoveries of the West during the post-Mao years have sometimes been as blinkered as Western views of China. Both sides have drawn too much from their own contexts in imagining nature of the other. But this is natural, and we should not be discouraged. Western writing on Communist China, while still flawed, is immensely better today than it was sixty years ago. The moon has regained its lead as the lesser-known terrain.

Originally published in the inaugural issue of *China Books Review*, October 2023

LEARNING

Dawn in China

⟡

(2011)

THE FIRST TIME I tried to go to China was in 1967, the year after I graduated from college. Rosy images of an ideal Chinese socialism were in my head, largely from magazines like *China Reconstructs* and Western writers like Felix Greene. I was living in Hong Kong, on a fellowship from Harvard, and wrote a plea to Beijing. A few months later I received a charming reply: two sheets of paper that appeared as if a Red Guard with weak English and a faulty typewriter had spent days laboring over them, composing a letter in which it was explained that the Chinese people had nothing against me, but that I was from a predatory imperialist country and could not visit the People's Republic. Before I left Hong Kong I bought four volumes of *The Selected Works of Mao Zedong*, and, grandiloquently, ripped the covers off of them so that I might carry them safely back to the imperialist U.S.

Meanwhile, though, I found a corner of Hong Kong that was still legally part of China, and I settled for going there. The "walled city of Kowloon," formerly an outpost of the Qing empire, had been abandoned for decades by both Nationalists and Communists and had been disowned by the British as well. It had become a fetid labyrinth of alleys and tunnels, the lawless bailiwick, I was told, of drug dealers, prostitutes, and gangsters. A group of Baptists ran a primary school there—and yes, there were children. I volunteered to teach English at the school. I knew this wasn't socialist China, but it was "China."

The first time I set foot in socialist China was May of 1973. A year earlier, in April 1972, a Chinese Ping Pong Delegation had visited the U.S. to break the diplomatic ice of twenty-three years, and I had served as an interpreter traveling with the Chinese and American teams. Chinese officials on that tour got a good political impression of me, in part because I led four of the six American interpreters in a boycott of the teams' meeting with President Richard Nixon at the White House. (Nixon had ordered a bombing of Haiphong just the day before; to me, small talk in the Rose Garden just didn't seem right that day.)

A year later, we U.S. interpreters asked if we could visit China, and the answer was yes. Over four weeks, we visited Guangzhou, Shanghai, Suzhou, Xi'an, Yan'an, Beijing, and Tangshan. The bill for the trip—room, board, airfare, rail, sightseeing, everything—was five hundred and fifty USD. A "friendship" rate.

But it was during that trip that cracks began to form in my ideal image of the People's Republic. I carried a small camera and took walks on my own, in search of "real life." I had learned in graduate school that there were no flies in China after the "Four Pests" campaign of 1958. When I saw a fly on a white stone table in Suzhou, I photographed it. I thought I had a real find.

In Yan'an, when four of us foreign guests boarded a crowded bus the driver shouted "*waibin!*" ("foreign guests!"). Immediately four seated passengers stood up, offering us their seats. The old man who stood up next to me did not, in my impression, seem to want to. I said, "Please, you sit," but he said nothing and remained standing. Embarrassed, I remained standing, too, and for the rest of the ride the people on the bus endured the ludicrous spectacle of an empty seat on a crowded bus.

We foreigners always rode "soft sleeper" class on the railroad, while most people on the same trains were riding "hard seat" class. I asked our guide about it.

"Why is there a soft-sleeper class?" I asked, my socialist principles in mind. "Who rides in it, besides us?"

"The leaders," the guide replied.

"Why?" I asked, unaware that it was a stupid question.

"They are busy. They have many burdens. They need soft-sleeper."

My image of a classless society had suffered a blow, and it suffered a few more before the tour was over. The example that sticks most in my mind happened in Tangshan, where we visited the huge Tangshan coal mine. We descended by elevator far beneath the earth's surface. (This was three years before a Richter 7.8 earthquake buried countless workers in that same mine.) Riding small railroad cars through a maze of tunnels deep underground, I noticed various signs: "slow!", "sound horn!", etc. The signs were in traditional Chinese characters, not simplified ones, and I also couldn't help noticing that there were no political slogans among them. All the signs were bluntly practical. This contrasted sharply with the surface of the earth, where slogans and quotations from Chairman Mao, on splendid red-and-white banners, or giant red billboards with gold writing and trim, were everywhere.

After emerging, I asked our guide: "Why are there no quotations from Chairman Mao down there with the miners?"

Her immediate reply: "Oh, it's too dirty!"

She seemed a bit irritated at me for suggesting such an inappropriate location for the Chairman's thoughts. To me, though, it was a hard fact to swallow: the dirt of the mines was OK for the working class but not for the thoughts of its leader?

The inner insecurity of the guides became apparent to me in something that happened in Hangzhou, when I bought a souvenir of my trip for my mother. My mother was born on a farm in Nebraska and was a salt-of-the-earth type. Her name was Beulah, she ate wheat germ, and brown was her favorite color. In a small shop I found hand-brooms that I knew she would like. They were crafted of sorghum stalks, light brown with dark flecks. Lovely. And symbols of the dignity of labor—which I knew she also would like. I imagined that she might hang it on a wall in her home, so I bought one.

Afterwards one of our guides, very nervous, approached me. He seemed torn between handling an emergency and trying to maintain politeness.

"Why did you buy this?!" he asked.

I explained about my mother.

"Let me get you a better one!" He took the broom back to the shop and returned with another—not much better or worse, to my eye, but in his view more nearly perfect. Then, sitting next to me on the mini-bus ride back to our hotel, he began a deeper interrogation.

"Doesn't your mother like silk? ...China has silk. China has jade carvings, China has cloisonné. Why do you buy a farmer's broom to represent China to your mother?" I began to realize that the guide saw what I had done as "unfriendly." He saw my mother and me as looking down on China.

This set me wondering: did this guide, deep inside, respect China's working people, the wielders of brooms—and want my mother to have the impression that "China is silk" only because he guessed that she, from a bourgeois society, would respect silk but not brooms? Or was it maybe worse than that? Was he participating in a societal hypocrisy that pretended to value brooms over silk but in reality did not?

From time to time during the trip I tried to strike up conversations with ordinary citizens, people with whom meetings had not been arranged. This was not easy. Foreigners were rare sights in China at the time, and people constantly formed crowds to look at us, but kept their distance and stayed quiet. I have a vivid memory of one man—I would guess he was about thirty—who was part of a crowd but made eye contact with me. When I tried to address him personally—"What's your name?" "How are you?" etc.—his lips and eyebrows contorted wildly, from what seemed to me like intense anguish, so I stopped.

Children were a bit less inhibited. Any walk of ten minutes or more on a city street attracted a long train of them, as if we were pied pipers. I was amused to note, one day as we were walking past the gates of the Beijing Zoo, that some children who already held tickets to go see hippos and giraffes chose instead to come out of the zoo and follow us.

During one meeting with children—this was in Xi'an—a number of them gathered around us and seemed willing to talk. I asked a boy what he wanted to be when he grew up.

"I want to go to the toughest place and serve the people!" He pronounced the words in a sharp, confident, high-pitched voice.

"And you?" I asked another.

"I want to go to the toughest place and serve the people!" Another sharp, confident, high-pitched voice—and exactly the same words.

I asked three or four more, of slightly different ages and of both sexes. Their answers were identical. I do not believe our handlers had prepared this scene for us; it had come about in too casual a manner. And I don't know how much of the conformity resulted from training in how to answer this question and how much may have come just from others seeing that the first boy had produced a good answer and wanting to play things safe by doing the same. In any case, it left me with a deep impression.

In the years since 1973 I have learned much, much more about how wrong I was in the late 1960s to take Mao Zedong's "socialism" at face value. I could not have been more mistaken. I am a bit puzzled that others among my leftist-student friends from the 1960s sometimes seem reluctant to face this obvious fact. Is it embarrassing? Why should it be? We were naïve, yes. We believed lies. But we were not the ones who spun the lies.

Besides, I have felt no need to explain any reversal in my underlying values. What changed my views of the CCP was not a value shift, but simply better access to facts. In the late 1960s, I admired Mao because I felt strongly about things like peace, freedom, justice, truth, and a fair chance for the little guy. Today I detest Mao and his legacy. Why? From considerations of peace, freedom, justice, truth, and a fair chance for the little guy.

Originally published in the *Hong Kong Economic Journal*'s
"My First Trip To China" Series, 2011

The Anaconda in the Chandelier

(2002)

I N CHINA'S Mao years you could be detained and persecuted for talking with your neighbor about your cat. The Chinese word for "cat" (*mao*, high level tone) is a near homonym for the name of the Great Leader (*mao*, rising tone), and a tip to the police from an eavesdropper who misheard one for the other and took you to be disrespectful could ruin your life.[4] Such things no longer happen. The importance of the Chinese government in the daily lives of ordinary Chinese people has receded markedly over the last quarter-century. The space in which unofficial life takes place has expanded, and informal speech is much freer than before. Although there are still no barbed political cartoons in newspapers, sarcasm no less biting is rampant in jokes and rhythmical ditties on oral networks throughout the country. Some of these sayings flatly blame the Communist Party ("If we don't root out corruption, the country will perish; if we do root out corruption, the Party will perish"). Others dare to satirize Jiang Zemin, Li Peng, and other top leaders by name.

Yet repression remains an important problem, and its extent and methods are still poorly understood in the West. To appreciate it, one must revisit a dull but fundamental fact: the highest priority of the top leadership of the Communist Party remains, as in the past, not economic development, or a just society, or China's international standing, or any other goal for the nation as a whole, but its own grip on power. Thus it continues to ban any public expression of opposition to itself and continues to crush any

4. See "Mao" ("Cat"), a story by Cao Guanlong in *Anhui wenxue*, No. 1 (1980), translated by John Berninghausen in *Roses and Thorns*, edited by Perry Link (University of California Press, 1984), pp. 123–130.

organization that it does not control or could not easily control if it needed to. The fate of *qigong* breath exercises is a good illustration. In the 1980s the Party encouraged *qigong* as an expression of Chinese essence and a symbol of national pride. The central government even set up a national *qigong* association, complete with its own bureaucracy. But in the 1990s, when some *qigong* masters (Li Hongzhi of Falun Gong was not the first) decided to build their own organizations outside Party control, the same Chinese-essence breath exercises overnight became an "evil cult" and a target for brutal repression. The founders of the Chinese Democratic Party, all of whom are in prison today, ran afoul of the same principle. Their crime was not the word "democratic" in their group's name (China has long had eight "democratic parties," all subordinate to the leadership of the Communist Party); their crime was to declare that their organization was independent.

Censorship in intellectual matters broadly follows the same pattern. Nearly anything can be said in private, which is a big advance over the Mao years. And because academic journals have such small circulations, they are given somewhat more latitude than other publishing media. As long as scholars don't confront the top leadership head-on, they can write pretty much as they choose in scholarly journals. Moreover, in recent years, what many of them have chosen to write has been more favorable to the Party leadership than what they were inclined to write in the 1980s.[5]

But when an intellectual does want to express a politically sensitive idea in public, it remains the case that he or she must take a risk. As in the past, taking risks is not just a matter of personal courage, although courage of course is important. It helps, as well, to have allies or backers with whom to share the risk. It can also help to use indirection, such as pseudonyms, surrogates, or Aesopian expression. Even highly placed people, such as the sponsors of *The Tiananmen Papers*, a collection of internal documents on the genesis of the 1989 Beijing massacre,[6] choose to be indirect when going public.

Although repression under Jiang Zemin has applied to a narrower range

5. The reasons for this shift are complex—some have to do with government pressures, others with shifting perceptions of China's place in the world; to probe this topic properly would require a separate essay, beyond my scope here.
6. Public Affairs, 2001. Reviewed in *The New York Review*, by Jonathan Mirsky, February 8, 2001.

of expression than it did under Deng Xiaoping, its essential methods have changed little. These methods have "Chinese characteristics"; they have always differed, for example, from those of the Soviet Union. The Soviets published periodic handbooks that listed which specific phrases were out of bounds, and employed a large bureaucracy to enforce the rules. China has never had such a bureaucracy or published such handbooks. The Chinese Communist Party rejected these more mechanical methods in favor of an essentially psychological control system that relies primarily on self-censorship. Questions of risk—how far to go, how explicit to be, with whom to ally, and so on—are to be judged by each writer and editor. There are, of course, material punishments that anchor a person's calculations. If you calculate incorrectly you can lose your job, be imprisoned, or, in the worst case, get a bullet in the back of the head. If you live overseas, you can run the risk of being cut off from your family and hometown. But most censorship does not directly involve such happenings. It involves *fear* of such happenings. By "fear" I do not mean a clear and present sense of panic. I mean a dull, well-entrenched leeriness that people who deal with the Chinese censorship system usually get used to, and eventually accept as part of their natural landscape. But the controlling power of the fear is impressive nonetheless.

Outsiders to this system can be puzzled by its use of vagueness. The puzzlement was rife, for example, in the well-publicized cases of the sociologists Gao Zhan and Li Shaomin, one a legal U.S. resident and the other a U.S. citizen, who were arrested last year during research trips to China. They were accused as spies and charged with collecting classified "internal" documents. But particulars remained unclear. What did they actually do? What line did they cross? How does the government define "spying"? Why were these two people arrested for using "internal" materials (of which there are many kinds and levels, some of which are openly available in bookstores) while so many other scholars both inside and outside China routinely do the same thing and are not bothered?

The answers to these questions in the cases of Gao Zhan and Li Shaomin indeed remain a puzzle, but the "vagueness" of the charges is hardly new. Such vagueness is purposeful and has been a fundamental tool in Chinese Communist censorship for decades. It has the following four advantages:

1) A vague accusation frightens more people. If I, like Gao Zhan, am

a Chinese scholar working in the U.S., and I don't know why she was arrested, then the reason could be virtually anything; therefore it could be what I am doing; therefore I pull back. (Result: many people begin to censor themselves.) If, on the other hand, I could know exactly why Gao Zhan was nabbed, then I could feel fairly confident that my own work was all right—or, if not, how to make it all right. (Result: few people would pull back.) Clarity serves the purpose of the censoring state only when it wants to curb a very specific kind of behavior; when it wants to intimidate a large group, vagueness works much better.

2) A vague accusation pressures an individual to curtail a wider range of activity. If I don't know exactly why I was "wrong," I am induced to pay more attention to the state's strictures in every respect. This device has been used in literary and social campaigns in China since the 1950s. Who can say—or ever could—what exactly is meant by "spiritual pollution," "bourgeois liberalism," or other such terms for ideological misbehavior? (Is long hair "spiritual pollution"? How long? Why were some people with long hair punished in the 1980s and others with the same length not? And so on.) The cognitive content of key terms is purposefully vague; only the negativity is unambiguous. To be safe, a person must pull back in every respect, and, moreover, must become his or her own policeman.

3) A vague accusation is useful in maximizing what can be learned during forced confessions. When Li Shaomin was arrested, he asked his captors the reason and they answered, "You yourself know the reason."[7] It was up to Li to "earn lenience" by "showing sincerity" through "confession." This word game is standard. The police routinely say that they already possess an exhaustive amount of information on your crimes and that the purpose of interrogating you is not to get information but to measure your sincerity by observing your confession. In fact, though, this is often a lie. Usually, the point is precisely to extract new information, which can then be used either against you or against someone else. Clarity about the accusation would obviously destroy this tactic.

4) A vague accusation allows arbitrary targeting. Leaders who exercise arbitrary power like to disguise the real reasons for their actions. In a culture like China's, where the leader's "face" represents his morality, which in turn is the basis for his political legitimacy, the need to pretend that

7. Lecture at Princeton University, October 1, 2001.

one is acting legally and morally is especially important. The need for pretense only increases as a leader's moral behavior worsens. In this context, the availability of vague and even self-contradictory laws can be extremely useful to a leader. For example, a rule might state "It is forbidden to collect internal materials" at the same time that at least some internal materials, such as government reports, are easily available and it is well known that many people collect them. This situation makes it possible for me, the authority, to use the rule to arrest Gao Zhan or Li Shaomin or whomever I like—*for who knows what reason*—and at the same time to have a ready, face-saving justification for my exercise of arbitrary power. China's constitution itself illustrates this handy flexibility. It provides that citizens have freedom of speech, of assembly, and of the press. But its preamble also sets down the inviolability of Communist Party rule, Marxism-Leninism-Mao-Zedong-Thought, the dictatorship of the proletariat, and the socialist system. The huge space between these two contradictory poles (both of which, by the way, are poor descriptions of the actual patterns of life in China) gives leaders immense room to be arbitrary while still claiming to be legal.

But the big story in Beijing's pressuring of overseas scholars is not in the high-profile cases of Gao Zhan, Li Shaomin, Wu Jianmin, Xu Zerong, and others. The pressures penetrate far deeper than those cases taken individually would suggest. The great majority of the other cases never come to light. Kang Zhengguo, writing in *The New York Review*, estimates that "hundreds and thousands" of Chinese who return to their homeland are invited for "chats" in which the police warn and threaten them in various ways ("Do you want to come back to China again?" "Do you wish the best for your friends and relatives?"). The police also specifically warn people not to say anything about these threats when they go back to the West. ("Let's not have any loose tongues"; "Remember to preserve the positive image of State Security"; etc.)[8] I cannot corroborate Kang's estimate that there are "hundreds and thousands" of such "returnee interviews," but would note that just within my own circle of friends I have heard a dozen or so such stories in recent years.

For example, I am acquainted with a woman—a well-known critic of the Chinese government—who lives in the West but recently went back to

8. "Arrested in China," *The New York Review*, September 20, 2001, pp. 6–8.

China under a pseudonym so that she could visit her ailing mother. (Use of pseudonyms for this purpose is common among overseas dissidents.) When she arrived in her Chinese hometown the police knew who she was, and let her know that they knew it, and yet both sides played the language game of pretending that her "returnee interview," where specific threats were delivered and received over tea and snacks, was simply a social event. Back in the West, she still abides by certain rules, one of which is not to reveal the very threats that she is obeying.

In addition to the number, whatever it may be, of Chinese people who are directly affected in this way, a far larger number feel the pressures indirectly. For every person who is threatened with forced exile or mistreatment of relatives, many more hear about such threats and censor themselves accordingly. In summer 2001, after the Gao Zhan and Li Shaomin arrests, probably a record number (my surmise; statistics are not available) of overseas Chinese scholars canceled research trips to China. At one major university a young professor made this decision even though her research was on the Tang dynasty (618–907 AD). Her problem was not that she thought her topic would cause trouble; it was that she had no idea what behavior did cause trouble. Could it be one's friends? One's itinerary? In such cases, active fear is rare. Conservatism and self-censorship are merely practical. With the passage of time, threats and prohibitions come to seem normal, even natural. Most Chinese wend their ways through the political landscape without questioning all of its boulders and ditches, but simply skirting them, getting where they want to go with minimum trouble. By contrast, the dissident who does raise questions, or states principles, can seem a bit blockheaded and even, in a sense, deserving of the trouble he or she gets into.

China scholars from non-Chinese backgrounds are affected as well. For example, in 1999, when the quasi-religious Falun Gong organization suddenly made itself felt in China and the world, a major U.S. news organization invited one of the U.S.'s top scholars in a relevant field for a television interview. The scholar, a Caucasian American, declined. He didn't want to lose access to fieldwork in China by publicly discussing a politically sensitive issue. He knew that foreigners who displease Chinese authorities can be denied visas, or, even if allowed into China, denied interviews or access to archives. He faced no specific threat in this regard, but chose to comply voluntarily under the same kind of general and vague guidelines that affect overseas Chinese. (It is unusual for anyone, Chinese or not, to receive a specific demand from the Chinese government, but this does happen. For example, a number of the Americans who worked to bring out *The Tiananmen Papers* are now denied visas to travel to China. But one of them, after requesting a reason for the denial, received a letter from a PRC official who explained that he could not help because he was "unable to guarantee to the relevant authority that you will extend certain apologies on your involvement in *The Tiananmen Papers* so as to clear your visa problems." Unusual specificity is used when the aim is to achieve a specific result—in this case, apparently, the discrediting of a troublesome book by one of its supporters.)

How often such things happen and what kind of self-censorship results are difficult things to measure. The problem is most salient, and unusually complex, for political scientists who study the Chinese government and need to nurture their contacts among Chinese officials. The effects are hard to measure not only because people are reluctant to speak about them (no scholar likes to acknowledge self-censorship), but because the crucial functions are psychological and sometimes highly subtle. They happen within the recesses of private minds, where even the scholar him- or herself may not notice exactly what is happening.

I do not say this to denigrate my fellow scholars. Over the years I have noticed the phenomenon in myself as well. It is always somehow more difficult than it should be for a China scholar to write or speak in explicit contradiction of what the Beijing government has pronounced to be a "fundamental principle." Beijing's "one-China principle" is an example. It somehow causes the very phrase "Taiwan independence" to take on negative connotations in discussions among contemporary China specialists. In a similar way, analysis of human rights often tiptoes around Beijing's principle "not to interfere in internal affairs." As in the case of overseas Chinese, China scholars who bear these taboos in mind for an extended length of time eventually feel them to be natural. To violate them comes to seem not just politically incorrect but somehow culturally insensitive, as if one does not pay due respect to the "other side" in a meeting of cultures. But the taboos are not cultural in their origins so much as political, indeed political in a partisan way.

In sum, the Chinese government's censorial authority in recent times has resembled not so much a man-eating tiger or fire-snorting dragon as a giant anaconda coiled in an overhead chandelier. Normally the great snake doesn't move. It doesn't have to. It feels no need to be clear about its prohibitions. Its constant silent message is "You yourself decide," after which, more often than not, everyone in its shadow makes his or her large and small adjustments—all quite "naturally." The Soviet Union, where Stalin's notion of "engineering the soul" was first pursued, in practice fell far short of what the Chinese Communists have achieved in psychological engineering.

For years the intimidation was aimed only at Chinese citizens, but now it has been projected overseas. As China's international involvements continue to grow (soon maybe faster than ever because of the country's entry into the World Trade Organization) it becomes important for the rest of the world to notice this problem. What are the effects of censorship—and induced self-censorship—on the flow of good information between China and other countries? I do not wish to argue that Chinese censorship is the only, or even the main, problem in this regard. (The slowness of Westerners to learn the Chinese language, for example, is at least as big a problem; today the ratio of Chinese who study English to Americans who study Chinese is several thousand to one.) But regardless of what else is involved, the role of Beijing's censorship is demonstrably harmful. It contributes to distortions both in Chinese perceptions of the West and in Western perceptions of China.

When the World Trade Center was destroyed, some Chinese—primarily young, male, and educated—exulted on the internet and cheered the flaming images. Later a group of twenty Chinese scholars issued a statement in which they decried this reaction and then sought to explain it. Chinese young people, they wrote, choosing their words with great delicacy, had been "led astray by certain media themes and education guidelines in recent times."[9] They were referring to how, when the Deng Xiaoping regime began to stoke Chinese nationalism in the early 1990s as a way to recoup its popularity after the debacle at Tiananmen, it employed images of the U.S. as a swaggering hegemon. The U.S., it was said, set out to frustrate China's Olympic hopes, interfered in China's domestic affairs in human rights,

9. Wang Dongcheng et al., "Guanyu '9 11' shijian de san dian gongshi" ("Three Items of Common Understanding on the September Eleventh Incident"), September 14, 2001.

sought to "contain" a rising China, and so on. The unsubtle images were not, for the most part, intended as accurate portrayals. They were caricatures produced and spread by Chinese journalists who, themselves living beneath an anaconda in the chandelier, may or may not have agreed with what they were writing—and indeed may not even have put the question of accuracy to themselves in exactly this way. What they wrote was by no means the only factor in why some Chinese youths cheered the collapse of the World Trade Center towers, but it had a part.

The costs in the other direction, in Western perceptions of China, are harder to measure but perhaps even more far-reaching. Scholarship is affected more than journalism. When a Chinese-American scholar cancels a research trip to China, and therefore does not write as much, or perhaps as well, about China's society, or economy, or even its Tang dynasty, how much is lost, in both the short and long runs? When certain questions are avoided, or written up in less than fully candid ways, how much less well informed is the Western public? When a leading scholar chooses not to share what he knows on a topic, how much does the public lose by listening instead to second-best answers from other sources?

A similar problem affects the international business world. While scholars, journalists, and overseas Chinese can be threatened with being cut off from their access to China, for businesses the primary threat is exclusion from China's huge potential market. (Grand hopes in the West about this market date from the late nineteenth century. The hopes have yet to be realized, yet the allure, understandably, persists.)[10] The threats against businesses seem, if anything, even more effective than those against scholars and even more shrouded in sensitivity.

After Li Shaomin was imprisoned in China, for example, faculty members at Princeton University, where Li had finished a Ph.D. in sociology in 1988, urged their university president to write to Chinese officials asking fair treatment of Li, and the university president complied. Around the same time, some of Li's former colleagues at AT&T, where he had worked for seven years after finishing his Ph.D., asked their company to join in the effort to free him. They received only a brief reply from Public Relations:

10. See Joe Studwell, *The China Dream: the Elusive Quest for the Last Great Untapped Market on Earth* (England Profile Books, 2002).

"We appreciate your commitment to this cause, but we believe it is not appropriate for AT&T to take an active role in publicizing it."[11]

Such regard for the sensitivities of Beijing is not unusual. When an analyst at a leading international investment firm last year released a financial report on the China Petro-Chemical Corporation, a large Chinese oil company run by the Chinese state and now listed on the New York Stock Exchange, Chinese officials found the report excessively negative and demanded an apology. Two executives of the investment firm, with the writer of the report unhappily in tow, traveled to Beijing to deliver it. Will that analyst, next time around, again write the truth as he sees it?

Gordon Chang, formerly a lawyer at the prestigious American law firm Paul, Weiss, Rifkind, Wharton & Garrison, worked for many years introducing U.S. businesses to China and grew accustomed to what he saw as a double standard between what Westerners said about the Chinese economy in private (that it was mired in corruption, bad loans, triangular debt, and bureaucratic excess, had no effective recourse to law, and faced more labor unrest than was generally known) and what the same people wrote for public consumption ("analyses from major investment banks and other businesses...are bland, uninformative, and generally too optimistic").[12] At the end of 1999 Chang withdrew from his law practice to write a book called *The Coming Collapse of China*,[13] in which he dramatically contradicts the rosy predictions of China's prosperity and at the same time flouts the taboos against frank talk in public. Chang has decided to retire from law practice, and this may be for the best because, he estimates,

> I would not be able to practice in a major firm because I would be too controversial.... I know many lawyers, fine and upstanding individuals otherwise, who refuse to utter a critical word about the regime except in private conversation. I know that they would not hire me now, and I would not even think of putting them in the position where they would have to say "no."[14]

11. Email letter from Dan Lawler, AT&T Public Relations, to Salvadore Cordo, June 15, 2001.
12. Email to Perry Link, November 20, 2001.
13. Random House, 2001.
14. Email to Perry Link, November 20, 2001.

Here we see just how far that anaconda in the chandelier can project its power. Not only can it induce scholars to lie low, businessmen to pull punches, and lawyers to mince words, but even a whistle-blower like Gordon Chang can "understand." He steers clear of causing more problems for others who are already steering clear of problems. So does Perry Link, by the way. Why, in the above, do I not name my scholar friends who canceled research trips to China or declined to appear on the evening news? Or my associate whom Chinese officials urged to denounce *The Tiananmen Papers*? Or the dissident who holds her tongue so that she can continue to visit her family? The anaconda reaches me through these friends, and I give in. The subtlety of how it all happens masks the super-sensitivity of the feelings that are at stake. People can get extremely nervous. At least one of my friends will almost certainly be angry with me for mentioning him in this essay, even anonymously. (I don't believe the reference hurts, or wouldn't make it.) In the case of the investment company that obliged its analyst to apologize to Beijing, I withhold the names involved because I would rather not risk a lawsuit, even though I have no doubt about the facts. The anaconda, itself outside the law, can ride on the law of others. And in the end it intervenes even between you and me, dear reader, on this very page.

Originally published in *The New York Review of Books*,
April 11, 2002

Why We Should Criticize Mo Yan

⊰⑊|⑊⊱

(2012)

A T A RECENT conference at Princeton University, I met a Chinese language teacher whom I had not seen since 1989 in Beijing. Trying to recall our first meeting, she asked me, "Was that before or after the *dongluan* [turmoil]?" Teasing her, I asked, "What do you mean by *dongluan*? Student *dongluan* or government *dongluan*?" She replied reflexively: "Student *dongluan*, of course." Then she peered at me for a moment, realized what I had meant, and said: "Oh, yes! Government *dongluan*. The massacre!" Then she went into a long apology to me: she herself had been a student protestor in 1989, had been in Tiananmen Square in the days before the massacre (but not during it); she was on the students' side; she agreed with me. And yet the phrase "student turmoil" now rolled off her tongue as easily as "Wednesday."

How much does this kind of induced linguistic habit reinforce state power? How much does it matter when writers toe the Party line when they choose words? And how much do the choices affect the thinking of readers?

In a recent essay in *The New York Review of Books* on Mo Yan, the winner of the 2012 Nobel Prize for literature, I objected to Mo Yan's way of presenting twentieth-century Chinese history. I noted that when he arrives at catastrophic episodes like the Great Leap famine, he deflects attention from true horrors by resorting to what I called "daft hilarity"—shooting sheep sperm into rabbits or forcing someone to eat a turnip carved to be a "fake donkey dick"—while making no mention of starvation that cost thirty million or more lives.

In a lengthy response, Charles Laughlin took issue with me, arguing that "Mo Yan's intended readers know that the Great Leap Forward led to a catastrophic famine, and any artistic approach to historical trauma is inflected or refracted." Laughlin sees Mo Yan as doing satire, not cover-up, and when the point is put this way, I can, in a narrow sense, accept it (even though my personal taste in satire does not extend as far as donkey dicks). The problem, in my view, turns on Laughlin's phrase "intended readers." Mo Yan has said that he does not write with any particular readers in mind, so "intended readers" here needs to be understood not as actual readers but as the kind of reader that is implied by the writer's rhetoric. In this meaning, "implied reader" is a well-established term in literary studies, and it is fair enough to analyze things this way.

But I worry about actual readers. How does "daft hilarity" affect them? I hope Laughlin will agree with me that Mo Yan's actual readers are numerous, mostly young, and not very well schooled in Chinese history. To reach the level of what Laughlin sees as Mo Yan's ideal "intended reader," a young Chinese must leap a number of intellectual hurdles that Communist Party education has put in place: first, that there was no famine, because the story is only a slander invented by foreigners; second, that if there really was a famine, it was "three years of difficulty" caused by bad weather; third, that if the famine indeed was man-made, it still wasn't Mao-made, because Mao was great; fourth, that if it was Mao-made, people died only of starvation, not beatings, burnings-alive (called "the human torch"), or brain-splatterings with shovels (called "opening the flower"), as Yang Jisheng's book *Tombstone* documents.

How dangerous is it that Mo Yan's giddy treatments of history divert attention from things that are hard to look at? Escape of this kind may be welcome to some readers, perhaps most. In any case it is certainly welcome to the regime. Can Mo Yan be unaware that the regime welcomes it? How could he be? Laughlin writes: "Surely Link doesn't mean to imply that Mo Yan, by writing in this way, is trying to whitewash history out of loyalty to the Communist Party?" But I do, I'm afraid, mean something very close to this. I would use the word "distort" instead of "whitewash," and instead of "loyalty to the Party," I would say "in order to preserve his career prospects under Party rule."

I worry, too, that finding excuses for deference to the regime's sensitivities (Mo Yan is by no means the only writer who does this) illustrates what in Chinese is called *xifangzhongxinzhuyi*. This phrase does not translate easily, so please pardon my awkward rendering as "West-centrism." The late Chinese physicist and human rights advocate Fang Lizhi was good at pointing out double standards in Western attitudes. When Communist dictatorships fell in Europe, the Cold War was declared "over." But what about China, North Korea, and Vietnam? If the reverse had happened—if dictatorships had fallen in Asia but persisted in Europe—would Washington and London still have hailed the end of the Cold War? What if Solzhenitsyn, instead of exposing the gulag, had cracked jokes about it? Would we have credited him with "art" on grounds that his intended audience knew all about the gulag and could appreciate the black humor? Or might it be, sadly, that only non-whites can win Nobel Prizes writing in this mode?

Pankaj Mishra, in an essay in *The Guardian* called "Why Salman Rushdie Should Pause before Condemning Mo Yan on Censorship," acknowledges that the support Mo Yan has offered to China's rulers is deplorable. But the main point of Mishra's essay is that Western writers have also been the handmaidens of powers that oppress people in distant places. He asks, therefore, that people like Rushdie (and me, whom he also mentions) "pause." I have long admired Mishra, and his essay in *The Guardian* offers penetrating observations; for example, that "Jane Austen's elegantly self-enclosed world" depended on unseen "hellish slavery plantations" in the Caribbean. But why does that mean that I should "pause" before criticizing Beijing or those who wink at it?

A certain kind of argument is often heard in debates over human rights. It has several versions but they all fall into this pattern:

A: Country X has problem P.
B: On the contrary, country Y also has problem P.

In most of these exchanges, people overlook B's logical flaw because his or her real point is not to supply facts but to give advice. If A is a citizen of country Y, he or she should be quiet about country X.

But why? Must Salman Rushdie hold his tongue about Beijing until London is squeaky clean? My guess is that Mishra, if shaken by the shoulders, would say (as I would) that any citizen of any country should be free to criticize any government anywhere that oppresses anyone.

Authoritarians in China and elsewhere regularly take the position that foreigners should keep criticisms to themselves. The reasons for their position are obvious. The reasons that Western liberals often take the same position are far less obvious but well worth probing. The kinds of problems in China that, in different ways, both Mo Yan and Liu Xiaobo (the 2010 Nobel Peace Prize winner) bring to our attention—suppression of speech to protect state power, harassment and prison for "offenders"—can also be found, to lesser degrees, in democratic societies. But to stand on that discovery and say "look, the whole world is the same, so let's calm down" is not only intellectually feeble but also, when uttered by people who live at comfortable distances from true suffering, morally indefensible. How do you think a Chinese liberal, sitting on a bench in a drab prison, would feel to hear an American liberal, sitting on a couch reading *The Guardian*, say "You and I both live under oppressive governments, my friend; I must pause before criticizing yours"? Actually, we don't need to guess at the answer. Former political prisoners from many places—China, Czechoslovakia, South Africa, Myanmar, and elsewhere—have made it abundantly clear that during stays in prison they craved any support they might get from the outside world.

I find the condescending attitude of some Western liberals especially distasteful when its main purpose is to comfort the condescender. American liberals can feel good in expressing criticism of their own society. It shows "critical thinking," "independence," and a generous broad-mindedness, all of which one can congratulate oneself for having. (True independence, in fact, is rare; the "critical" views one hears often show great conformity, and one major source of the comfort I am referring to is the confidence that one's conforming expressions will be safe from attack by peers.) Comfort is a good thing; I am not opposed to it. But to make the mental comfort of someone in an armchair a higher priority than the spiritual and physical torment of a prisoner is disgusting.

Laughlin notes that I do not answer the question posed by the title of my *New York Review* essay: "Does This Writer Deserve the Prize?" Fair enough. The title was written by editors of the *Review*, and I did not see it until the piece came out. Let me address the question now.

Measures of excellence in the natural sciences are objective enough that the question "Did X really deserve a Nobel?" can be answered with some confidence (if never certainty). For the literature and peace prizes, though, the question is so beholden to subjective impressions that consensus is impossible. Henry Kissinger won a Peace Prize. If that happened, what is not possible? I can answer only the question, "Would I personally have chosen Mo Yan?," and I would like to restrict it further by adding the phrase "among living Chinese writers." (Only living writers are eligible.)

My answer is no. Mo Yan would not have been at the top of my list. For authenticity and control of language, I would rate Zhong Acheng, Jia Pingwa, Wang Anyi, and Wang Shuo more highly; for mastery of the craft of fiction, Pai Hsien-yung and Ha Jin are clearly superior to Mo Yan; for breadth of spiritual vision, Zheng Yi is one of my favorites. I would also have put Yu Hua or Jin Yong (the Hong Kong writer of popular historical martial-arts fiction) above Mo Yan. But these are only my views. Please help yourself to your own.

Originally published in the *NYR Daily*
December 24, 2012

Life on a Blacklist

(2016)

ONE OF THE questions I am asked most often is what it feels like, as a China scholar, not to be able to go to China. I have been denied visas since 1996. I do not know the reason (the authorities won't specify), although I can see that the number of possibilities is large.

On the evening of July 8, 1996, I arrived at the Beijing Capital Airport after a long, two-stage flight from Newark, New Jersey. I was ready to see friends who were waiting for me outside the airport, but more than anything I needed sleep. In those days the Beijing airport still bore some of the quaint flavor of China's Mao era: drab walls, ceiling fans, luggage carousels built of wooden slats. The spanking new construction that came with the city's hosting of the 2008 Summer Olympics had not yet arrived.

Passport control did have new computers, and when my turn in line came, a young officer squinted at his monitor, rather longer than one would think he had to, and then told me in halting English to take a seat and "wait a moment." About an hour later, another uniformed man, middle-aged with a long, serious face, returned to say, in Chinese (apparently, research on me during the hour had revealed that I could speak Chinese), that "we have checked with our superiors and you are not welcome in our country." I mumbled that I had a Chinese visa and asked what the problem was. He said nothing. He pointed an index finger toward the ceiling and fixed me with a look.

It was late in the evening, and there were no return flights to the U.S. until the next morning. This made me a problem for him and his colleagues, whose need to come up with a solution can explain at least part of my hour-long wait. In the end, four young plainclothes policemen accompanied me to the United Airlines ticket counter. One of them, with a crew cut and bushy eyebrows, was the leader, and showed some enthusiasm for that role. He seemed new in it. He told the United agent on duty that the airline had brought into China a passenger whose papers were unacceptable and that the airline would have to provide a hotel room for one night. United, which apparently had a policy of just giving in when such matters arose, paid for a room at the nearby Movenpick Hotel, and the four young policemen and I went there to spend the night. Officially, I had not entered China.

The young policemen smoked, and I do not, but other than that I suffered no mistreatment. As I was brushing my teeth the bushy-browed leader read to me in English the formal police language that it was his duty to read: "You cannot leave the hotel, you cannot leave our company, you cannot make a phone call," and so on—about eight items in all. The phone-call rule was the relevant one, because my only request to the police had been to call my friends who were waiting for me outside the airport. I wanted to tell them to go home and not to worry. But the policeman said this was not permitted and, to emphasize the point, had the others unplug the telephone in the room and place it beneath the pillows on one of the beds.

After the official rules had been read, the speech of the four young policemen shifted to an informal register. We switched to Chinese, which seemed to relax them. They expressed puzzlement that my Chinese tones were correct ("How did *that* happen?") and then moved on to questions like how much my watch cost. They were glad to be with me in the Movenpick, because the police system provides meal coupons for overtime work, so tonight they had a special opportunity to eat in the fancy restaurant on the ground floor. It was past 11:00 p.m., but never mind; they wanted dinner. They asked me to come down with them. I teased them by asking whether they had a free-meal coupon for me, too. "Oh, no sir!" they said (when speaking informally, they were deferential), "but you can buy your own." I was not hungry and told them I did not want to eat. That created another problem. I was not allowed to leave them, which meant they were not allowed to leave me, either. They solved the matter by taking turns. Three of them went down to eat, while one, smoking and chatting, stayed with me. When the three came back, that one went down.

The next morning they took me back to the airport and to the United counter for check-in.

"The flight is full," said the agent.

"If this passenger is not on the flight, the airplane will not leave the airport," the leader said. I doubt that this was an idle threat. In any case, United did find me a seat, and I headed back to Newark.

"Congratulations," said Liu Binyan, the distinguished Chinese journalist who was living in exile in New Jersey at the time, when I told him of my turn-around in Beijing. "Now you know what it feels like to be Chinese." He said that my rejection at a physical border had actually ushered me across a cultural border. For decades, the authorities in China had been telling intellectuals whom they wanted to control that "you are wrong and here is your punishment; it is now up to you to reflect on your errors and to write a confession." Liu saw me in that position as well.

I began searching my mind. Which of my "errors" might be the one that precipitated the regime's decision? I had written about censorship and repression in China, had translated dissident writers, and had joined human rights groups. But exactly what line had I crossed, and where? I asked Liu Binyan and other Chinese friends to help me guess. Some said it must have been because, the day after the Tiananmen Massacre in June, 1989, I had given a ride to the U.S. Embassy in Beijing to Fang Lizhi and Li Shuxian, professors of physics and a married couple, whom the government viewed as "black hands" behind the pro-democracy movement. Fang and Li were offered refuge in the embassy and stayed for thirteen months. This was an embarrassment to the Chinese authorities, who blamed the U.S. for "meddling in its internal affairs." All this would have made me a major meddler, my friends said.

This theory makes good sense except that it does not explain why I was able to travel to China six times between 1989, when the massacre happened, and 1996, when I was turned around at the airport. I spent the entire summer of 1994 in China as field director of *Princeton-in-Beijing*, an intensive summer Chinese language program that my Princeton colleague C.P. Chou and I had established the year before. When I left Beijing at the end of that summer, four policemen met me at the airport to give my luggage a thorough inspection for twenty minutes. (They were especially interested in my address book). But other than that, I had no political trouble that summer, and I visited Beijing again in 1995.

So the question becomes: what happened in 1994 or 1995 that caused a change? Some of my friends have guessed that it was because 1994 was the year when I agreed to serve as Chair of the Board of the Princeton China Initiative (PCI), an umbrella organization that had raised funds to provide temporary homes, physical and intellectual, to refugees from the 1989 crackdown. The group included some who were still on Chinese government wanted lists. My position as board chair was pro forma. I felt like a figurehead accepting the title—but I did accept it, because the group needed an American for legal purposes. Was I blacklisted because, in Beijing's view, I was now head of a counterrevolutionary camp? Some of my friends in PCI thought so.

Others noted that 1994 was the year President Bill Clinton decided to "de-link" human rights from trade in his China policy. In the early 1990s, the U.S. had used the granting or withholding of "most favored nation" trading status to pressure Beijing for human rights concessions; after 1994, Beijing was given Permanent Normal Trading Relations, and the pressure disappeared. It might be, my Chinese friends speculated, that Beijing now saw that they could handle small fry like American human rights advocates pretty much as they liked, with no fear of consequences. Still others of my friends thought (and this would be my guess, too) that the 1989 incident with Fang Lizhi was still the reason, or at least the main reason, and that it had taken the Chinese leaders a few years to decide to punish me for it. In 1989 I had been director of the Beijing office of the U.S. National Academy of Sciences (NAS), and the Beijing authorities, thirsty for Western science to bolster its catch-up efforts in technology, and for that reason not wanting to jeopardize its relationship with the NAS, probably held its nose and tolerated me until, in 1994 or 1995, it seemed safe to levy punishments.

After 1996 I tried and failed several times to get visas. I never tried just for the sake of trying. I tried only after receiving invitations to attend conferences or to give lectures. In each case my Chinese hosts issued invitations, after which I applied and then was rejected.

In 1999, a highly-placed Chinese official who used the pseudonym Zhang Liang carried out of China a trove of government documents that related to the June Fourth massacre in 1989. He gave them to my friend Andrew Nathan, a professor of politics at Columbia, and Nathan asked me to help translate and edit the documents into an abridged English version. I agreed, and the book appeared in 2001 as *The Tiananmen Papers*. By the time it was finished I had become friendly with Zhang Liang (who does not want his real name publicized, even now), and I asked his advice about my visa problem. He said that a matter like this would need to be addressed at the highest levels in China. If I would write a letter to China's premier, Zhu Rongji, he could get it into Zhu's hands.

In December, 2002, I addressed a letter to Mr. Zhu in both Chinese and English versions. I explained who I was and said that I would like to travel to Beijing in summer 2003 to work on the *Princeton-in-Beijing* language program. I wrote that I hoped that he would share my view that "to train young Americans to speak Chinese, write Chinese, make Chinese friends, and understand Chinese daily life is an extremely meaningful mission." A few months later Zhang Liang called me on the telephone. He was ready to give me an oral report on the response to my letter.

Zhu had read it, he said, and had written at the bottom (the following words are not a direct quote; they are based on my memory of the phone call), "Please check to see if Perry Link really is a scholar, and if he is, my opinion is that he should be allowed to come to China." Then, said Zhang Liang, Zhu forwarded the letter, with his opinion appended, to China's Ministry of Foreign Affairs (MFA) and Ministry of State Security (MSS). MFA relayed the matter to the Chinese Embassy in Washington, D.C., where officials looked into the matter. MFA's reply to Zhu was that, yes, Link is a scholar and MFA has no objection to his coming to China. The reply from MSS was much lengthier and ended by saying (again, from my memory of the phone call) that "in view of the continuing complexity of the international situation, it is our view that Link and the seventeen others should for the time being not be allowed into China." This told me two things. First, somewhere in the world, seventeen others were on the same blacklist as I. Second, the MSS outweighed China's premier on such questions.

In fall, 2013, the Chinese government inadvertently allowed me a glimpse into how the Ministry of Culture, too, defers to MSS. I was doing research at the Academia Sinica in Taiwan when, out of the blue, I received an email from a man named Zhou Yong, First Secretary of the Cultural Office of the Chinese Embassy in Washington, D.C., who was inviting me, all expenses paid, to a "Forum of Overseas Sinologists" that was to be held in Beijing in December of that year. The Ministry of Culture was host. A number of first-rate Chinese intellectuals were also being invited, so I was interested. I wrote an email, in Chinese, directly to the forum organizers in Beijing, reminding them that I had been denied visas for many years—were they sure they could invite me? That email brought no response, which I took as neither good news nor bad. I then followed up with Zhou Yong, who responded with enthusiasm and urged me to attend. I told him I was in Taiwan and asked how I could get a visa (one cannot get mainland visas in Taiwan). Zhou suggested that I go to Hong Kong for one. But I did not want to do that, because I remained skeptical that a visa would actually be forthcoming and did not want to spend time and money in vain. I asked if I could send my passport to Washington by express mail and let him and his colleagues stamp the visa there. Mr. Zhou looked into the request and wrote back, "though it's tricky, finally it could be handled as you wish." He even offered to fill out parts of the visa form for me and to pre-pay the fee, saying that I could repay him later. So I mailed my passport to Washington. Later that same day, November 8, Mr. Zhou sent another email: "After review, I'd like to inform you that you will not be invited to the forum. I'll have your passport sent back to you as soon as possible."

I replied that I would be sorry to miss the forum but would like to maintain my visa application anyway, because I would like to do some interviewing in Beijing and Tianjin on my current research project on Chinese comedians' dialogues (*xiangsheng*). (I was indeed doing research on comic dialogue—not delivering a satiric comment on our email exchange.) I actually felt some sympathy for Mr. Zhou. He had, after all, only been doing his job. A mistake inside his government's bureaucracy—someone's failure to check with State Security—had blindsided and embarrassed him. The evaporation of my invitation must have been more surprising to him than to me.

Zhou had always answered my emails promptly, but this last one—about my request to maintain my visa application anyway—brought no reply. Nine days later, November 17, I still had no answer, and no passport, so wrote again: "Dear Mr. Zhou: Have you received my passport? Please tell me where things stand." Still no answer. By chance the passport did arrive the following day, so I wrote once more, "Dear Yong, I understand that you work for an authoritarian government and do not have the freedom to answer my emails once you have been told to cut off. This is not your fault, and I do not blame you for it. My passport has been received. Thank you for sending. Best, Perry."

I can understand why Chinese authorities do not like my opinions and the candor with which I sometimes state them. But there is something else they don't like as well. It is a subtle matter, but is telling in its implications and therefore worth a short detour here.

Chinese culture usually welcomes outsiders in proportion to how much they are willing and able to look, sound, and act Chinese. It is, from one point of view, a presumptuous attitude, because it seems to assume that being Chinese is the best way to be human. But it is also a generous approach in that it offers any human being the route to Chineseness if he or she wants to take it. A white Caucasian like me cannot easily look Chinese; but to sound and act Chinese remains possible and can make a big difference in how well a person fits into Chinese daily life. I was born with a knack for imitating sounds, and my first teacher of Chinese, at Harvard in 1963, took advantage of that knack to drill Chinese tonal pronunciation into me. On the telephone, Chinese people are sometimes dubious when I tell them that I am not Chinese. I have even been accused of lying about it. Face-to-face, it is obvious that I am not Chinese, but the boundaries between "you" and "us" melt away faster when oral exchange begins. This effect is visible whether or not the context is happy. It made a difference when I met in Princeton with Chinese refugee-dissidents who were seeking Princeton's help; it made a difference, too, when I was in the Movenpick Hotel with four policemen whose job it was to watch me.

The issue matters for the blacklist question because China's Communist authorities, differently from the culture at large, are strongly averse to seeing foreigners get "inside" their world. They want the borders of their world to be impenetrable, and foreigners who sound too Chinese make them nervous. They would rather deal with foreigners who either speak no Chinese or, if they do speak it, speak it badly enough that the line between "you" and "us" is obvious. Once, at a luncheon for a visiting Chinese delegation at UCLA, where Americans and Chinese were speaking through interpreters, I decided to ask a question directly in Chinese, without the interpreter. The head-of-delegation from China was visibly discomfited. He was on the spot. What should he do? After an awkward moment he turned to his interpreter and waited for her near-verbatim repetition of my question. In form, after all, she was the person who was supposed to be speaking Chinese to him. Waiting to funnel the message through her was not done to improve clarity; it was a more nearly a political reflex, whose purpose was to maintain the border between "our side" and "your side."

In short, I believe that for people in the CCP regime, who do not like it when I do things like help Fang Lizhi or co-edit *The Tiananmen Papers*, it only makes things worse that I sound like a Chinese person orally. It makes me seem slicker, more sinister, and more likely to have been trained in the CIA. (The latter point is ironic, because it is well-known in the Chinese-teaching field in the U.S. that CIA schools do not stress training in tonal pronunciation.)

People ask if being blacklisted ever makes me regret my choice to spend my life studying China, the country that bars me. Do I feel at some level betrayed? Oddly, perhaps, I have never felt that way in the slightest. I am so distant from that feeling that I almost cannot understand it. Most obviously, this is because I have never thought of the people who have blacklisted me as representing China. They are only one small (and especially ugly) part of a much larger and more various entity. Do farmers in Guizhou view me as *persona non grata*? Miners in Anhui? I can't imagine it. Even the list-makers minions—the young policemen who detained me at the Beijing airport or the hapless Mr. Zhou in the Chinese embassy in Washington—are different from the list-makers themselves. Would these people have barred me, if it had been up to them? I doubt it, but they are "China" just as much as the men they work for.

China is history, language, fiction, poetry, food, humor, scenery—and on and on. My wife and most of my best friends in this world are Chinese. The harm that the blacklist-makers have done to them, and to countless others whose fates I have been able to observe, directly or through writing, makes the harm done to me about as heavy as garlic skin. Without, of course, intending to, leaders of the CCP have given me deeper understanding of certain human values—truth, freedom, integrity—than, perhaps, I could have reached in a world lacking the CCP.

There are two main reasons why I wish I were not on a blacklist. One is that I miss China's life on the ground: the sounds, sights, and smells of the streets, the charming snacks that can be had there, and the lively, authentic speech. My 2013 book, *An Anatomy of Chinese: Rhythm, Metaphor, Politics* is about contemporary Chinese language and draws examples not only from published writing but also from T-shirts, graffiti, slang, jokes, and other ephemera that I could collect easily during times I spent in China but since then can gather only second hand. I also miss face-to-face encounters with writers, scholars, activists, booksellers, and people on the street. But such losses are not as severe as one might fear. I can meet people when they come out of China, and, thanks to email and the internet, can stay in touch intellectually without much difficulty.

The second cost of being blacklisted troubles me more. It is that blacklisting turns me into a tool of the Chinese government in its efforts to impose self-censorship among Western students and scholars. My blacklisting became well known in China studies after 1996, and since then I have had many inquiries about it, especially from younger scholars. In one way or another they ask, although always politely, "How, Professor Link, do I not end up where you are?" A bright Princeton undergraduate, who had studied Chinese language with me, was delighted to tell me that she had secured a summer internship with Human Rights Watch. A few days later, after hearing of my blacklisting, she came back to ask, "What did you do?" I told her the truth, of course, which was that I did not exactly know, but I also tried to assure her that something as innocuous as a summer internship at HRW should be no problem. She came back a few days later to tell me that she had declined the internship. She thought it too big a risk; she might want a China career later. Around the same time, a Ph.D. student came to consult me about his dissertation topic. He wanted to write on Chinese democracy, but his advisers in the politics department were cautioning him that this might not be a smart move. What if it cost him his access to China? The young man chose a different topic. Were his advisers wrong? From one point of view, no, they were not. Unclarity about where red lines exactly are, when magnified by fear, makes self-censorship even more constricting than conventional censorship. Another Princeton student—a president of the undergraduate student body, who had been invited to China along with other Ivy student presidents—came to ask me whether, while in China, he could even utter the words "Dalai Lama."

I could tell many other stories of how China scholars, including senior figures, stay away from public comment on topics that Beijing considers "sensitive." When they do need to touch on them, they choose their phrases carefully. A term like "Taiwan independence," anathema to Beijing, is avoided in favor of "cross-strait relations" or "the Taiwan question." The June Fourth massacre of 1989 is demoted linguistically to an "incident." Liu Xiaobo, the Nobel Peace Prize winner who sits in prison, is not mentioned at all, if possible.

It is not quite accurate to say that China scholars are either naïve or cowardly in accepting these verbal accommodations. Their ways of speaking are a sort of professional code that the field understands as code and that does not color—at least not very much—the underlying grasp of issues. The costs of using the code are most heavy when experts turn to address students or the public. Audiences not privy to the code can be given the impression that a massacre was only an incident; that Taiwan independence really isn't much of an issue; and that a Nobel Prize winner in prison may not be worth mentioning.

The avoidance of straight talk with the public is, in my view, a violation of the tenure system. A tenured professorship is a wonderful job: a person gets respect, social status, and a guaranteed upper-middle-class lifestyle all the way to the grave. Why does society give us such a good deal? Because we are nice people? Because we have already worked hard and so deserve guaranteed groceries for life? No. Society gives us the good deal so that we can tell the truth as we see it, without fear or favor. Tenure protects us so that we can do that. What we owe society in return is candor. If we hem and haw, pull punches, and are otherwise "prudent" about telling the truth, we renege on the tenure deal.

People who ask me about my blacklisting usually don't imagine that there are benefits to the status, but there are. Again, I will name two.

One is that a person gets undeserved credit. It embarrasses me to hear people say, "You were so courageous to help Fang Lizhi on the day of the massacre." The events of that day had stunned me into a state of mind where my decisions were neither courageous nor cowardly but simply reflexive. "We need a ride; can you help?" "I think so; let me try." That was it. No courage involved.

The congratulatory views can be surprising. In 2008, shortly after I arrived at the University of California at Riverside to teach, I was walking across campus one day when a young blond male on a skateboard came careening my way. He jumped off in front of me and neatly flipped the board upward with his foot to catch it in his right hand.

"Professor Link!" he said.

"Yes...?"

"I hear you're on a Chinese government blacklist!"

"Yes, that's right..."

"Dude!" he shouted, gave me a thumbs up, and skated off.

The second benefit of being blacklisted is more important. It is that blacklisting leaves a person freer than before. This is because once a blacklisting happens, the fear that it *might* happen disappears. After all it is dread of the event—not the event itself—that causes people to self-censor. Relieved of the pressure, it becomes much easier to say what one thinks. My favorite expression of this principle is the Chinese farmers' proverb *sizhu bupa kaishui tang* "dead pigs aren't afraid of hot water." A dead pig not only enjoys maximal latitude to comment but can be of service to others. In 2015 the Dalai Lama was interested in having a small meeting with American China scholars, and the scholars whom the Dalai Lama's office approached showed strong interest. But the question of who would host the meeting became a problem; to do it would be to risk blacklisting. Someone called me to see whether I could help. I would not need to raise money or do any organizing—just be the official host. I agreed. Why not? A second death would be redundant.

Some people have tried to help me get off the blacklist. I have already noted how the compiler of *The Tiananmen Papers* tried. In 2010 a reporter named Shi Feike, from China's liberal-leaning Southern News Group in Guangzhou, interviewed me in depth during a trip to the U.S. He did an excellent write-up of the interview, but it had to be cut by more than half before it was published. He knew that the cutting would happen, but felt that just to have my name, photo, and some of my words appear in the mainland press would be a worthwhile step forward, both for China and for me. He wanted, he said, to help me *tuomin*, literally "depart sensitivity" in the mainland press. Americans have tried to help, too. In 2008 a group of eighteen prominent China scholars wrote a private letter to the Chinese government advising that the blacklisting of American scholars is harmful to both the U.S. and China.

When is it right to make some compromises in order to get off of blacklists? Exiled Chinese dissidents have sometimes agreed to terms in order to make home visits for pressing reasons, such as the funeral of a parent. Americans, too, have sometimes succeeded in getting off blacklists, with or without making concessions. I would make concessions if I had a reason as strong as the death of a parent, and I find it hard to make blanket judgments about how any person should or should not play Beijing's unpalatable game. For me personally, though, the prospect of remaining on a blacklist has so far been preferable to acceptance of made-in-Beijing adjustments.

Reality Deeper than Fiction: The Truth of Sun Weishi

$\iff$

(2023)

A review of *The Woman Back from Moscow: In Pursuit of Beauty* by Ha Jin.

THIS BOOK will be denounced in Beijing. Ha Jin's *The Woman Back from Moscow* is a novel based on the life of Sun Weishi, an adopted daughter of Chinese premier Zhou Enlai, whose brilliant mind and intensive study in Moscow of the Stanislavski acting method brought her to the pinnacle of China's theatrical world during the Mao years. Her beauty and effervescent personality attracted powerful men—not only Zhou, who doted on her, but also Lin Biao, the Chinese Communist Party's leading general, who divorced his wife in order to propose marriage to her (unsuccessfully), and Mao, who apparently raped her during a long rail trip. She had several other suitors and eventually married the film star Jin Shan.

Ha Jin, a former soldier in the Chinese army who came to the U.S. in 1985 at age twenty-nine to do graduate study, has written ten novels in English as well as poetry, short stories, and essays. In *The Woman Back from Moscow*, he conveys in supple prose what Beijing inevitably will regard as too much truth about the history of the CCP. Perhaps anticipating trouble, Other Press offers a publisher's note at the book's beginning:

> This is a work of fiction. Names, characters, places, and incidents either are the product of the author's imagination or are used fictitiously, and any resemblance to actual persons, living or dead, events, or locales is entirely coincidental.

In an author's note at the book's end, Ha Jin lists five works of nonfiction that were his main sources. Although he imagines dialogue and invents some connective tissue, he writes, "Most of the events and details in this novel were factual.… Reality is often more fantastic than fiction, so I did my best to remain faithful to Sun Weishi's life story." He calls her Sun Yomei, a name she used in personal correspondence, because the name Weishi "is hard to pronounce in English and might upset the cadence of sentences."

Scandal is popular everywhere, of course, but in Communist China historical truth-telling carries special weight, because it questions the legitimacy of the regime. Although the CCP's "red families" (offspring of the original Mao-era revolutionaries) heavily influence elite politics, they do not enjoy a formal right to rule of the kind that, in imperial times, was passed from father to son. Nor does legitimacy derive from elections, because the CCP does not allow them. Legitimacy depends crucially on the historical record of how the rulers have performed. Some observers, including Cui Weiping, a prominent Chinese public intellectual, have argued that history has taken on an almost religious significance in Chinese politics. Religions project ideals into the future and offer followers the hope of reaching them. China's history-religion projects ideals onto the past and cites them as the reasons why a regime should continue. But a serious problem arises for this history-religion. The future has not yet happened, so religious promises cannot be falsified. The past has happened, so it can be.

It thus becomes a matter of utmost importance that the appearance of political virtue be preserved in accounts of events such as the Communists' Long March to Yan'an in the mid-1930s, their establishment there of an idyllic community, their founding of a "people's" republic in 1949, and much more. Of course there must be no mention of mass political executions or a huge famine. A whitewashed version of history becomes a kind of religious idol. It is placed beyond the public's questioning and can be tweaked only when a leader needs support for a current policy.

Guarding official history becomes the métier of a group of state-sponsored "historians" who construct versions of the past and are not bothered by any discrepancies between their accounts and what actually happened. "It does not even enter their thinking," says Cui Weiping. They and their superiors measure the quality of their work not by its degree of truth but by its likely effectiveness in selling the history-religion. This is why Beijing's red royalty will see Ha Jin's book rather as a convention of manicured cats might see an approaching bulldog. What he writes is fiction, but it is far closer to truth-telling than what the regime calls history.

Talk in China about elite politics has long made use of stage metaphors that originally come from popular opera. A leader gaining power "ascends the stage," in losing it "leaves the stage," and while on it plays roles. Actual life is covered up. "Mao" is a fabricated Mao, "Lin Biao" a fabricated Lin Biao. Ha Jin's novel removes the masks. He presents human beings enmeshed in thoughts and emotions that other human beings will recognize.

The culture we glimpse in the novel is the special culture of the Communist superelite, which differs greatly from the way most ordinary Chinese live. For example, socialist ideology notwithstanding, members of the elite keep servants. From the dusty caves of Yan'an in the late 1930s to the red-hot "class struggle" of the late 1960s in Beijing, there are always maids to peel pears, orderlies to deliver lunch boxes, and guards to watch doorways, and when a child arrives the family goes out and hires a nanny. Ha Jin does not spotlight this aspect of life. I am doing that, plucking details from a narration within which they are unobtrusive, which adds to their credibility. We learn that Mao's wife Jiang Qing enjoys a villa, a yacht, and a "flock of servants" in Hangzhou only because these facts happen to appear as Ha Jin is relating a story about her resentment of a rival.

The sufferings of the elite are of a special kind, different from the sufferings of "the masses." Sun Yomei and her colleagues know about the attack in 1951 on the film *The Life of Wu Xun,* which Mao, in an apparent effort to control the film industry, instructs his underlings to denounce as a "model of reconciliation with feudalistic and reactionary forces." His words are, to be sure, a harsh blow. But during the same years (1949–1953), putative "landlords" were being executed by the millions in a land reform campaign. Yomei and her artist colleagues make no mention of that. They likely are unaware of it. They also do not remark upon the Anti-Rightist Campaign of 1957, in which hundreds of thousands of intellectuals were killed, jailed, or persecuted, or the Mao-induced famine of 1959–1961 that took at least 30 million lives, except when such events tangentially affect a person in their lives. They are ethical people; we trust that they would be concerned by such matters if they were aware of them.

They live in a cocoon, but the culture inside is hardly protective. It is tense and bereft of trust. Familial affection is present, but it gives way to politics whenever necessary. President Liu Shaoqi is willing to derail the marriages of two of his children, who have non-Chinese partners, because of "revolutionary needs." Zhou Enlai clearly cares for his adopted daughter. He coaches her in how to survive: "Just be careful about what you say in your letters. Always assume that some other eyes will read your letters before they reach me." But during the Cultural Revolution, when Zhou is faced with the dilemma of whether to sacrifice Yomei in order to protect himself from Jiang Qing, he signs a warrant for her detention that leads to her torture and death in prison. An aunt of Yomei's, observing Zhou's maintenance of a suave exterior, calls him a "smiling snake."

Zhou is no anomaly. He lives in an environment where, in the end, people can trust only themselves. The distinguished Australian Sinologist Simon Leys once observed that comparisons of the CCP elite to the mafia are in a sense unfair to the mafia, in which a certain loyalty to "brothers" does play a part. Losers of political battles at the top of the CCP generally are not relegated to comfortable retirements—they go to prison or worse. Zhou did not wish to seal Yomei's fate; he was forced to when it became clear that it was either him or her.

Political power so infuses personal relations that the question "How might I use this person?" is almost always in the background. As Mao awakes in his railroad car, lying next to Yomei, whom he has raped during the night, he lights a cigarette, blows "two tusks of smoke out of the edges of his mouth," and says, "I could tell you were not a virgin…. Please join my staff. I need your help and will be considerate to you." Shocked and in tears, Yomei bolts from the car, but not before Mao adds, "Even though you don't want to work for me, keep in mind that I'll be happy to help you when you need me."

Many years later, she does need him. Red Guards are torturing her brother Sun Yang, who has written a laudatory biography of Zhu Deh, Mao's rival in the claim to be the founder of the People's Liberation Army. Yomei appeals in person to Mao to intervene for her brother. He listens and says that "we should look into" the matter. In fact he does no investigating, but neither he nor Yomei finds it extraordinary that a rape victim is asking her rapist for a favor.

This is within the culture. The "scar literature" that followed Mao's death in the late 1970s offers many credible accounts of how victims had to defer to the very people who had once harmed them. This problem was not just in elite culture; it reached as deep into society as Party rule did. The writer Zheng Yi records the case of a woman whose preschool son was killed because his father had been a "class enemy." Three men tied the boy by a rope to the tailgate of a truck and dragged him until he was dead. Fifteen years later the three murderers visited the mother's home, accompanied by a Party official, to perform a ritual "apology." She was obliged to pour tea for them.

During Yomei's final days—she died in prison in 1968—police grill her on her personal connections. It is their job to gather intelligence that can be useful in future political combat. Yomei is annoyed at one point with their persistent questions about sex. They wonder whether Zhou's affection for his adopted daughter was in part sexual. To find evidence of this would neither raise nor lower Yomei's political standing but would be immensely useful to Jiang Qing in her bitter rivalry with Zhou. Yomei asks her tormentors, "Why are you so interested in what happened inside the top leaders' pants?"

For reasons that are unclear to me, under China's Communist regime sexual misbehavior came to be considered a strong indicator of depravity. In imperial times, a man's wealth could be measured by how many women (both wives and concubines) he accumulated and how many children they produced. Sexual prowess was admired. Dalliance outside the home was not exactly favored, but it was seen more as a profligate use of time—like chatting in teahouses or listening to singsong—than a moral transgression. In the Communist years, however, extramarital sex came to be seen as an unambiguous sign of foul character and was often used as a weapon in political struggle.

In 2016 Xu Zhangrun, a distinguished professor of law at Tsinghua University, began publishing essays that criticized Xi Jinping's national policies in fundamental ways. Xu's essays were erudite, broadly conceived, and written in an elegant semiclassical Chinese. Xi needed to fight back, but how? He was no literary match for Xu, so his weapons were limited to firing the professor from his post, depriving him of his pension, blacklisting him, and detaining him. And what else? Charging him with visiting prostitutes in Sichuan. The accusation was sufficiently aggressive that its falsity did not seem to matter.

Accusations of sexual excess could be potent weapons against the powerful as well as their victims. In the mid-1990s, after Mao's personal physician Li Zhisui published his book *The Private Life of Chairman Mao*, Chinese people focused quickly on its revelations of Mao's lifelong appetite for young women. Slower and more sober readings of the lengthy book showed in detail how Mao treated people heartlessly and caused the unspeakable suffering of millions. But what grabbed public attention was his rampant lust.

Was there no sign of Maoist ideals in Yomei's milieu—of serving the people or building a new socialist China? In Ha Jin's telling, such ideas rarely enter the thinking of top leaders. Jiang Qing wants to create a "new" Chinese opera, but her goals are personal fame and power, not benefit to society. Mao never mentions to Yomei any rationales for collectivizing agriculture, which his regime was pursuing in the 1950s, but when she shows him a Soviet film of an atomic bomb explosion he is smitten by the "typhoon of fire" and becomes obsessed with getting a bomb for himself.

And yet there were people who did embrace the new ideals and did devote their lives to them. The main theme of Ha Jin's book is what happened to these people, and Yomei is his main example. Sent to Moscow in 1939 with Zhou Enlai, who needs medical treatment there, Yomei stays, learns Russian, studies theater, and becomes deeply enamored of Stanislavskian principles: actors must internalize the characters they play— their thoughts, feelings, and fears, both onstage and off—and must focus intently on the drama they are participating in whether or not they have speaking roles. She finds that the best way to pursue this approach is through directing, not acting, and after she returns to China in 1950 has great success as a director and eventually begins to write her own plays.

But she soon encounters a problem that only grows larger as her work continues. She directs *Pavel Korchagin*, a stage adaptation of Nikolai Ostrovsky's classic 1936 Soviet novel *How the Steel Was Tempered*. The art flows from within her, the critical reception is enthusiastic, and the success leaves her euphoric. Then she hears Mao's encomium, in which he states she has "won honor for China and for our Party." This shocks and disappoints her. She had not felt a political motivation in staging the play and finds Mao's assertion of state sovereignty over her work inappropriate and awkward.

Years later she arrives at the view that "any extraordinary talent that emerged in arts would get noticed by the powers that be and would be harnessed to serve a cause or a political purpose." In such circumstances, pursuit of creativity is futile. Worse, it could be dangerous. Innovation could cause a person to stand out from a group, whereas "in this country, it was always safer to remain common and average."

I was reminded of an exchange I had with the Chinese writer Cao Guanlong in June 1980. Cao worked in a bicycle factory in Shanghai. When he asked me if American bikes were different from Chinese ones, I commented that most of ours had gears. I felt apprehensive that my words might embarrass him on behalf of his country and was surprised to hear his quick response:

> We know how to install gears. I can do it. My friends can, too. But we don't dare. Anyone who added gears would be stepping out of line, upsetting the uniformity. The leaders don't like that. So we don't do it. Not worth it.

During the Cultural Revolution Yomei moves to an oil field in remote Heilongjiang Province, where she lives among ordinary workers and learns of their lives and ordeals, especially those of the women. She writes a play called *The Rising Sun* that becomes a major success in Beijing and other cities. It is an excellent example of what Mao, ever since his famous Yan'an talks in 1942, has been demanding that Chinese writers do: go among the workers, farmers, and soldiers, "directly experience" their lives, and bring their struggles and triumphs into art. In the end, though, the political authorities reject Yomei's work as "bourgeois and reactionary." At the cost of her life, she learns that what Mao has actually wanted from artists all along is not the autonomous pursuit of ideals but political fealty. An artist's job is to support the Party. Her or his work is to be poured into Party molds and presented as Party products.

In an art class at a primary school in May 1973, during my first trip to China, I saw a young boy drawing a picture of an airplane crashing in flames. The student sitting next to him was drawing the same thing. Then I saw that all the students in the class—thirty or so—were drawing the same scene in the same way. The teacher had provided a model. The drawing showed the fate of Lin Biao, who in September 1971, it was said, had attempted a coup against Mao and fled to the Soviet Union, but died when his plane crashed on the way. The youngsters' drawings were an example of how artistic effort from below fills molds prescribed from above. This was the system that stifled Yomei and ultimately destroyed her.

Yomei's experience in the theater exemplifies a broad pattern in the fate of "new socialist art" in the 1950s. Writers and artists of many kinds supported the new regime and were eager to promote its ideals. If this meant changing their work, that was all right—it was a welcome challenge. China's most popular performing art at the time was the comedic dialogue form known as *xiangsheng*. Long disparaged as low-class, xiangsheng performers were keen for the laurel of "socialist worker" and ready to work to deserve it. The regime's instructions to them were to transform their intrinsically satiric art into one that praised the new society. But that was a puzzle: How could satire be used to praise? One could satirize class enemies, but that approach quickly grew dreary. One could satirize men who believed that "the new woman" could not drive trucks, but problems arose when audiences didn't get the joke or laughed at the wrong things.

Despite the challenges, by 1956 a number of xiangsheng experiments had succeeded, and it appeared that a new socialist art indeed was at hand. But as with Yomei and the theater, the regime was not seeking autonomous efforts at anything. It wanted control. Independence of any kind was a threat. In 1957 He Chi, the most brilliant *xiangsheng* innovator to that point, was labeled a "rightist" and sent to a labor camp for twenty-two years. Others in the *xiangsheng* world noticed, and the experiments ended.

These examples from art illustrate a condition of life in Communist Chinese society that, although it is omnipresent and substantial, foreigners seldom notice. From the beginnings of the Communist regime until the present, there have always been popular thoughts, feelings, and initiatives that have been distinct from political labels and prescriptions. A concept like "ordinary life values" deserves a much larger scope in analyses of China than it normally gets. In the 1950s, when factories, schools, hospitals, and other institutions were converted into Party-led "work units," people did not ask, "How can I contribute most to the collective?" but "How can I get the most for my family from the new system?" Today a farmer getting out of bed in the plains of Gansu Province will be thinking not about "the thoughts of Xi Jinping in the new era" but about things like the day's weather and food, clothing, medicine, and shelter for his or her family. If a political thought does occur to the farmer, it will likely be about a local bully, not about the "cult" of Falun Gong or the traitorous Dalai Lama.

This distinction between unofficial and official life holds from the bottom of society to the top. The actual life of the red elite that Ha Jin depicts could hardly differ more from its officially projected images of giving speeches, doing inspection tours, and in other ways focusing on "service to the people." The questions "What best fits the system?" and "What best serves my interests?" are asked in parallel by people at all levels, and they seldom have the same answers. In his memoirs the dissident physicist Fang Lizhi recalls how Teng Teng, vice-chair of China's State Education Commission in July 1989, summoned American ambassador James Lilley to berate him about how the U.S. was allowing Chinese students who had spoken out against the Tiananmen massacre to remain in the U.S. indefinitely. An hour after returning to the embassy, Lilley got a telephone call from Teng Teng's secretary asking him to give special attention to Teng's wife and children, who were seeking that same "indefinite residence" status in the U.S. There are plenty of other examples like this. The "split consciousness" of Chinese people in recent times has been widely noted.

Increasing repression under Xi, who came to power in 2012, has made it difficult for Chinese writers to present unapproved history. A few try, though, and with admirable success. Ian Johnson's *Sparks: China's Underground Historians and Their Battle for the Future* (2023) shows how a dozen or so writers and filmmakers, in loose association and using rudimentary tools, have been uncovering evidence of labor camps, famines, massacres, and other inglorious historical events that the government claims to be nonexistent. Johnson's "underground historians" work as if with hand chisels in salt mines, digging out, with great effort and at great risk, empirical results that have unchallengeable solidity.

Ha Jin is a comrade in their mission but uses different tools and reaps a different kind of harvest. Replacing the hand chisel with a deft pen fueled by reading, imagination, and empathy, he reveals mental life. He and Johnson write of history that lies "beyond the seam," as it were, and for Westerners this offers rare value. Most books by Western experts on China, including a few recent ones, are written as if there were no unofficial China to speak of.

People living inside China already know about the border between official and ordinary life, but they still could gain much from reading both these books. We should hope that good translations will appear. Ha Jin's accounts of actual life at the top would come as revelations to many, especially the young. A centuries-old Chinese literary genre called *yanyi*—"historical fiction"—survived into the Mao years in oral storytelling and underground "hand-copied volumes." These works recounted adventures, both true and imagined, of Mao, Zhou, Lin Biao, and other top Communists. Skulduggery abounds and the halos are gone, but the characters themselves are flat. There is no view into their inner lives—as there richly is in Ha Jin's novel. A reader in China today might find his accounts explosive. Oddly, we might say that the most extraordinary achievement of the novel is its brilliantly credible evocation of the ordinary.

Of course the regime will ban any translation. But still it would reach many people. Today perhaps 80 million or more internet users in China use virtual private networks to jump the government's firewall—and that doesn't count tens of millions of overseas Chinese.

Originally published in *The New York Review of Books*,
December 7, 2023

TEACHERS

People who have helped me to understand China are far too many to count. In this section I list nine and feel guilty for omitting so many others. Rulan Pian and Ezra Vogel taught me when I was an undergraduate at Harvard. Liu Binyan, Fang Lizhi, and Xiao Qiang I later came to know quite well; Chen Ruoxi and Kang Zhengguo are admired friends; Eileen Chang I have known only through letters and Liu Xiaobo only by telephone.

My Teacher Rulan Pian (1922–2013)

⊰)||⊱

(2014)

WHEN I WENT to college in 1962, I knew that I liked languages, English as well as others. In high school I had taken French, and I thought that in college I would try Chinese. I had lived two years in India as a boy, and might have taken Hindi, but Harvard didn't offer Hindi. It did offer Sanskrit, but I wanted to talk to people who were still alive.

"Don't do it," said the undergraduate adviser for "Far Eastern Languages," as the department was known in that era. "In your freshman year you should get started in a basic discipline. Chinese takes a lot of time. You can do it next year."

For this reason, I did not meet Rulan C. Pian until fall of 1963, at the beginning of my sophomore year. I took her course "Chinese B." It was a beginning course, but "B" didn't stand for "beginning." (I never did learn what the B stood for.) The adviser a year earlier had been right about one thing: the course took a lot of time. I split my time 50-50—half on Chinese B, half on everything else.

There were twelve students in Chinese B that year. A few had had some Chinese before, but none had had R.C. Pian before, so it was fair. She started us with tones, and then went to the *gwoyeu Romatzyh* romanization that her father Chao Yuen-ren had helped to invent. People have always said that I have good tones (for a foreigner), and here is the reason: *gwoyeu Romatzyh* + R.C. Pian. Later in my life I taught beginning Chinese about thirty times, and I always used the *gwoyeu Romatzyh* + R.C. Pian formula. It works. More importantly, lots of other things don't work.

It may seem odd to say that a nineteen-year-old boy from upstate New York fell in love with a forty-one-year-old Chinese lady who was married, but that is sort of what happened. Rulan did not seem forty-one. She bounced around the classroom as if there were springs in her shoes and spoke in a voice so charming and clear that you wanted to learn Chinese only because she spoke it. Some students called her "Dragon Lady," but that was based on a confusion. She was not frightening, only meticulous. If your "h" was insufficiently guttural, she told you, and you had to do it again. People talk about "tough love." In her, some students felt the "tough," but I felt the "love." I wasn't alone, either. There was another student in Chinese B, a sophomore like me and, as it happened, a dorm mate of mine, named Tom Schaefer. Tom and I liked our Pian classes so much that we would walk back to our dormitory together playing a game of how much real-world talk we could actually do using the limited vocabulary of Chinese B. I have lost track of where Tom went in life.

Besides me, quite a few other professors in China studies—Frederic Wakeman and Andrew Nathan, to name two—began Chinese with R.C. Pian. I don't want to continue trying to name names, because I inevitably will miss many, and I would not want the many who are missed to feel they are less important in my view than the many who are named.

In my junior year I took second-year Chinese, also with Rulan, and continued to do well in everything except memorizing how to write characters. I still split my time 50-50. In my senior year, though, I could not afford a 50-50 split, because I was majoring in philosophy and wanted to write a senior thesis on ethics and epistemology. When I graduated, Harvard gave me a "traveling fellowship" that let me go anywhere in world I liked, so I chose to go to Taiwan and Hong Kong (Americans couldn't go to mainland China in 1966). In preparation for that adventure, I took a third-year summer-intensive Chinese course at Middlebury College. Rulan's friend Liu Chün-jo was the school's director.

When I landed in Taiwan a few weeks later, my first big shock was that nobody on the island sounded like R.C. Pian. I don't mean that most people were speaking Taiwanese, although that was true; and I don't mean that the minority who spoke Mandarin had heavy "southern accents"—no retroflex initials, and so on—although that, too, was true. I mean that even the few who spoke northern Mandarin did not have that clear, bell-like voice that, to me, was what "Chinese" was supposed to sound like. I wished that Rulan could come over and straighten everybody out for me. That was impossible, of course. So I wrote to her asking for advice. What should I do amid all these imperfections? She wrote back: "Stick with what I taught you."

After a year abroad I went back to Harvard, but switched from philosophy to East Asian Studies for an M.A., and then to Chinese history for a Ph.D. In my second year in graduate school, Rulan hired me as a Teaching Fellow in Chinese, and that was the beginning of a forty-year span in which I taught Chinese, on average, every other year, and participated in writing two Chinese-language textbooks. When the Vietnam War heated up and it looked like I might be drafted, Rulan and her colleagues figured out how to hire me as a full-time teaching assistant in Chinese. That got me a "teaching deferment" from the draft and let me stay at Harvard, albeit not enrolled in graduate school, until I turned twenty-six and was exempt from the draft.

I wrote my dissertation on the rise of popular fiction in Shanghai in the early twentieth century, and I dedicated the work to R.C. Pian. Some of my fellow students—and, I fear, some of my graduate-school advisers as well—found it odd that I was honoring a "language teacher" in this way. They wondered if it was because Rulan had helped me with the dissertation. She indeed had given me a bit of advice on it, but the reason for the dedication was Chinese B. I felt that Chinese B was the most important course I had ever taken. Getting started well in Chinese language seemed to me the key to everything else. I wanted to get "inside" Chinese culture, and to the extent that I had succeeded, it was because of language, and my grasp of language was because of Chinese B. I couldn't imagine trying to understand Chinese without tones, and she had given them to me. I have the same view today, thirty-seven years later.

I finished the chapters of my dissertation during a seven-month marathon from July through December of 1975. On half-year leave from Princeton, where I had begun teaching, I rented an apartment in New York city and barely left it. One of my few diversions was to listen to audiotapes of Hou Baolin performing *xiangsheng* 相声. At first I couldn't understand the routines very well, but I loved them anyway, and eventually did figure some of them out, memorized a few, and finally even performed one at a CHINOPERL "frolic." Rulan was among the listeners, and I could tell that she was delighted. I could almost hear her saying to herself, "Look what I did!"

A few years later her friend Liu Chün-jo invited me to Minnesota to give a talk on *xiangsheng*, with performance. Rulan was there, and she agreed to be my "straight man" *penggen de* 捧哏的. This was okay with me, because, as everyone knows, the *penggen de* is the actor who is really in charge; my role was to be the "funny man" *dougen de* 逗哏的, who blabbers all over the place, very much out of control. So, we performed together. I remember that Rulan's only question was, "So I'm the straight man, am I? What's the opposite of straight man? Crooked woman?"

She understood irony, as this question of hers shows. In fall of 1989, the first time she saw me after I had brought Fang Lizhi and Li Shuxian to the U.S. Embassy in Beijing the day after the June 4 massacre, she said, "So, I read in the newspaper how you are causing trouble again!"

When Rulan retired in 1992, I went to her retirement party in Cambridge and brought my eleven-year-old daughter Monica with me. Monica had learned Chinese pretty well during a year in China in 1988–89, and she, like me, liked *xiangsheng*, so we performed a piece for Rulan. We also dressed up like a walrus and a carpenter to perform a recitation of "The Walrus and the Carpenter" that Rulan's father had translated and included as Lesson 20 in his classic textbook *Mandarin Primer*, whose every page I had studied in college. Rulan had always required us to memorize the lesson texts, and I had done that for Lesson 20 in 1965, so in order to do it again in 1992, I did not have to start from scratch. To make tusks for the walrus, Monica and I melted two white candles sufficiently to bend them into tusk-shape.

The last time I saw Rulan was in March, 2013. I had gone to Colby College in Maine to give a lecture, and on the way home stopped in Cambridge to see her. Monica was teaching philosophy at Tufts, so she came along. I had just published *An Anatomy of Chinese: Rhythm, Metaphor, Politics* (Harvard, 2013) and had dedicated the book to her father, so wanted to give her a copy.

At age ninety her long-term memory was still good. She knew exactly who I was, and was obviously pleased that I had come to see her again. But her short-term memory was not so good. She asked me, "What are you teaching?" and I explained. I was teaching Chinese literature and a course on human rights in cross-cultural perspective; I had also volunteered to do a freshman course on writing English. After my explanations, she smiled sweetly and we changed the subject back to her father and my book. About five minutes later she turned to me again: "So! What are you teaching?" Before Monica and I left that day, she asked the same question two more times, clearly with no sense of revisiting covered ground. In that respect she had declined. But where she had not declined was that each time she asked the question her voice, although a bit hoarse now, was still warm and sincere, and still had a glint of that bright-eyed, bouncy spirit that I had found so alluring in 1963.

Originally published in the newsletter of the Department of East Asian Languages and Civilizations, Harvard University, January 6, 2014

My Teacher Ezra Vogel (1930–2020)

⊰⊱

(2022)

E ZRA WAS GENTLE. Agreeable, considerate, humble, a good listener, and famous enough to wear a stuffed shirt but utterly lacking any desire to do so. He shook hands limply, and at first might give you the impression of "soft." But the Chinese idiom 外圆内方 "round outside and right-angled inside" is more like it. He was rigorous inside. In the spring semester of 1966 I had a tutorial with him on Mondays from 4:00 p.m. to 4:30 p.m. We started every Monday at exactly 4:00 and he dismissed me at precisely 4:30. No wobble. The purpose of the rigor was as much to discipline himself, I felt, as to train me.

His use of language was the same: on the surface were plain, simple words that a high-school student could follow, but inside was packed content that experts envied. As I later moved into literary studies and had to cope with the discourse of constructed subjectivity and its imbricated topoi (in short, with emptiness), the plunk-plunk-plunk of Ezra's style, each meek word carrying its own freight, became a model.

In the early 2010s, on a visit by Ezra to California, Dick Madsen, Paul Pickowicz and I invited him to dinner. He started bemoaning the way young sociologists became overjoyed when they found huge data sets at hospitals, police departments, or wherever. Working out one's theoretical contribution had become essential for professional advancement, and it had become a real coup to lay hands on a stash of fresh data that one could use to illustrate one's point. What's wrong with that?, we asked Ezra. "Intellectually, it's upside-down," he said. "You learn from your data; you don't teach it." A provocative view, trenchantly put. Here, too, was rigor inside softness.

Rigorous never meant brittle or narrow. Ezra's expansive intellect was the very opposite of that. I want also to point out his political breadth. He was strongly supportive of me from my undergraduate years on, even though we both knew that my views of the Chinese Communist Party came to diverge sharply from his. (In brief: I see Deng Xiaoping less as a beneficent "architect" of reform from the top down and more as a savvy ship-captain who kept the CCP boat on top of a sea of demands for reform that pushed from the bottom up.) I once visited Congress to testify about Confucius Institutes and was very harsh on the CCP. (Properly, of course.) I denounced, among other things, its practice of spending billions of yuan to promote its image around the world while kids in the hills of Guizhou still didn't have desks and blackboards. A couple of weeks later I got an email from Ezra; he told me he had seen my testimony and liked it. I wrote back that he doesn't have to be polite. He is my dear teacher and I his ever-grateful student, and it's OK if we disagree on some questions. He wrote back quickly: "No, no, no, I really *do* like your testimony." I had been wrong to guess that he was being polite. His broad intellect could take in a wide range of viewpoints and think about all of them. This ability also allowed him space to tell me, with nothing but kind intentions, when I had gone astray. When Andy Nathan and I edited *The Tiananmen Papers*, he told me I shouldn't be so confident in the "compiler" of the papers until I got to the bottom of who he was.

The last time I saw Ezra was in June 2017, when my family and I were visiting Cambridge on our way back from a short stay in Maine. My wife Tong Yi had served as an assistant to Wei Jingsheng during Wei's seven-month respite from prison in 1994, and for that offense she had spent two and a half years in a labor camp. She knew about Ezra because of the Deng Xiaoping book. She loathed Deng, and so, at first, I was swimming upstream in getting her to understand my affection for Ezra. We were walking near Sumner Road when I pointed to number 14. "See that house? That's where Ezra Vogel lives." "Let's go!" she said. I had to say "No, we can't just crash in uninvited. We can send an email first." But it's not easy to stop an ex-convict with an idea. Tong Yi walked straight to the house and knocked on the door. Ezra and his wife Charlotte were at home, extremely warm, asked us in, and gave us tea—using about an hour, right in the middle of Ezra's work day. He was doing his China-Japan book at the time and explained that he wanted to do a Hu Yaobang book next. In his mid-eighties, he had two more books in mind—Hu Yaobang and his memoirs.

My peppery spouse put the key question, "Why do you do this? Why are you working so hard even at your age?" Any other person might have taken this as a rhetorical question and given a pro forma answer. Not Ezra. He took it as a serious question that deserved a responsible reply. Visibly, he started introspecting: WHY do I do this? After a moment or two he was talking about his hometown in Ohio, where his parents had made him feel that it was his duty to be "a good boy." He grew up, he said, always wanting to be a good boy for them. They died, but the habit had become rooted in his character. His duty to parents just shifted to be a general duty toward the world. He was still trying to be "a good boy," he said. This reminded me of the late-Ming ideal of *tongxin* 童心 "the childlike heart." A person who has such a heart grows old while preserving the sincerity of a child's outlook. *Tongxin* is not the same as naiveté. It absorbs experience and strife while maintaining full authenticity. The trait is truly rare, but Ezra had it.

Reproduced by permission of the Harvard University Asia Center from Martin Whyte and Mary C. Brinton, eds., *Remembering Ezra Vogel*, pp. 311–313 (Cambridge, Mass.: Harvard University Asia Center, 2022)

Liu Binyan (1925–2005)

(2006)

LIU BINYAN, the distinguished Chinese journalist and writer who died of cancer on December 5, 2005, in exile in New Jersey, at the age of eighty, had a powerful analytic mind and was an inveterate defender of the poor and the oppressed. But the trait that most determined his course through life was his bent for speaking out, combined with his utter inability to say anything that he thought to be false. This was so even in small matters. During his last visit with me he said, "Perry, you're a Sinologist, but I have never tasted really good Chinese tea at your house."

In an authoritarian political system like China's, this sort of candor is dangerous. In 1956, Liu published stories about how officials controlled the press and engaged in industrial corruption; the next year the Chinese Communist Party, whose underground organization he had joined in 1943, expelled him for "anti-Party, anti-socialist" activity. He was denounced, banned from print, and sent to a remote mountain village. Twenty-two years later, during the thaw after the death of Mao, authorities "reversed the verdict" on him, readmitted him to the Party, and restored his right to publish.

While this sort of treatment made many other writers meek, Liu returned to his work with even more passion, exposing injustice and analyzing corruption in more depth and detail than before. He spoke of "two kinds of truth," one that floated down from "the policies of the higher-ups" and another that forced its way up from below, from "the longings of the common folk." He wrote stories about corrupt officials, who, for example, diverted coal supplies to their cronies in exchange for kickbacks, and then could say with a smile that this was "serving the people," while arranging life sentences for anyone who dared to object.

By the mid-1980s he had earned the nickname "China's conscience." People from throughout China lined up at his door, asking him to help them right wrongs. In 1985, when Chinese writers were allowed (for the first and only time) to hold free elections for posts in the Chinese Writers' Association, only the elderly Ba Jin, famous since the late 1920s, got more votes nationwide than Liu.

That same year, though, Liu published a long article in which he argued that loyalty to socialist ideals must sometimes take precedence over loyalty to the leaders of a socialist system. Soon thereafter Deng Xiaoping labeled Liu a "bourgeois liberal," and in 1987 he was expelled from the Party for a second time. He was a Nieman Fellow at Harvard in 1989, at the time of the June Fourth massacre in Beijing, and he went on U.S. television to denounce the killings. After that he was never allowed back in China. A complete ban on his work inside China has left a younger generation of Chinese with little idea of who he was. Ill with cancer during his final three years, Liu sent letters, hand-delivered by sympathizers, to Jiang Zemin and Hu Jintao, asking for permission to go home. The letters got no response. The day after Liu's death a spokesman for China's Foreign Ministry had no comment on Liu except that "we have already reached our conclusions about him."

If it seems odd that the government of the world's largest nation should fear one ailing, elderly man, we need only remember that Liu was never the sole creator of the tremendous power that his writings generated. That power came from inside China. Liu was a popular hero because he wrote and said publicly things that hundreds of millions of Chinese dared to say only in private, if at all. That Party leaders in 2005 were still afraid of him shows that they were aware of the fragility of official truth inside their country.

After Liu died in a hospital in New Brunswick, New Jersey, had funeral in Princeton, New Jersey, and was cremated in Trenton, New Jersey, his daughter Liu Xiaoyan, who had traveled from China to be there, took possession of his ashes and would tell no one what she was doing with them. Liu Binyan had made clear that he wanted the ashes to go back to China and be buried beneath a stone that bore the epitaph: "Here lies a Chinese person who did some things that were right for a person to do, and said some things that were right for a person to say."

Liu Xiaoyan kept her handling of the ashes secret because she wanted to get them back to China and was afraid of police at the border. Even the ashes of a regime critic as powerful as Liu Binyan might be viewed as "destabilizing" and therefore confiscated. With careful planning Liu Xiaoyan did get the ashes back to China and got them buried in a graveyard on the western side of Beijing. The Liu family then asked the cemetery staff if they could erect a tombstone bearing the words: "Here lies a Chinese person who did some things that were right for a person to do, and said some things that were right for a person to say." The staff agreed, but returned a few days later to tell the family that the words could not be put onto the tombstone. The "superiors" had said no. Only Liu's name and dates could appear on the stone. There was no explanation, but fears of "instability" were clearly the reason. (What if someone were to lay flowers? What if several people did? What if a group formed?...) After deliberation the family decided to withdraw its request for the inscription, bide its time, and hope for a day when the stone might be able to appear as Liu Binyan wanted it. They decided, for the time being, to leave the stone blank. Inadequate as a monument to Liu, it stood, in another sense, as a telling comment on the Chinese regime. How could one capture, in brief, the odd combination of its visible power and its inner weakness? A wordless stone, in the end, said it best.

Originally published in *The New York Review of Books*,
February 9, 2006

On Fang Lizhi (1936–2012)

(2012)

Fang Lizhi, a distinguished professor of astrophysics and a luminary in the struggle for human rights in contemporary China, died suddenly on the morning of April 6, 2012. At age seventy-six he had not yet retired, and he was preparing to leave home to teach a class when he commented to his wife that he did not feel quite right. She urged him to stay home and he agreed, saying he would call his department secretary to explain. A few minutes later he had died in his chair at his home office.

News of his passing spread quickly on the Chinese internet. Students whom he had taught in the 1980s and admirers of his eloquent championing of human rights wrote their accolades. State Security officials noticed, and within hours ordered internet police to delete all messages that mentioned the words "Fang Lizhi." After that, tweets about Fang on *weibo* (a Chinese version of Twitter) disappeared about a minute after posting.

Fang's father was a postal clerk and he grew up in modest circumstances. His brilliant mind and outstanding work as a student led him to the Physics Department of China's elite Peking University in the early 1950s. The campus atmosphere of optimistic socialism attracted him, and he joined the Communist Party. In courting his girlfriend (a fellow student who later became his wife, the physicist Li Shuxian), he once invited her to "watch me grow into a good Communist." During Mao Zedong's Cultural Revolution in the late 1960s, he was persecuted and confined in a reeducation camp at a coal mine in southern Anhui province. It was this treatment that led him to specialize in theoretical astrophysics, which he later told me was "the only field of physics I could pursue without equipment." After Mao died Fang's star rose again, and in 1984 he became vice-president of China's prestigious University of Science and Technology in Anhui.

By then he had shed his attachment to Marxist dogma and, in addition to teaching physics, began delivering trenchant speeches on human rights and democracy. For example, when the government began using the slogan "modernization with Chinese characteristics" (i.e., modernization except for monopoly power for the Communist Party), Fang responded satirically by asking students if they believed in physics with Chinese characteristics. Students were charmed; the authorities were not. In January 1987, they fired him from his university job (for this and other speeches), expelled him from the Party, and compiled excerpts from his speeches that they then distributed to campuses all across China as examples of "bourgeois liberalism" that students should avoid. But students found the excerpts themselves far more attractive than the warnings, with the result that Fang suddenly became famous everywhere in China. He became the spirit behind the nationwide pro-democracy demonstrations in the spring of 1989. He lived on the outskirts of Beijing at the time, but purposefully stayed away from Tiananmen Square. He wanted to make it clear to everyone, including the authorities, that the students were acting autonomously.

After the June 4 massacre that ended the protests, the government published a list of people wanted for arrest. Fang Lizhi and Li Shuxian were numbers one and two. On June 5 they took refuge in the U.S. embassy in Beijing, where they lived for thirteen months in a basement apartment that had no windows. On being told that Deng, in a conversation with Henry Kissinger, had said he wanted him to write a confession, Fang wrote one in the form of a forthright statement of human rights principles. In June 1990 the Japanese government negotiated the release of Fang and Li by offering economic concessions to China, and for the next nearly twenty-two years they lived in exile.

Fang's path through life observed a pattern that is common to China's dissidents: a person begins with socialist ideals, feels bitter when the rulers betray the ideals, resorts to outspoken criticism, and ends in prison or exile. Liu Binyan, Wang Ruowang, Su Xiaokang, Hu Ping, Zheng Yi, Liu Xiaobo, and many others have followed this pattern. Most have been literary figures—writers, editors, or professors of Chinese—who base their dissent in the study of Chinese society and culture. Fang was a natural scientist, and this made him different in important ways.

He was good at explaining how, for him, concepts of human rights grew out of science. He named five axioms of science that had led him toward human rights: 1) "Science begins with doubt," whereas in Mao's China students were taught to begin with fixed beliefs. 2) Science stresses independence of judgment, not conformity to the judgment of others. 3) "Science is egalitarian"; no one's subjective view starts ahead of anyone else's in the pursuit of objective truth. 4) Science needs a free flow of information, and cannot thrive in a system that restricts access to information. 5) Scientific truths, like human rights principles, are universal; they do not change when one crosses a political border.

Science was not only the origin of Fang's thinking on human rights; it remained for him the grounds for authority on the issue. When he began speaking on human rights in the 1980s, his audiences paid him special attention because of his high position in Chinese academic life. No Chinese intellectual who has chosen to speak out on human rights has ever been as high "within the system" as Fang was when he began. To Fang, though, authority that derives from bureaucratic position was quite beside the point. His authority in human rights was the truth, discoverable by science, that lay within the patterns of the universe. This kind of grounding gave him confidence to confront any Party official—who, by the same logic, would be weakly positioned to answer him. Fang had science, and no Party leader could belittle science. Science was part of the Four Modernizations, the guiding policy of the day. Moreover, it was in Marxism, which claimed to be a "science" of human history. The leaders of the regime no longer believed in Marxism, but had to pretend that they did. Fang's challenge from science frightened them more deeply than anything a writer or a professor of Chinese might do.

Of the many comments from Fang's Chinese admirers that I heard in the days after his passing, here are three of my favorites:

> Some call him China's Sakharov, and that's fine. But to me, Fang and the Communist Party are more like Galileo and the Roman church. An astrophysicist against powerful and arbitrary authority; the authority persecutes the physicist, but the physicist gets the truth right.

> In the 1980s the words "human rights" could hardly be uttered in China. Today they can, and the term *weiquan* ("support rights") is everywhere. No one person made this change. But no one person had more to do with it than Fang Lizhi.

Fang shows us a better way to be Chinese in the modern world. To be Chinese does not have to mean "supports Bashir al-Assad at the UN" or "puts a Nobel Peace Prize winner in prison." We can be better. Teacher Fang is our example.

Others of Fang's friends have noted his literary talents. He occasionally wrote charming essays on topics such as his courtship with Li Shuxian, or about how, as a boy, he and his friends rigged the doorbell of a famous opera singer so that it wouldn't stop ringing, then hid to watch the fun from a distance. His wry wit was a constant joy to friends as well as a stiletto in political debate. I remember watching a Western journalist interview him during the student protests in spring 1989. When the interview was over the reporter asked if there were a way he could ask follow-up questions, if necessary. Fang said "sure," and gave the reporter his telephone number.

"We've heard that your phone is tapped," the reporter said. "Is it?"

"I assume so." Fang grinned.

"Doesn't that...bother you?" the reporter asked.

"No," said Fang, "for years I've been trying to get them to listen to me. If this is how they want to do it, then fine!"

Borrowing Fang's wit, we might note that the authorities did more than listen. They "wanted" him. The 1989 warrant for his arrest was never dropped, so that when he died he was still officially wanted: for "the crime of counterrevolutionary incitement" and as "the biggest black hand behind the June Fourth riots."

Originally published in *The New York Review of Books*
May 10, 2012

Mao's China: The Language Game

(2015)

This essay is about something I learned from the famous writer Eileen Chang—not in person, but from one of her novels.

IT CAN BE embarrassing for a China scholar like me to read Eileen Chang's pellucid prose, written more than sixty years ago, on the early years of the People's Republic of China. How many cudgels to the head did I need before arriving at comparable clarity? My disillusioning first trip to China in 1973? My reading of the devastating journalism of Liu Binyan in 1980? Observation of bald lies in action at the Tiananmen massacre in 1989 and in the imprisonment of a Nobel Peace laureate in more recent times? Did I need all of this to catch up to where Chang was in 1954 in her understanding of how things worked in Communist China, beneath the blankets of jargon? In graduate school I did not take Chang's *Naked Earth* (published in Chinese in 1954 and translated by Chang into English in 1956) and its sister novel, *The Rice-Sprout Song* (also published in 1954 and translated by Chang into English in 1955), very seriously. People said the works had an anti-Communist bias. How silly.

In *Naked Earth*, Chang shows how the linguistic grid of a Communist land-reform campaign descends on a village like a giant cookie cutter. There are Poor Farmers, Middling Farmers, Landlords, Bad Elements, and more. When actual life doesn't fit the prescriptions, so much the worse for actual life. Make it fit. A "cadre" (a technical term for a functionary in the Communist system) complains that the farmers have "always been back-ward. . . . All they ever see is the bit of material advantage right in front of them." This leaves them "afraid to be active." Perhaps they don't want to be active? No, answers the Organization, they are reticent only because they fear "the revenge of the Remnant Feudal Forces." When finally coaxed to complain, they sometimes—oops!—complain about the cadres, not the Landlords.

Eventually the farmers, like everyone else, figure out that their personal interests depend on correct verbal performance. There are certain things you are supposed to say and certain ways you are supposed to say them. "Tell the truth!" is a command that you recite your lies *correctly*. An unimpeachable exterior becomes everyone's goal.

In this novel, Chang was turning her attention to the years 1949 to 1953 and writing about parts of China—agricultural villages, a Communist newspaper office, soldiers in the Korean War—that were new to her. She is best known in the West for her stories from the 1940s, finely translated by Karen Kingsbury and collected in *Love in a Fallen City*. These earlier stories are delightful for their evocative language, psychological insight, moral acuity, and close observation of Chang's own social milieu, the Chinese urban elite. Given her background, one might ask how she could make such a transition as smoothly as she did.

Certainly her skill in imagining the private thoughts of people as they interact, so expertly honed in her earlier fiction, continues to serve her well in *Naked Earth* and *The Rice-Sprout Song*. In addition, she seems, like George Orwell, to have almost a sixth sense for immediate comprehension of what an authoritarian political system will do to human beings in daily life. She looks past the grand political system itself and focuses instead on the lives of people—how they feel and behave as they adapt to what the system forces upon them.

Still, readers may wonder how Chang could know about land reform in the Chinese countryside or about the Korean War without firsthand experience of those events. Perhaps sensing a need to address this question, Chang writes in prefaces to both *The Rice-Sprout Song* and *Naked Earth* that the novels are based on true stories. (She had never offered similar assurances about her earlier stories.) Chang did travel to rural China, at least briefly, in the years immediately before and after 1949, but most of the material for her novels seems to have come from secondhand accounts or from published sources. "Self-criticisms" by officials and descriptions of famines had appeared, after being combed for political correctness, in the state-run press. Chang could read past the propaganda overlay and infer what had actually happened.

She also appears to have learned from *The Sun Shines over the Sang-gan River*, the Chinese writer and Communist Party member Ding Ling's Party-approved long novel (published in 1948 and winner of the Stalin Prize in 1951) about land reform in Communist-held areas in the 1940s. The Chinese literary scholar Zhang Qianfen has noted a broad range of "intertextuality" between *Sanggan River* and *Naked Earth* on questions that range from how farmers wash their hands to what public "struggle sessions" look like. The main difference is that Ding Ling feels a continual need to invent "model behavior," while Chang does not.

In *Naked Earth*, one young woman suffers a torrid criticism session, ends it with a self-denunciation, and then steals away to weep in solitude. Someone discovers her and accuses her of "only pretending to accept criticism." Thinking quickly, she explains that, no, hers are tears of gratitude: "Everybody was so concerned about me, so enthusiastic in helping me to make Progress." Does her explanation pass muster? Yes, but less because it is credible than because it reinforces the exterior mask that says "I submit to the Organization." To the powers that be, that demonstration is more important than what she actually thinks.

Over time, the need to maintain a correct exterior turns public political language into a kind of chess game. You make moves in order to get what you want, and you avoid bad moves that would bring punishment. During the Three-Anti Campaign in 1951, when nearly all Communist cadres are scrutinized for corruption, waste, or bureaucratism, Ko Shan, a Party member and newspaper manager in public but a "tubercular nymphomaniac" (in C.T. Hsia's apt phrase) in private, is forced onto a stage for self-criticism:

> I have nothing to say in my own defense. I feel very much ashamed that even now—after so many years spent in the very nucleus of the struggle—even now there still exist in my consciousness certain bad traits of the petit-bourgeoisie. I have this Tendency toward Freedom and Looseness. And then when I fought in the guerillas I got into the Guerilla Style of behavior. Ever since then I've found it hard to Regularize my life. Now the matter of man-woman relations. My starting point was comradely love. But, it has gone out of bounds and has led to Obscure Behavior.

The crowd who is listening to her is aware that her oration is only a series of chess moves aimed at minimizing punishment. There is prurient interest, though, in the question of her illicit lovers. People heckle her to name them. Trapped before the Masses, Ko Shan needs to betray at least one lover, but which one? Liu Ch'üan, the young protagonist of *Naked Earth*, whom Ko Shan has recently seduced (despite their difference in age), is in the crowd listening and is terrified that he will be named.

"It's Chang Li," Ko Shan finally says, choosing not to name Liu Ch'üan. Chang is a slick official whom the reader already knows to be contemptible. We feel relief that Ko Shan, however cynical, retains at least enough humanity to protect the naïve Liu Ch'üan.

But no, it turns out. When Liu later visits Ko Shan's house to thank her, she explains that, "I mentioned Chang instead of you because I could trust him not to get me into a bigger mess than what I am in already. Which is more than I can say for you." She had named Chang because he was better at manipulating the language game, that's all. It had simply been another chess move on her part. Liu then asks her why Chang, who was also present at the meeting, had not shouted out "Liu Ch'üan too!" in order to split the blame. Could it be that Chang, for his part, had a bit of humanity somewhere inside him?

"What good would that do him?" Ko Shan responds. He would "just make an enemy without making things any easier for himself." Chang, too, had made a cold chess move, and nothing more.

Eileen Chang's acute observation of political language in China in the early 1950s reveals patterns that have persisted ever since. Maoist extremism has passed, but it remains true that an incorrect word-performance in public can be costly to a person's interests, and it is still the case that one person can earn credit by reporting the misstatements of another. When Liu Ch'üan volunteers to fight in Korea (escaping the political cauldron of Shanghai), he notices that he feels watched even after moving abroad. He "wondered if anybody who had lived under Communist rule could ever feel unwatched again." And indeed, in the Xi Jinping era, Chinese students in California still keep nonstandard political views under wraps when speaking in the company of other Chinese students. Only among well-trusted friends does one venture to "live in truth," in Václav Havel's phrase. In the early 1950s Liu Ch'üan and his girlfriend Su Nan inhabit "the cozy little igloo of their love, made of ice but warm and homey within." Today, the igloos are not so frozen to the ground, but are still there.

The distinguished journalist Dai Qing has suggested that the Communist Party failed to buy off Eileen Chang, even with lures like "member of the Political Consultative Conference or Vice Chair of the National People's Congress." I cannot vouch that such offers to Chang were made, but Dai Qing, who grew up in the family of Marshal Ye Jianying, who was a confederate of Mao Zedong, has considerable credibility on such topics. What we do know is that Chang accepted a grant from the United States Information Service (USIS) to write *The Rice-Sprout Song* and *Naked Earth* after she left China in 1952. This fact has been widely noted, and its significance sometimes exaggerated. It is far-fetched to imagine that the USIS distorted Chang's writing. She is too powerful a writer for that—too "immune from being tricked," in Dai Qing's phrase. Indeed, there is irony in the fact that the U.S. government still has not collected what it paid for: Its understanding of the language and politics of Chinese communism still lags far behind what Chang offered it sixty years ago.

If nothing else, the beauty of Chang's writing makes it hard to view it as anyone's propaganda. After a rain squall on a dusty loess plateau, trees "were still sniffling and shedding big tears." At a nearby river, "Long wisps of yellow mud trailed sluggishly in the current, like half-beaten egg-yolk...." On the whole, *Naked Earth* has less of this than Chang's 1940s novellas do, but it would be a mistake to view this change as a compromise with USIS style. Chang has matured in this novel to a sparser naturalism, to a plane where "the shimmer of the unsaid," in Marianne Moore's phrase, can say even more than brilliant metaphor does.

Near the end of *Naked Earth*, Liu Ch'üan reflects that "As long as one man like him remained alive and out of jail, the men who ruled China would never be safe. They're afraid, too, he thought, afraid of the people they rule by fear." Did Liu foresee that in the Xi Jinping era those "men who ruled China" would still be spending hundreds of billions of yuan annually on "stability maintenance"? Chang seems even to anticipate the paradoxical connection between communism and luxury that has emerged recently in China. After normal human values have shriveled, only material scales remain, and in *Naked Earth*, we see already how officials in the regime have begun to take this route: villas, banquets, concubines. Chang died in 1995;

how surprised would she be to see the stupendous wealth of the Communist super-elite today?

Originally published as the "Introduction" to Eileen Chang,
Naked Earth (New York Review Books, 2015)

Beijing Protests a Lab Leak Too Much

(2021)

I AM AS eager as anyone to follow the world's virologists as they try to determine how COVID-19 emerged in Wuhan, China. But as a long-time student of Chinese Communist political language, I will need considerable persuading that the disease came from bats or a wet market. The linguistic evidence is overwhelming that Chinese leaders believe that the Wuhan Institute of Virology was the source—or, at a minimum, fear that this is what the world will believe.

Many years ago a distinguished Chinese writer, Wu Zuxiang, explained to me that there is truth in Communist Party pronouncements, but you have to read them "upside down." If a newspaper says "the Party has made great strides against corruption in Henan," then you know that corruption has recently been especially bad in Henan. If you read about the heroic rescue of eight miners somewhere, you can guess that a mine collapse might have killed hundreds who aren't mentioned. Read upside-down, there is a sense in which the official press never lies. It cannot lie. It has to tell you what the Party wants you to believe, and if you can figure out the Party's motive, *which always exists*, then you have a solid piece of information.

A few years ago another outstanding Chinese writer, Su Xiaokang, brought me one step deeper. You Westerners, he explained, are too hung up on the question of whether propaganda is true or not. For the regime, truth and falsity are beside the point. A statement might be true, false or partly true. What matters is only whether it works. Does it advance the interests of the Party? The top leaders hand out words and phrases for their minions to use, like trowels in a garden. The minions dig with them.

After the Communist Party locked down the city of Wuhan in winter 2020, a local writer named Fang Fang began recording the conditions and moods of the people around her and posting entries on the internet. "Fang Fang's Diary" quickly attracted a large following, and the author became known as "the conscience of Wuhan." Michael Berry, a UCLA professor of Chinese literature who was translating one of the author's novels, went to work on her posts as well. They were published by HarperCollins as *Wuhan Diary: Dispatches from a Quarantined City.*

The book consists of simple, unadorned, language that stood out in Wuhan only because no one else dared to write anything at all. But the regime's response was to attack Fang Fang more ferociously than any Chinese writer has been attacked since Mao Zedong's Cultural Revolution in the late 1960s. In his day, Mao had made "struggle" a transitive verb: to struggle someone was to surround him or her, in the street or on a stage, and hurl taunts, insults, threats and demands for confessions; no bystander would dare speak for the struggled for fear of becoming the next target. Verbal abuse often led to physical beatings, sometimes even to death.

Xi Jinping has revived struggle in a form that might be called "cyberstruggle." The young zealots of Mao's era, called Red Guards, have been replaced by equally frenetic strugglers nicknamed "Little Pinks." In spring of 2020, Little Pinks and others struggled Fang Fang: "Down with the imperialist running dog and traitor to China, Fang Fang!" To them, the diary was a "pile of messed up garbage and fabricated rumors [that] should be called 'Fang Fang's Sexual Fantasies'!" She received death threats. A witch hunt identified her supporters and began to struggle them, too. Mr. Berry, her translator, wasn't spared. Hundreds of text messages arrived on his cell phone: "You ugly white devil, feasting on the flesh of man and drinking human blood, the eighteen realms of hell were created especially for you!"; "If you ever set foot in China again I will kill you"; and others.

The invective might tell us something about the origins of COVID. Two facts are worth noting. First, the attacks are coordinated, not a random explosion of vitriol. Second, they are much stronger—orders of magnitude stronger—than other verbal attacks on individuals in China recently have been. These two facts, taken together, make it all but certain that the campaign against Fang Fang came from the top.

Borrowing Wu Zuxiang's technique of reading "upside down," what the Fang Fang campaign tells us is that Xi Jinping is extremely worried that the world will hold his regime responsible for the pandemic. The most radioactive question has been where the virus originated. Fang Fang made no mention of whether the virus originated in a wet market or a lab; she merely documented all of the suffering that began in Wuhan. The regime's focus on the origins question alone all but screams a truth.

The Chinese Communist Party's official account of the virus is that it "jumped" from bats to humans at a wet market not far from the Wuhan lab. The city government was quick to close down that market, seal it off, and provide the world with photos showing that the sealing had been done. Why were the authorities so swift and conspicuous? Because they suspected the wet market or because they wanted the world to? If they were certain that Mother Nature was the culprit, why silence their scientists and seal laboratory records? And why begin a vicious cyber struggle against someone who records daily life as she sees it?

We cannot fault HarperCollins for not seeing the full import of these dynamics in the background. But we should note that the publisher did agree, after a strong protest from Beijing, to alter the book's subtitle, which had referred to Wuhan as the "origin" of the pandemic, in favor of calling it simply a "quarantined" city.

Originally published in *The Wall Street Journal*,
June 13, 2021

Censoring the News Before it Happens

(2013)

Xiao Qiang, a physics student of Fang Lizhi's, a champion of human rights, and founder of China Digital Times, *has taught me much.*

EVERY DAY in China, hundreds of messages are sent from government offices to website editors around the country saying things like, "Report on the new provincial budget tomorrow, but do not feature it on the front page, make no comparisons to earlier budgets, list no links, and say nothing that might raise questions"; "Downplay stories on Kim Jung-un's facelift"; and "Allow stories on Deputy Mayor Zhang's embezzlement but omit the comment boxes." Why, one might ask, do censors not play it safe and immediately block anything that comes anywhere near offending the rulers? Why the modulation and fine-tuning?

For China's Internet police, message control has become complex. Local authorities have a full toolbox of phrases, which are fairly standard nationwide, that they use to offer guidance to website editors about dealing with sensitive topics. The harshest guideline is "completely and immediately delete." But with the rapid growth of difficult-to-control social media, a need has arisen for a wide range of more subtle instructions. For stories that are acceptable, but only after proper pruning, the operative phrase is "first censor, then publish." For sensitive topics on which central media have already said something, the instructions might say "reprint Xinhua [the government information authority] but nothing more." For topics that cannot be avoided because they are already being widely discussed, there are such options as "mention without stressing," "publish but only under small headlines," "put only on back pages," "close the comment boxes," and "downplay as time passes."

Directives are sent out by email or internet text-messaging. This is not ideal, because such messages can be traced or leaked. When traditional media such as newspapers, radio, and television are censored, directives normally arrive via unrecorded telephone calls that cannot be easily traced or leaked.

We know all this thanks, in large part, to Xiao Qiang, an adjunct professor at the School of Information at Berkeley, who leads the world in ferreting out and piecing together how Chinese internet censorship works. Xiao and his small staff have collected and organized a repository of more than 2,600 directives that website editors across China have received during the last ten years. Some are only a line or two long; others run to many pages. Some of the entries are verbatim copies, while others are paraphrases. Some were collected from Twitter, Sina Weibo (China's domestic Twitter), and internet forums, while others were sent to Xiao by editors in China who were frustrated or angry—either at what the directives said or at the fact of censorship itself.

The government's censorship strategies show its growing awareness of the power of social media. Informal news stories—often accompanied by photos from smart phones—now spread widely and quickly enough that official media lose credibility if they do not at least mention them. In such cases, "put on the back page" is often the best option. Under the scrutiny of web users, propaganda officials face the unwelcome task of censoring the internet while trying to appear as though they are not doing so—or at least not doing it "unreasonably." A balance must be sought. In one example, a story about two policemen who were killed in an auto accident got out on social media; censors anticipated an outcry if they "completely and immediately deleted," so they allowed the story to appear but added the instruction "close comment boxes"—apparently from fear that the boxes might fill with cheers of the kind that often spring from generalized resentment of the police.

Here, as an example, is a summary of directives that government officials in Beijing sent to Hunan Province in June 2011 (and that was leaked five months later):

All websites should conscientiously grasp the relevant principles and use them to purge any material that:

1. blackens the image of Party and state leaders or obfuscates the great historical achievements of the Party;
2. attacks our system or advocates the Western democratic system;
3. incites illegal assembly, petitioning, or "rights support" activity that harms social stability;
4. uses price rises, corruption cases, or other controversial events to spread rumors and incite hatred of officials, of police, or of the wealthy that could lead to activity offline;
5. incites ethnic hatred [of Han Chinese] that harms national unity;
6. attacks the Party's systems of managing the media and the internet by using the slanderous claim that we limit free speech.

If these are the regime's instructions about what *not* to do, Xiao's research shows that at least as much effort goes into the parallel task of "guiding" expression in pro-government directions. When a story reflects well on the Party, web editors receive instructions like "place prominently on the home page" or "immediately recirculate." Authorities also organize and pay for artificial pro-government expression in chat rooms and comment boxes. Provincial and local offices of External Propaganda and Party Propaganda hire staff at salaries of about one hundred USD per month (or less for part-time work) to post pro-government comments. It is hard to say how many salaried commenters exist nationwide, but estimates run to the high hundred-thousands. Some of this commenting is outsourced as piece-work. A few years ago, people who agreed to do this work were given the satiric label "fifty-centers" because they were said to be paid fifty Chinese cents per post. By now there are commercial enterprises that contract for comment work. Even prisons do it; prisoners can earn sentence reductions for producing set numbers of pro-government comments.

The "fifty-cent" initiative has met with some problems, however. Posts for pay have become so repetitive and mechanical that Web users spot them easily—leaving them with no credibility. Such posts run the risk of undermining opinion that might be genuinely pro-government, because they make any pro-government comment subject to the suspicion that it was done for money. In some circles, mockery aimed at fifty-centers has expanded to include regime apologists of any kind. Someone who thinks that External Propaganda might actually be doing some good by watching the internet is called a "self-employed fifty-center." Westerners who praise the CCP are "foreign fifty-centers."

On his website at Berkeley, Xiao Qiang protects his informants by slightly altering dates, names, and word-orders. He needs to do this: in 2005 the journalist Shi Tao was sent to prison for ten years for sending an unapproved document overseas. Xiao and his staff check the authenticity of what they receive against evidence of actual censorship. Occasionally they detect fake directives, which they toss out. The work is tedious and time-consuming, but sometimes they get lucky. One day in spring 2012, for example, as Xiao was using keywords to validate directives, a Google search turned up an item that was oddly labeled "save for evidence." He opened it to find a very large file that contained a full year of directives to a major province-level news forum. Normally such material is guarded behind firewalls in government servers, but Google found this one in someone's personal space. Xiao did not know the person, but the label "save for evidence" seemed a hint that the person might be a website editor who had become disgusted with government directives. Xiao's archive contains this and three similar large, comprehensive sets of directives.

In late June of 2013, ten scholars of Chinese law, politics, society, and language attended a workshop at Berkeley to join Xiao and his staff in analyzing Xiao's archive. The day sparkled with insights, a few of which were these:

- One of the principal aims of the government directives is to prevent unapproved groups from organizing through the internet (noted as "incitement," "gatherings," etc.); some of the scholars argued that the goal of stifling unapproved organizations is even more fundamental than prevention of negative comment about the Party.
- Because political power and commercial interests are commonly intertwined in China, censorship often merges with something that resembles commercial "reputation management" in the West. In 2008, when a scandal broke over melamine found in the baby formula of the Sanlu milk company, government censors sent out dozens of directives trying to play down the matter. To protect Sanlu? To tamp down general "incitement"? Both? In any case, it is

easy to find examples of censorship that protects both political and commercial interests.

- In some cases, a directive to block an item of news comes out even before the news itself appears. This seems to happen because of worry over what public reaction will be. In August, 2010, web editors in Hunan received this directive: "The trial on the June 21 murder case in Guizhou will open tomorrow; no medium of any kind is to make any report about either the trial or the sentencing."

- In its attempts to garner popular support for censorship, the regime still lumps political speech together with pornography. (The two are similarly "unhealthful to society," according to the government.)

- Officials tend to be protective of their own jurisdictions, but not necessarily of others. News of a scandal in Henan, blocked in Henan, might appear in Shanxi. While local officials rarely oppose the central government, that, too, can happen. After Xinhua reported that a military official in Guangzhou had assaulted a flight attendant in 2012, the Propaganda Department for Guangdong province ordered that Guangdong websites "not republish related Xinhua copy."

- Directives aimed at improving the popular image of courts are of mixed quality. Some instruct editors to refer to people who face trial as suspects rather than criminals, and this seems a step forward; but others seem to revert to an earlier mindset, telling editors to "report on the upcoming trial but not on the execution to follow."

- The government seems to have concluded that news of suicides should be blocked, not only to protect the overall image of a "harmonious society" but also to reduce the credibility of suicide threats, which can be used to leverage concessions from officials.

- Until about ten years ago, more than half of the reporting in the Xinhua information system was "internal reference" (classified) reporting to the leadership on what people in society were actually doing and thinking. With the dramatic growth of the internet, this function of Xinhua has shrunk. The internet makes it far more readily apparent—to anyone—what people are doing and thinking.

In the end, though, none of the parts of Xiao Qiang's project are as important as the whole that it seeks to reveal. In recent years China's rulers have been building a gargantuan internet censorship system. It is many times larger than any comparable effort, in any era. Soviet-era censorship and China's own Mao-era approach to the press were tighter and also included elements of both guiding and suppression. But no system in the world has been remotely as large in the number of details attended to or in the number of people involved in the work. The secret interception of telephone metadata by the National Security Agency in the U.S. is comparable in scope but not in detail and it involved only listening, not blocking, manipulating, or "guiding."

Most of the Chinese system remains obscure; Xiao's 2,600 directives show only a corner of it—or, more precisely, several small corners. On June 17 and 18 of 2013, Xiao attended an international "Freedom Online" conference in Tunis. One of his hosts brought him to visit the nearby Bulla Regia ruins of an ancient Roman city. They observed some walls here, some columns there, a mosaic over there—remnants that spoke of something much grander. Xiao was reminded of his research project—except that, in his case, the huge mysterious picture was slowly coming together, not deteriorating.

Originally published in the *NYR Daily*
July 10, 2013

Introduction to *The Execution of Mayor Yin and Other Stories from the Great Proletarian Cultural Revolution* by Chen Ruoxi

(Indiana University Press, 2004)

W HEN EDITORS AT Indiana University Press told me that they planned to re-publish Chen Ruoxi's "Mayor Yin" stories, the idea immediately felt good. Indeed, there was something strange about how good it felt. Why, I wondered, are these stories still so important decades after they were written? In the mid-1970s, when they first appeared, the excitement about them was easier to understand: they were then unique windows into a mysterious China; they were also among the first signs the outside world had of the catastrophic failure of the Maoist experiments of the 1950s and 1960s. Later, however, there was a flood of writing on such themes. In the late 1970s "scar literature," followed in the 1980s by works of "reflection" and "root-seeking," overran Chen Ruoxi's early trickle of truth with a river of it. Criticism of the Mao years became so commonplace in the 1980s that writers began to view it as passé. So haven't the "Mayor Yin" stories been superseded?

No, oddly. They continue to stand out, and not only because they were chronologically first. They stand out because no Chinese fiction has yet exceeded them in looking squarely at the heart of the Maoist calamity.

It is not easy to "look squarely" at disaster in one's national past. Shock, pain, confusion, and shame can all erect barriers. As other cases in the twentieth century make clear, the effort to look and to come to terms can take time—or, to put it more precisely, can require the psychological distance that passage of time can provide. Anne Frank wrote a diary during the Holocaust, recording what she saw, heard, and thought in her immediate environment, but "Holocaust literature" of a kind that looks at history, that tries to see it squarely, to encompass it, to understand the un-understandable and somehow to come to terms, took decades to appear. Primo Levi's writing, which began as a survivor's notes about a death camp in the 1940s, reached its maturity, indeed achieved a remarkable poetic grace, in 1986 with *The Drowned and the Saved*.[15] Alexandr Solzhenitsyn and Václav Havel not only exposed political prisons in Soviet Russia and Czechoslovakia but helped their readers to address moral issues of an entire system of oppression. In Japan, "Atomic Bomb Literature" has sought to absorb the disasters of August 6 and August 9, 1945, into the Japanese national psyche, but again, although poems and witness accounts appeared soon after the bombs fell, humanist transcendence came only with Ōe Kenzaburō's *Hiroshima Notes* in 1965,[16] while relatively full literary address of the devastation awaited Ibuse Masuji's *Black Rain* the following year.[17] Pol Pot's killing fields in Cambodia during 1975–79 are recorded in several literary memoirs, but, as yet, only rarely do these show enough regaining of balance to address the unfathomable questions of "how could it happen?" and "what does it mean?"[18]

Human disasters caused by humans are incomparable in many ways. They involve genocide, class warfare, world warfare, empire and colonialism in complex and differing patterns. But human recoil from extremity has its commonalities, and to ignore these might be as big a mistake as to ignore the historical differences. Let me proceed, with caution, to suggest three broad commonalities: 1) human societies seek psychological recovery from disasters, 2) literary expression can play an important role in this effort, and 3) the passage of time is important in gaining perspective. By these measures, China's Maoist disasters—primarily the Great Leap Forward and the Great Proletarian Cultural Revolution—present some awkward questions: Is China able to look squarely at the worst of

---

15. *I sommersi e i salvati* (Torino: Einaudi, 1986); translated by Raymond Rosenthal as *The Drowned and the Saved* (New York : Summit Books, 1988).

16. *Hiroshima noto* (Tokyo: Iwanami Shoten, 1965); translated by Toshi Yonezawa as *Hiroshima Notes* (Tokyo: YMCA Press, 1981).

17. *Kuroi ame* (Tokyo : Shinchosha, 1966); translated by John Bester as *Black Rain* (Tokyo and Palo Alto: Kodansha International, 1969.

18. Parts of Someth May's autobiography called *Cambodian Witness* (London and Boston: Faber and Faber, 1986, ed. James Fenton) achieve remarkable perspective.

what occurred? Is the culture seeking to interpret those facts and "come to terms"? What are writers doing to help?

The Mao nightmare continues to haunt China's modern self-conception and subtly to undermine its national self-respect. Those frightening times loom in the not-so-distant background like a fetid fog that neither dissipates nor forms itself into a cloud coherent enough to be named and understood. And, inside China, the problem is not just with the past but with its extension to the present: the collapse of Mao's promises to China left the country with a deep public cynicism that has hardly diminished through the ensuing years. It is true that in today's China the spirit of money-making diverts attention from past troubles, especially among the young; but the prevalence of deceit and corruption in public life and the ruthless competition to gain advantage at any cost show that China has yet to recover from the disillusionment that Mao caused, from the sting of realizing that "Serve the People" turned out to be a fraud. All of this calls for literary address. The saga of Maoism in China is certainly enough to allow hope that a Chinese Primo Levi, Ōe Kenzaburō, or Václav Havel might appear, but so far none has. Time of course is necessary; but it has been nearly thirty years since the beginnings of the unraveling of Maoism, and thirty years should be enough. It is sad, and for a Sinophile like me even a bit embarrassing, to look through China's voluminous literary output of the past three decades and have to admit that, for an honest look at Mao's subversion of Chinese life, nothing appears to have gone much beyond those first, limpid sketches by Chen Ruoxi. The reasons for this lack are worth exploring.

Soon after Mao's death, "scar literature," led by Lu Xinhua's story "Scar,"[19] uncovered patterns of official hypocrisy and corruption and showed how politics had devastated family and social life. Nearly all problems were attributed to only a "Gang of Four" and its followers; there were clear limits on how much unpleasantness one could put down on paper. You could say Red Guards "struggled" people, but not that they gouged their eyes out; you could mention Mao, but not implicate him. Still, the opportunity for public discussion of Mao-era pain was so exhilarating, and had been

19. "Shanghen" *Wenhuibao* (Shanghai) 11 August 1978; translated by Bennett Lee as "The Wounded" in Lu Xinhua et al, *The Wounded: New Stories of the Cultural Revolution*, 77–78 (Hong Kong: Joint Publishing, 1979).

bottled up for so long, that public enthusiasm for scar literature skyrocketed. The circulations of literary magazines reached levels that have not been matched before or since. The appetite for national self-examination was strong. It was just the kind of trend that might, if left alone, have led to a mature "coming to terms" with China's Maoist episode.

For several reasons, this did not happen. First, the perennial prohibition against criticizing the Communist Party proved to be especially debilitating to scar literature because it not only ruled certain comments out of bounds but had a distorting effect on nearly everything that did get into print. The underlying spirit of scar writing was to protest the basic direction that China had taken during late Maoism. Yet writers could target only miscreant officials—not the Party, the system, or the current top leadership. One had to say—or allow it to be reasonably inferred—that the original system was sound and the current top leadership clean. This requirement induced in scar writing a pervasive attitude of supplication. *If only* the true path of socialism had been followed, *if only* Zhou Enlai could have lived longer and done more, *if only* intellectuals had been seen as sincerely patriotic, etc., then the catastrophes would not have happened—and, therefore, we the writers of scar literature appeal to you in the leadership to keep the rudder of the Party in the right direction from now on. In a number of works, such as Wang Meng's *Bolshevik Salute*,[20] this "supplicatory attitude" was the main point, and was set out explicitly. Yet, in a larger sense, supplication underlay virtually all of scar literature. It did not have to be forced upon writers; many of them actively sought re-acceptance by a chastened Party. In Chen Rong's *At Middle Age*,[21] no censor required that a Party Secretary send a car to pick up the heroine from the hospital at the story's end. The author said she wanted it that way; appreciation of intellectuals had not been a pattern in recent Chinese life, and she was making an appeal that it now become one.[22] Other writers added "happy tails" to their stories perhaps less willingly, but few broke out of the pervasive mode of supplication. For a reading public that stood in need of a thorough, probing look

20. "Buli," *Dangdai*, March 1979, pp. 4–39; translated by Wendy Larson as *Bolshevik Salute* (Seattle: University of Washington Press, 1989).

21. "Ren dao zhongnian" *Shouhuo* 1980.1.52–92; translated by Yu Fanqin and Wang Mingjie in Shen Rong, *At Middle Age* (Beijing: Panda Books, 1987), pp. 9–85.

22. Interview with Chen Rong, August 7, 1980, Beijing.

at the Maoist debacle, this approach had obvious limitations. (Chen Ruoxi, who was grounded in a different context, was quite free from it. She did not need to appeal to the Party and did not even think of doing so. More on this below.)

A second problem in the "scar" era was that even the limited freedom writers had gained was trimmed back beginning in 1980, less than three years after it had arisen. Deng Xiaoping had needed a public outcry in order to justify his abrupt turn away from aspects of Maoism, and scar literature had served his purposes. Once his policy departures were secure, any deeper probing by Chinese writers would only have undermined his renovated regime—and so were dangerous, and therefore were repressed. Writers were told to stop exposing social problems and to join hands with the public at large to "look forward"—neither to pardon the past nor to condemn it, but just to let it go, to pretend it did not matter, to set it aside and to concentrate on the future. It is hard to imagine any guideline that could contradict more directly a writer's effort to "look squarely" at a national disaster or try to interpret it. In addition to the intrinsic difficulties of such a project, now there were government penalties for even trying. Most Chinese writers, whether willingly or not, bent under this wind—and this, I believe, is the main reason why, in all the vastness of ink on paper that has appeared in China since the early 1980s, there is not much to rival the work of Chen Ruoxi. We cannot survey everything here, but let us look at some examples—each of which, in a different way, illustrates the problem of coming to terms with the Maoist past.

Zhang Xianliang has written tens of times—maybe a hundred times— as many words as Chen Ruoxi, and is justly famous for revealing life and psychology in Maoist labor camps.[23] No Chinese writer, in my view, has done more than Zhang to examine the daily grind of camp life and the ways in which hunger, thirst, deprivation of sex, isolation from family, and enforced mendacity can affect a person's mental life. On these topics Zhang is in a league with Solzhenitsyn writing on the Gulag, Someth May writing

23. Especially in his later novels such as *Xiguan siwang* (Taibei: Yuanshen chubanshe, 1989), translated by Martha Avery as *Getting Used to Dying* (New York: Harper Collins, 1991); *Fannao jiushi zhihui* (Vexation is wisdom) (Beijing: Zuojia chubanshe, 1994), abridged and translated by Martha Avery as *Grass Soup* (London: Secker & Warburg, 1994); and *Wo de puti shu* (Beijing: Zuojia chubanshe, 1994), translated by Martha Avery as *My Bodhi Tree* (London: Secker & Warburg, 1996).

about Pol Pot's camps,[24] or Bloke Modisane evoking South African town-ship life.[25] But Zhang differs from these writers, and from Chen Ruoxi, in his conceptual frame. He grounds himself in a fundamental loyalty to the system "before it went wrong." He seems (at least until his neocapitalist turn at the end of his life) to feel profoundly guilty about his Shanghai-banker family background and to wish, against all the evidence that he himself provides, that there truly had been, or could be, a "revolution" of the kind that his ideals have called for. Chen Ruoxi does not carry such baggage. Moreover, she writes better than Zhang, who, although an astute observer of human psychology, is not a literary artist. Yang Jiang, who has also written about the Mao camps,[26] is considerably more graceful, but Chen Ruoxi's best work exceeds even Yang's. In its artful structure, evoca-tive language, and generation of an almost excruciating poignancy, "Geng Er in Beijing," in my view, is one of the best stories in modern Chinese literature.

In a way very different from Zhang Xianliang's, the fractured narrative and violent descriptions of "experimentalist" writers who appeared in the late 1980s—Can Xue, Yu Hua, Han Shaogong, Bei Cun, and others—also seem to suggest a recoil from Mao. Where, we might wonder, were these writers inspired to write such unsettling unpleasantness as Can Xue's "The Things That Happened to Me in that World"[27] or Yu Hua's "One Kind of Reality"?[28] Some had read Western "absurdists" (Franz Kafka) or "magi-cal realists" (Gabriel Marquez). But they had also grown up during China's Mao-madness, had sometimes been literally orphaned by politics, and, as children, had been even less ready than adults for "rational" understand-ing of the bizarre cruelty that surrounded them. Perhaps no one, including

24. Someth May, *Cambodian Witness* (London and Boston: Faber and Faber, 1986, ed. James Fenton).

25. *Blame Me on History* (New York, Dutton, 1963).

26. Yang Jiang. "Ganxiao liuji" (Six chapters on cadre school) *Guangjiaojing* (Hong Kong) no. 103 (April 1981), translated by Howard Goldblatt as "Six Chapters from My Life 'Downunder'" in *Renditions* (Hong Kong), no. 16 (Autumn 1981).

27. "Wo zai neige shijieli de shiqing" *Renmin wenxue* 1986.11.92–94, translated by Ron-ald R. Janssen and Jian Zhang in *Dialogues in Paradise* (Evanston: Northwestern Uni-versity Press, 1989).

28. "Xianshi yi zhong" *Beijing wenxue* 1988.1.4–25, translated by Jeanne Tai as "One Kind of Reality" in David Wang, ed., *Running Wild: New Chinese Writers* (Columbia University Press, 1994), pp. 21–68.

they themselves, can precisely trace their jarring writing to its roots. But if, and insofar as, their upset does indeed stem from Mao experiences, their work can only be a first step in any larger cultural quest to "come to terms" with a national past. Can Xue's stories give us interesting pictures—and perhaps highly accurate ones—of mental phenomena that might be ripples from her own childhood trauma. But to move from those impressions toward a public understanding that can be useful in national recovery is a tall order.

Yet another way to look back at the Maoist past is in the ultra-direct style of Zheng Yi. Zheng is best known for his 1984 story *Old Well*,[29] a middle-length work of fiction set in a rocky village in Shanxi and later made into a prize-winning film. But in another vein of his writing, Zheng makes "facing up" his top priority. To authorities and to ordinary citizens alike, he seems driven to say, "*look at this*, dammit, even if you don't want to!" In 1979, when writers were encouraged to attack the Gang of Four without showing physical violence directly, Zheng Yi effectively said "no, I am going to show physical violence directly." His story "Maple,"[30] about Red Guards killing one another, was barely published (and an illustrated version was indeed stopped literally at post offices). In the mid-1980s Zheng got wind of reports that, in parts of Guangxi in 1968, Maoist fervor had reached the hideous height of inducing ritualized cannibalism. The ultimate sign of triumph over the "class enemy" became the act of consuming some of the enemy's body parts after killing him. Zheng sought counsel from Liu Binyan, the distinguished writer of literary reportage, and learned that Liu—although he had also heard of these reports, and found them credible—had decided not to pursue them. The story was "just too ugly," Liu said. But to Zheng it was not; he continued to feel a mission to seek out precisely the most ugly facts, the ones that defined the limits of how far things had gone wrong, and to force himself and his compatriots to face them. He traveled to Guangxi, where, from interviews and archives, he found solid evidence of sixty-four cases of political cannibalism. He then took three years to write them up, in careful detail and with much

29. *Lao jing* (Taibei: Hai feng chubanshe, 1991).
30. "Feng," *Wenhuibao* 11 February 1979; translated by Douglas Spelman in Perry Link, ed., *Stubborn Weeds, Popular and Controversial Chinese Literature after the Cultural Revolution* (Bloomington: Indiana University Press, 1983), pp. 58–73.

ancillary comment, in a 686-page book called *Red Memorial*.[31] If the world had a prize for the "squarest look" at disaster, it is hard to see how any book would beat this one.

Still, in terms of helping Chinese culture as a whole to come to terms with the past, *Red Memorial* has not achieved much. The book was banned inside China. Underground in China, and outside where available in book-stores, *Red Memorial* has not circulated very well. Some of the reasons are not hard to see. It remains difficult—as with the A-bomb, the Holocaust, and elsewhere—to look at things that are "just too ugly." But this is only part of the problem. Worries over national "face," exacerbated by a sense of a history of humiliation over the last two centuries in encounters with the West, lead many Chinese to fear that a book like Zheng's will cause foreign-ers to form negative opinions not just of Maoism but of Chinese culture as a whole. In the 1990s China's leaders deliberately stimulated nation-alism in order to re-coup their battered legitimacy after the 1989 Beijing massacre had brought it to a low, but this whipped-up nationalism is not what I mean here. The reaction to *Red Memorial* was grounded at a deeper level. Even liberal intellectuals feared that Zheng Yi's book, when read by foreigners, might do more harm than good. The question led to spirited debate in literary circles, with Liu Binyan and others favoring publication, but equally eminent figures, such as the literary critic Liu Zaifu, demur-ring. No one doubted the truth of Zheng Yi's reports. The question was whether the nation's shame should be exposed to the world.

The examples above, ranging from Zhang Xianliang to Can Xue to Zheng Yi, show very different kinds of responses to Maoism. I have chosen them with this variety in mind, because the variety itself helps to illustrate how difficult it has been for Chinese writers, no matter how they come at Mao, to actually "get there"—to actually help their fellow Chinese take a square look. Chen Ruoxi shows the suffering of ordinary people without, at any level, needing to supplicate a still-reigning political authority. She uses plain, undistorted language, with no need to leave readers guessing about where violence fits in. And, as an overseas Chinese, she has other places to invest her national pride than in the "face" of a brutal government. (Here, though, we must give special credit to Chen; not every overseas Chinese

---

31. *Hongse jinianbei* (Taipei: Huashi wenhua gongsi, 1993); abridged and translated by T. P. Sym (pseud.) as *Scarlet Memorial* (Boulder: Westview Press, 1996).

can see the wisdom of this simple point. It is far too common that, in looking for something on which to pin their national pride, overseas Chinese
look past all the splendors of China's history, philosophy, poetry, painting, calligraphy, food, etc. and opt for a squalid political regime to be their
emblem.) In short, the art of Chen's "Mayor Yin" stories, had she continued
to write in their vein, might have matured into something much fuller. I
will not chide Chen for failing to become "the Chinese Primo Levi" or "the
Chinese Václav Havel," because her literary art is unique and would certainly have continued to differ from that of others had she gone on. And,
of course, her decision of what route to take through life belongs to her,
not to a cheering bystander. I dare to mention my thought only because
she herself does. In an email to me in summer, 2003, she writes that, "Now,
I...wish that I had done more, i.e. written more and better." Yes, I want to
reply. Yes, and all of China might have been better off if you had.

Chen Ruoxi's stories are referred to in English as "fiction," but the term
can be misleading. They are not spun from imagination, curious though
some of their details might seem. In Chinese they are called *xiaoshuo*, or
writing about "small" affairs, which traditionally meant stories about love,
family life, and the passions and problems in ordinary people's lives—
standing in implicit contrast to *dashu*, or the "great" stories about emperors, ministers, generals, and the other events that were worthy of historical
records. In contemporary terms, Richard Nixon's visit to China was a great
story, while accounts of how ordinary citizens were obliged to dismantle their clothes-drying racks in order to prettify an apartment building
in anticipation of Nixon's visit (in the story "Nixon's Press Corps") were
xiaoshuo. But both kinds of writing were *true*—or, if embellished here and
there, at least largely true.

All the "Mayor Yin" stories should be read as true accounts. In the mid-
1960s Chen Ruoxi and her husband, who were originally from Taiwan but
had gone to the U.S. for graduate study, joined political movements among
left-wing overseas Chinese students. In 1966 they made the courageous
decision to put their ideals into practice and headed to China to support
the Chinese revolution and to serve the people. From 1966 until 1973 they
lived in Beijing and Nanjing, where they endured, and watched others
endure, the brunt of Mao's Great Proletarian Cultural Revolution. What
they saw and heard of daily life indeed brought revolutionary change to
their outlook, but not of the kind they had anticipated. Like George Orwell,

Arthur Koestler, and other socialists who admired the idea of Soviet Communism up until the point when Soviet realities kicked them in the teeth, Chen Ruoxi drew her subsequent creative energies not only from human sympathy for victims but from the sting of disillusionment at the hands, in Koestler's phrase, of "the God that failed."[32] Her view of Mao completely turned around, but not because her values had gone anywhere.

The "Mayor Yin" stories stay close to the ground of daily experience and offer life-like touches not often seen in other stories of the time. In the early and middle 1970s, China's published short stories, which were sometimes written by committees, could be so flat and cliché-ridden as to be almost funny. Post-Mao "scar literature," while a big improvement, was still dominated by one-dimensional characters. By contrast, Chen Ruoxi shows us twisting, turning, surprising life. Her characters are not only three-dimensional but alive. They are the little people of Maoland—its earthworms, as it were—and, like earthworms, each squirms, and even if something slices it to bits, the bits writhe. In "Residency Check" we meet Peng Yulian, cheerful and outgoing, yet apparently an adulteress, and in any case the target of a vicious rumor barrage. We also meet her husband, the broken victim of a political campaign, aged before his time and not a good match for his vivacious wife. He is victimized by her adultery and its attendant public scorn, but he forgives her, and she in turn decides to continue supporting him, and life goes on. We also see inside the story's narrator, who, reminiscent of Lu Xun's narrators,[33] shares with us the moral dilemmas of how those in the role of bystander should react.

In following her characters through life, Chen treads across political "forbidden zones" as if they were not there. ("Scar" writers could not do this. They did "break into" forbidden areas, but invariably were self-conscious about doing so, preparing in advance for both battle with opponents and the cheers of supporters.) Chen treats it as no big deal to tell us, for example, about Mayor Yin's KMT (Nationalist) background even when this background shows that the Communist armies of the 1940s

32. Arthur Koestler, et al., Richard Crossman, ed., *The God that Failed* (New York: Harper, 1949).
33. For example in "Guxiang" (My Old Home) in *Nahan* and "Zhufu" (The New Year's Sacrifice), and "Zai Jiuloushang" (In the Tavern) in *Panghuang*; translated by Yang Xianyi and Gladys Yang in *The Complete Stories of Lu Xun* (Bloomington: Indiana University Press, 1981), pp. 55–65, 153–183.

acted more treacherously than those of the KMT. Her story called "Ren Xiulan" is pretty much out-of-bounds from start to finish. Ren Xiulan is a Party secretary whose ultra-leftist "May 16th Group" loses out in a political struggle of arcane elite provenance; she is detained as a counterrevolutionary and held under 24-hour surveillance, from which she eventually "escapes," and everyone in the College of Hydraulic Engineering where she works, including the small schoolchildren, is mobilized to hunt her down. In the end, her body is discovered rotting in a cesspool into which she has thrown herself.

We do not know what the Communist Party's Department of Propaganda, behind its closed doors in the mid-1970s, said specifically about "Ren Xiulan" or others of Chen's stories, but here are some reasonable guesses: classic poisonous weeds, a crop of blatantly anti-socialist anti-Chinese slander, the frenzied jottings of an active counterrevolutionary who had slithered her way into the midst of the people. What, though, to do about it? Ban the stories inside China, of course; then, in the outside world, organize some "patriotic" overseas Chinese to expose the author as a bourgeois interloper. Invite some of these patriotic guests to China, bring them to the College of Hydraulic Engineering in Nanjing to hear that Chen Ruoxi is a snake, and then send them back to spread this message abroad.

One writer who accepted such an invitation, Ms. Yu Lihua, went to Nanjing with the aim of uncovering the actual people upon whom Chen's stories were based. Yu's plan made sense. By meeting the actual people, she could easily measure and then demonstrate Chen's class biases and unpatriotic motives. Life surprised her, though. According to an eyewitness at a seminar that she held with Chen Ruoxi's former colleagues, she seemed uneasy at hearing even more of the grisly details connected to the Ren Xiulan story. In a final effort to break through the fictional level and get at the truth, she asked, "What was Ren Xiulan's real name?" When the answer came back "Ren Xiulan," she seemed stunned. The story was *xiaoshuo*, but not fiction. There had been no fabrication, no embroidery, no class bias. What happened happened. Ren Xiulan was Ren Xiulan. The seminar ended.

Chen Ruoxi stands apart from other writers in the "scar" years for her *bidiao*, or literary "tone." For many it was normal to spill emotion onto pages as if there were no tomorrow (a mood that, given the uncertainty of Chinese politics, was not entirely unwarranted). Chen understands that the impact on a reader is most powerful not when a narrator wails "this is tragic, weep for it!" or "this is outrageous, shout at it!," but when she sets out key points, with parsimony, and lets the reader infer the terrible impact. When the long-suffering Mayor Yin is about to be shot, for example, he shouts "Long live Chairman Mao," causing his executioners, fingers on triggers, to feel a curious dilemma: to shoot the criminal is required, but to "open fire on such slogans"[34] is unthinkable. Here most "scar" writers would have expatiated: Imagine equating a human life with slogans! Just look at this distortion of values, of language, of life! But Chen Ruoxi's narrator is brief: here is what I saw; here is what I heard. The reader does some of the work of inferring the horror of the scene, and that extra work magnifies the impact. At the end of "Geng Er in Beijing," the iron-terse dialogue between the parting lovers is almost unbearable in the emotion it packs, and yet none leaks out. The tragedy of Geng Er's wasted life rises to transcendence.

If Chen Ruoxi differs from "scar" writers in making no appeal to the Communist Party, she does make an appeal, of a somewhat different kind, toward the West. Her exposure of Maoist facades that the Chinese government erects to deceive foreigners (in "The Big Fish" and "Nixon's Press Corps," for example) amounts to a plea to foreigners not to be so naïve. She reserves special contempt for Westerners who visit China on luxurious mini-tours and then go home to help spread the lies—either because they are blinded by the romance of their privileged roles or, more darkly, because they enjoy those roles too much to risk losing them. Chen names Han Suyin in this connection (in "Geng Er in Beijing"), and might have named Felix Greene, Paul Lin, or the latter-day Edgar Snow, among others. These names may seem relics from the past, sorry quirks of history that only an oddity like Maoism could have made possible. Unfortunately, this is not so. Although China today is more open, and many more outsiders get better looks at more of the country, the Han Suyin syndrome remains alive and well. Whole parts of Chinese life are still tucked away from the view of foreigners, useful lies are still prettily told and naïvely accepted, overseas Chinese are still simultaneously lured by "patriotism" and threatened with being cut-off from their families if they speak out, and foreign "friends of

---

34. *The Execution of Mayor Yin and Other Stories from the Great Proletarian Cultural Revolution* (Bloomington: Indiana University Press, 1978), p. 35.

China" are still cultivated, rewarded, and cajoled. Such "friends" often end in a muddle within which the pronouncements of top Chinese leaders and the lives of ordinary Chinese people can somehow become hard to distinguish—a malady for which a professorship in political science is not, alas, necessarily an antidote. It would be wonderful if the outside world no longer needed to hear Chen Ruoxi's appeal, but it does.

Chen makes her point about Han Suyin in her normal way—by showing, not telling. In clear, spare prose she relates an anecdote about Han and leaves the irony and disgust for the reader to figure out. Clear, spare writing is naturally powerful, of course, but many observers have noted that an authoritarian context magnifies this effect. To ban a bit of truth can turn it into a brick, or, as Simon Leys noted in his 1978 introduction to the first edition of this book, "In the empire of lies, the humblest truth is revolutionary."[35] And a web of lies not only has the odd effect of enhancing the value of truth; it simultaneously constricts itself by the need to maintain a crafted pretense. Václav Havel has noted that the Czech regime of the 1970s was "captive to its own lies" and thus always had to pretend. "It pretends to persecute no one. It pretends to fear nothing. It pretends to pretend nothing."[36] And it needed, of course, to guard the appearance of consistency among its pretenses.

How does such a system handle an obdurate plain-speaker like Chen Ruoxi? The fact that the Chinese government's Chen Ruoxi problem has not melted away during a quarter century of "reform and opening" is one more piece of evidence that essential features of the political system have been continuous from Mao Zedong to his successors. Chinese government views on Chen Ruoxi have flipped and flopped. Confrontation has alternated with cajolement. In the late 1970s, the regime banned Chen's work and tried to discredit it. For two years she was on a visa blacklist. In the early 1980s, Party General Secretary Hu Yaobang decided that Chen was "patriotic" after all and invited her to China. She visited in 1984, and in the late 1980s was again regularly published in Guangzhou and other Chinese cities, although her Cultural Revolution pieces remained under ban. In 1989, after she denounced the Tiananmen Massacre, she was again banned

35. Introduction to *The Execution of Mayor Yin* (note 18), p. xxi.
36. Václav Havel, "The Power of the Powerless," in *Living in Truth* (London and Boston: Faber and Faber, 1989) p. 45.

and blacklisted. (What did they expect from her? one wonders. A Brent Scowcroft, ready to dine with the architects of the massacre in order to preserve good relations?) In 1993 the visa ban was lifted, but not the ban on her writing, which remained in place.

In any context, when one party's judgments of another change as fitfully as this, we have to suspect that somebody, either the judging side or the side that is judged, is confused, or perhaps even has lost bearings. Which side might that be? Is Chen Ruoxi flopping about, trying this and trying that, looking for what works? Or is it a frightened government in Beijing that is still groping, still wondering if Ren Xiulan is Ren Xiulan, still pretending to pretend nothing?

Originally published in *The Execution of Mayor Yin and Other Stories from the Great Proletarian Cultural Revolution* and re-published with the permission of Indiana University Press

Introduction to *Confessions: An Innocent Life in Communist China* by Kang Zhengguo

⟨⟩||⟨⟩

(New York: W.W. Norton, 2007)

THIS MAY BE the best account of daily life in Communist China that I have ever read. It stands out not because the broad outlines of history that it mentions are anything very new, but because of the extraordinary lifelike quality of the writing and the credibility of what is said. Hundreds of writers of both fiction and non-fiction have given accounts of "the people" (a.k.a. "the masses") during China's Mao years, but nearly all use an ideological lens that flattens the dialogue and homogenizes the background—indeed starches the clothing, tidies the town square, re-colors the sky, and, most important, tells you what to think about a social problem in terms that are usually over-simplified and often grossly false.

After Mao there was a quick literary reaction against much that Mao had done, but not so much against the Maoist style of writing. The "scar literature" of 1978–80 reversed direction on some key points. (Mao's top lieutenants, once infallibly correct, now included the all-evil "Gang of Four"; the Cultural Revolution was not glorious, but violent and bloody; corruption, formerly unmentionable, was now acknowledged as a big problem.) But the colored-lens problem persisted; only some of the colors had changed. Maoist literary style survived as a habit even among writers who consciously sought to pull themselves free from Maoist ideology. For a few who became aware of this problem, the quest for self-extrication itself became a sort of obsession—and this, too, created problems when they tried to look squarely at history. Trying too hard to write naturally is another way of not writing naturally.

Kang Zhengguo, who never bought into Maoism, does not have to tell us how he got out of it. His writing is a powerful indictment of life under Mao, but not because he is pushing any alternative ideology. What he gives us is daily experience written from the ground up, as it were, and with a charming transparency that spares no one, including himself; the prose conveys a sense of authenticity that is extremely rare in accounts of life in Communist China. It is startling, when you think of it, that the world has so far had almost no honest accounts of daily experience in a country as large as China over nearly half a century of its modern history. Here, though, we do have one.

Although Kang reveals a great amount about ordinary life in China, his own path is not very ordinary. He is by nature a willful character, a square peg unsuited to the round holes laid out by authorities of any kind, be they his father, his school, his wife, or the Communist Party of China. He thinks for himself and is a bit too quick to assume that if something makes sense to him, it ought to make sense to everybody and therefore should be acted upon. His wife says of him, "You always stick your neck out when everybody else has the good sense to lie low." Yet Kang's blunt approach turns out to be an excellent lens for exposing the submerged textures of everything around him. While most of his contemporaries submit to authority, get used to doing so, and eventually regard this as so "normal" that they become entirely unaware of the patterns that their own lives are observing, Kang does none of this. He trundles his way through life rather like a good-natured rhinoceros, ignoring boundaries, inadvertently dislodging rocks, and occasionally trampling the tails of snakes that spring up to bite him. We follow him from college to brick factory to labor camp to prison and finally into rural exile. The odyssey is revelatory at every stage.

For the social historian, Kang's book opens the door on the mechanics of the Mao-era control system. We get to see, for example, how the use of the official stamp to coerce conformity had a power that went far beyond the particular issue at hand. You want a job? A residence permit? A marriage license? From the point of view of the omnipresent control system, exactly what it is that you want is almost irrelevant. The important point is that I, the official, have the power to withhold it from you, the supplicant, and this power gives me leverage over *every* aspect of your life, whether related to your request or not. You want that marriage license?—Behave better at work. You want a job assignment?—Submit to authority in your neighborhood. And so on. The "smart" way to handle such pressures is to learn to toady. Kang's way (and he was not alone here; a number of the inmates in the labor camps and prisons he inhabits are like him in this regard) is to reason on principle, to resist, and in consequence to be snared by the system and labeled a trouble-maker in a broad sense that follows one wherever one goes, year after year.

Once snared, miscreants are squeezed. After Kang is expelled from college and sent home, he finds that his ration coupons have been withheld. He has to impose on family members for rations, and this makes him feel an increasing pressure to move out. But then he finds—and this pattern repeats itself several times—that the only route *out* is *down*. You can leave home, but only by "volunteering" to live and work at a squalid brick factory. You don't like the factory? You can leave (further down the social scale) for a rural labor camp. Your counterrevolutionary record is getting the better of you? You can renounce your past, your childhood, your family name, your everything, and offer yourself as an adopted son to an elderly bachelor in the countryside. No problem! A few banquets and gifts to grease the wheels, and we in the system can arrange all this for you. The bizarre comes to seem so normal that the simplest of unapproved human expression resembles the derring-do of a spy: an old friend silently passes a note about where to meet, at a later time, for frank talk in a cornfield. Watching Kang spiral downward, the reader is led to muse on the mechanics of social mobility in the other direction: just what kind of behavior would help one to *rise* within a system like this?

Following Kang on his tour of the innards of the Mao years, we come to see the surface impressions of that era quite differently. Take the "Great Proletarian Cultural Revolution," for example. How much writing has there been about its radical zeal, its pushing of communist theory and practice to a new level? Kang does not bother to tell us that this writing is superficial. He just relates what he saw and heard in daily life, and, in passing, shows that much of the popular rage that burst forth during the Cultural Revolution was born of recoil from what the communists had already done—not from a demand, as the propaganda claimed, that they do more of it. The Cultural Revolution also brought Kang more, not less, access to "bourgeois" pleasures like reading non-communist books, smoking cigarettes, and chatting with friends.

Kang's free-range writing moves seamlessly between his external context and his inner world of thoughts and feelings, thereby showing us not only social patterns but the psychological ripples that accompany them. Fresh insights emerge. In official language, for example, the "collectivism" of the Mao years has always been officially presented as a kind of idealistic group-mindedness, and we do know from other memoirs, such as Liu Binyan's, that elite young people in the 1950s and 1960s did pursue group interests with enthusiasm. But in daily life at many other social levels, the Party's power-engineering created very nearly the opposite of group-mindedness. It focused sharply on the individual person: *you* are wrong; *you* are alone, *you* need to join the mainstream; and your only route to re-joining it is to submit to *me*, the one who holds power over you. Not just Kang, but most of the people in his memoir, are actually or potentially trapped by this kind of threat. They are isolated as individuals—or at most in families or small circles of friends—and they perceive the larger society as a majority that is arrayed against them, while in fact that majority is itself a sea of people who are similarly frightened and isolated. The collective consciousness of "the mainstream" is an illusion.

One important reason why the illusion can persist is that people fear guilt by association. When one person's political taint becomes known, everyone else keeps a distance. So-and-so is a counterrevolutionary? Has a prison record? Stay away! On the surface, the Party can claim that this reaction demonstrates collective political will: See? The Chinese people hate counterrevolutionaries! In fact, though, what everybody hates is the possibility that the political leprosy will spread to themselves. Thus each person's calculations about how to survive, when viewed alongside every other person's, produces the surface appearance of unanimous support for the Party. The Chinese people were (then as much as now) certainly smart enough to figure all of this out, and could have done something about it if public discussion and organization had been allowed. But they were not, and everyone knew that anyone who moved to claim these rights was only asking to become yet another political leper. The Party further suppressed such thoughts by seeing to it that errant individuals remained intensely aware of their own guilt. After his release from prison, for example, Kang was forced to reimburse the state "for the expense of imprisoning me."

Prohibitions against misbehavior eventually sank in as permanent and unquestioned features of life, as obvious as the rule that you get wet if you go out in the rain. This is why Kang's parents, and later his wife, find his resistance neither admirable nor courageous, but simply obtuse. Yet when Kang's fortunes hit rock bottom, he finds (and this has happened with other dissidents) that his spirits get an unexpected lift. When he learns that a friend has burned his diaries, "the thought that I had nothing to lose was strangely calming," Kang writes. The psychological pressure generated by the fear of loss dissipates when little or nothing remains to be lost. Later, after Kang recovers and eventually emigrates—and once again comes to feel that he has significant things to lose—he again is ready to compromise, albeit reluctantly. When he returns to China in 2000, he arranges his itinerary so as not to rile his hometown police during the "sensitive period" of the June Fourth anniversary of the Beijing Massacre of 1989.

In the 1970s, when Kang goes to live for several years in the Shaanxi countryside, he arrives there as a cultural outsider and immediately turns into a keen observer of rural life. His book, among its other virtues, offers some excellent anthropology. Other accounts of Mao-era commune life have too often bristled with one or another kind of jargon: either the political cant of Maoism, which paints a super-idealized picture that is grossly false, or, in more recent times, the puffy academese of certain strains of Western anthropology, whose language can leave the ground and ascend into clouds of splendid uninterpretability.

Kang the anthropologist, in his concrete and lively language, combines an acerbic eye with a good-natured respect for China's folkways. We see how the language of "commune" and "work team" overlay a daily life in which people in fact were acutely aware of private property; no one was in doubt about who owned what tools, grain, animals, or housing, and there was considerable jealousy over who got how many "work points." As in pre-communist China, the boredom of village life put a premium on every small distraction, so that, for example, when someone fell ill, the whole village had an opportunity to drop by, offering "unsolicited advice and expressions of feigned concern." Traditional notions of peasant egalitarianism had been strengthened by Maoist dicta, and villagers, even while covetous of their own hoes and work points, felt that anyone in the village who got a windfall should be obliged to share some of it. Hence, when Kang's parents in the city pay for a pile of pretty red tiles for Kang to use to put a roof over his head, a stream of villagers drop by to let it be known they would like to "borrow" a few. How to handle these requests and still have enough tiles for the roof became a problem for Kang, who concludes that "a stroke of good luck could be a nuisance in disguise."

The brilliant 1980s short stories of Gao Xiaosheng ("The Money Purse," "Fishing," and others)[37] reveal this same mentality among farmers in another part of China, Jiangsu Province; both Gao and Kang also show how the mental world of Chinese villagers, despite the blandness of daily life (or perhaps *because* of it?), could be surprisingly complex and sophisticated. Why, for example, do the people in Kang's village vote for his adopted father Li Baoyu to be Chairman of the Poor and Lower-Middle Peasants' Association? Li had a mixed reputation: "not greedy or dishonest," but often "mulish and stingy" and not very bright, indeed "practically the village idiot." Li's singular credential for office turns out to be that his house is the only one in the village that has no wall in front of it. With no wall, he can hide nothing. Unable to hide things, he will not pilfer from the group. And everybody knows that he is too poor to build a wall. So elect him!

Countryside people are forbidden from moving to the cities, where life is better, and for this reason they feel inferior; on the other hand, their envy of urbanites melds into feelings of rivalry, so that they sometimes regard urbanites "as monsters, a different species"—just as, Kang wryly notes, "Chinese people in general regarded foreigners."

But for all its good sociology and anthropology, the special virtue of this book is its fine writing. Kang's prose is supple, lifelike, vivid, graceful. His characters stand up and walk off the page, and his charming turns of phrase are an added treat: the stillness in his village is broken only by "the raucous braying of bored donkeys"; when he is forced to write yet another self-criticism, the blank page "mocked me like a funhouse mirror." The credit for capturing Kang's art in English belongs to Susan Wilf, his superb translator. Wilf understands, as many translators of languages as different as Chinese and English do not, that word-for-word reflection of syntax and lexicon can be a pedantic sort of fidelity, and that the life and art of a piece is more faithfully served by reading a whole sentence, or several, at once, and then contriving to give the reader the fullest and most natural re-creation of the original that one can manage—even if this means completely re-thinking the syntax and being "free" with lexicon.

37. *The Broken Betrothal and Other Stories* (Beijing: Panda Books, 1978)

My field of study is modern Chinese literature, and I have often felt puzzled by the difficulty Chinese writers have had in looking deeply into Maoism and its aftermath. For other modern societies that have endured severe trauma, literature has played a role in facing difficult truths and helping to transcend them, but in modern China, it's as if a huge reverse magnet lies at the core of the issue. Writers of several kinds have aimed at the heart of Maoism and begun to move toward it, but as they draw near are deflected in one direction or another.

The "scar" writers of 1978–80 denounced the Gang of Four and spoke of "ten years of catastrophe." But they told only a fraction of what they knew and felt. Deng Xiaoping's demand for "stability and unity" blocked their way forward, and most eventually passed from the literary scene after only, as the Chinese idiom puts it, "scratching the itch from the outside of the boot." A number of writers (Wang Meng, Zhang Xianliang, Cong Weixi, and others are examples) who were avid supporters of the Party in the early 1950s, then labeled "rightists" in 1957, then sent away for two decades, then "exonerated" in the late 1970s understandably did not like what happened to them but also did not want to say that the ideals of their youth had been mistaken. In them one sees what I call a "supplicatory" address to the Communist Party: *please, please go back to the ideals and get it right next time; please also recognize our sincerity and loyalty.* This is one way the reverse magnet has worked.

Some of the "modernist" literary works that appeared in China in the late 1980s and the 1990s can also been seen, in part, as post-traumatic symptoms of the Mao years. Worlds filled with murderous toddlers, incestuous fathers, belching grandmothers, horn-blowing deaf-mutes, hoodlums who grin as their electric drill penetrates someone's kneecap, sunlight so hot that it melts the sand underfoot, family history that gets more and more grotesque the deeper one digs, narrative dreaminess that blurs reality and nightmare, and more, were all the creations of a generation of writers who had grown up during late Maoism. However bizarre, these images bear a certain authenticity. Can Xue, whose stories are among the strangest of all, has said that she writes in a sort of trance-like state—allowing, as it were, content to vault from the back of her brain directly onto the paper before her—and then never revises. It may be hard to imagine a more honest way of writing, but for the reader it leaves daunting problems of interpretation. What does she mean by unexplained references to "the man locked up in the hut banging furiously against the door" or "dead moths and dragonflies scattered on the floor"?[38] If such images can be seen as ways of looking back at the Mao disaster, then they still seem to me responses to the power of that reverse magnet that deflects square looks. Twenty years after the death of Mao, after the purge of 1987 and the bloody crackdown in 1989, most Chinese writers had given up fighting the reverse magnet. Many turned around, plunged into the sea of innocuous topics, and, in terms of living standards and fame, found good careers.

We should note in passing that the reluctance to look squarely at the Maoist past is not only a Chinese problem. Westerners have also fallen into self-censorship and have been caught up in a variety of supplicatory poses. These have arisen in part from the same kinds of implicit threats and rewards that affect Chinese people, but also in part from the West's old romantic notion that the East is an exotic world and an appropriate receptacle for Western wishful thinking.

Now we have Kang Zhengguo, whose writing is free of self-censorship, supplicatory address, bizarre modernism, or other deflections of vision of the sorts just reviewed. Kang is free as well from the kind of distortion that, in some writers, grows out of conscious rebellion against such deflection. Kang seems, as he wanders through his memories, completely unaffected by questions of how close he may or may not be coming to politically radioactive turf. He tells us what he saw, heard, and felt, and uses the same tone whether or not he happens to be implying that the emperor is naked. For example, when local officials categorize him as "the dregs of society" (a technical term in communist jargon) and assign him to labor, he neither accepts the insult nor turns sarcastic toward it, but is almost childlike in his observation of a contradiction in how they have presented things to him: "if labor was so glorious, why did they give all the dirty work to us, the 'dregs of society,' instead of doing it themselves?"

Before the communist revolution, a few writers, like Xiao Hong in her wonderful *Tales of Hulan River* (1942), were also able to write in this tone of childlike lucidity. But since then, examples of the style have been extremely rare in mainland China, where guidelines, "forbidden zones," and required

---

38. These images are taken, almost at random, from Can Xue's story "Hut on the Mountain" as translated by Ronald R. Janssen and Jian Wang in *Dialogues in Paradise* (Evanston, Ill.: Northwestern University Press, 1989), p. 47.

jargon and conceptual categories have driven pre-communist writing styles deep into the crannies of society, far from the printed page. Bu Nai-fu's *Red in Tooth and Claw*, which Kang Zhengguo admires, is a rare example of writing that somehow survived in one of those crannies. Bu wrote as Wumingshi 'Anonymous'; his account of life in labor camps, which reveals Mao-era realities in unusual depth, reads as if sealed off from both Maoist literary influence and the recoil from it. Kang and Bu are similar in this regard.

It would be wrong, though, not to acknowledge and admire those Chinese writers who at one point did embrace Maoism—or were simply engulfed by it—and later consciously sought to pull their writing free from the Mao-mentality. This, too, was done in a variety of ways. Some—such as Zhong Acheng or Wang Zengqi in the 1980s—sought refuge in the language and narrative technique of traditional Chinese fiction and storytelling. In so doing they drew upon the latent power of Chinese cultural habit, which endured despite attempts during the Mao years to stomp it out. Other writers, such as the "misty" poets of the late 1970s and early 1980s, and some of the modernist fiction writers a decade later, borrowed Western literary form and technique to help with the self-extrication process. In this they had a powerful ally in the widespread assumption in China (whether stated or not) that the West is "advanced." Some writers went, as it were, all the way West-ward in literary terms by adopting Western languages as their very means of expression. Ha Jin writes in English, as, sometimes, does Zha Jianying, while Dai Sijie and Nobel laureate Gao Xingjian have written in French. It may seem odd that a writer's leap "out" of China and into a Western language can leave him or her more free than before to evoke the mood and subtleties of life in China. But this, in a few cases, has indeed been the case. I know of no fiction written in Chinese that reveals the mood of Chinese urban life in the 1970s better than does Ha Jin's *Waiting*. Readers of Kang Zhengguo's memoir will note a similarity between it and Ha Jin's prose. Both penetrate daily life in the communist period very effectively, even as neither carries the slightest hint of communist literary practice. This is rare.

Communist Party leaders, who have felt that their rule might collapse if its Maoist pedigree were challenged, have put teeth behind their demand that Mao's reputation remain at least seventy percent good. The teeth include censorship, which blocks unapproved ideas from publication, and enforced self-censorship, by which a writer withholds or alters his or her expression from fear of some kind of punishment. Both these deterrents have been important in preventing honest literary engagement with China's recent past, and Kang Zhengguo avoids both of them. But he avoids yet another important barrier, which is the controlling power of language itself. This is more subtle and insidious, and it may be worth a short diversion to try to make it clear.

To adopt the lingo of people one interacts with is natural, indeed so common that we might call it human nature. It happens even when one does not admire the terms that one's interlocutor uses, as, for example, when I as a professor talk with my registrar about "units" of coursework in literature even though I find a metaphor that suggests "measurable lump," like cheese or tofu, to be ridiculous when applied to literature. The pressure to adjust to someone else's terms grows stronger when the other party holds pervasive power over one. During China's Mao years the Communist Party's use of language caused certain patterns of expression to become entrenched within the public so deeply that people took them for granted. Eventually it did not seem strange, but only reasonable, to master the official language in order to protect oneself or to get what one wanted. In the late 1970s, for example, when it became a national policy to make amends with intellectuals who had been persecuted during the Cultural Revolution, professors who wanted better housing did not go to their local Party leaders and ask, "Can I have a bigger apartment?" They would say something like, "Could the recent policies of Party Central be concretized in my case?"

Eventually, moreover, official language seeped into unofficial contexts where it affected daily-life expression. "Annihilate" (*xiaomie*), for example, was prominent in the communist lexicon because combat was common in the Party's history and Mao Zedong became partial to this word. People who grew up in China in the 1950s through 1970s began to use the word metaphorically in daily-life contexts. When, for example, a bit of food is left on a serving plate at a dinner table, and might best be finished off, someone might say "let's annihilate it." (The usage is not idiomatic in Taiwan or in overseas Chinese communities.) In 1988 on a public bus in Beijing I heard a little boy say to his mother, "Ma, I gotta pee!" The mother said, "Persevere!" using *jianchi*, a term that had been used for decades for upholding one or another political line, but which had come to permeate daily life so thoroughly no one on the bus seemed to find it remarkable.

The seepage of political language into daily life affected literature. With the categories and concepts that it entails, political language has done at least as much to impede clear-eyed writing as editorial censorship and conscious self-censorship have done. Moreover, its effects have been harder to get rid of because most writers, most of the time, have been unaware of them. Writers in the 1950s were drawn into what Chu Anping called "the world of the Party," in which all public expression observed stylized norms that signaled—regardless of topic and even of viewpoint—that "I am part of this Party-world." When Miklos Haraszti observed that Hungarian writers in the 1950s were living inside a "velvet prison,"[39] he was referring not only to the system of material rewards that lured and held them but also to the velvet unreality of official language that cushioned their intellectual work. For China in the late 1950s, in my view, the metaphor of velvet is not quite strong enough. Chinese writers "inside the world of the Party" were then more like George Orwell's depiction of Henry Miller, swallowed like Jonah and "inside the whale," i.e., its stomach, "like a womb big enough for an adult." Orwell invites us to imagine:

> ...the dark, cushioned space that exactly fits you, with yards of blubber between you and reality, able to keep up an attitude of the completest indifference, no matter what happens. A storm that would sink all the battleships in the world would hardly reach you as an echo. Even the whale's own movements would probably be imperceptible to you. He might be wallowing among the surface waves or shooting down into the blackness of the middle seas..., but you would never know the difference.[40]

Were Chinese writers in the 1950s aware of where the great Maoist whale was headed? When the great famine began devouring tens of millions of lives, could they, from their position inside the whale, cushioned by yards of blubber, even begin to describe the sea and the storm? Did the public domain offer them adequate language for such an effort? Twenty years after the great famine, when writers could begin to address what had happened,

39. *The Velvet Prison: Artists Under State Socialism* (New York: Basic Books, 1987), translated by Katalin and Stephen Landesman.
40. "Inside the Whale," in A Collection of Essays by George Orwell (Garden City, N.Y.: Doubleday & Co., 1954), p. 249

they were still constricted—by continuing political guidelines and implicit threats, but also by language. They spoke of "mistakes," of "prices that were paid," and of how too bad it was, for example, that Mao Zedong had out-maneuvered Peng Dehuai in 1959. Their views were passionate, and worth a salute from us, but they still could not say plainly what needed to be said.

When we read Kang Zhengguo it can seem oddly striking that we find his outlook so commonsensical. How did such a sense-making approach emerge from such "crazy" times? Moreover, we see that Kang was not alone; we see other ordinary Chinese coping their ways through life, thinking and behaving not like Mao-models but in ways that human beings elsewhere in the world can relate to. That human beings in Maoist China were fundamentally the same as human beings elsewhere ought not to count as an insight, and yet, given the dearth of honest writing from the period, it does appear as one.

As we read Kang and get deeper and deeper into the non-Party-world that he unfolds, the Party-world seems correspondingly to shrink. It still dominates, to be sure, and is still frightening. But we see more and more that the Party-world is not coterminous with "China." Since the 1950s the Communist Party of China has always spoken of itself, both internally and to the international world, as if it *is* China: nation, state, and Party are all one. This rhetorical device of course has its political purposes: to suggest that support of the Party is support of China, that criticism of the Party is criticism of China, that to oppose the Party is to be non-Chinese, and so on. Perhaps the most life-affirming fruit of Kang Zhengguo's memoir is that it opens a small space around Kang's daily life and then, as Kang meets others and the space expands, pushes back the hegemonic claim that "Party and China are one." The Party eventually comes to seem not the whole of the country but a sort of private-membership group—albeit a very large one—that rides atop the populace. In 1991 Wan Runnan, the famous chief of the Sitong Company who was obliged to flee China after the June Fourth massacre, commented that "China belongs to the people of China; it is not the private property of the Communist Party." This assertion, obvious in one sense, was unutterable during the Mao years and still sounded radical in 1991. Kang Zhengguo does not repeat the assertion but just assumes it, and then tells us how the true owners of China made the best of their lives during difficult times.

The Passion of Liu Xiaobo

(2017)

I N THE LATE 1960s Mao Zedong, China's Great Helmsman, encouraged children and adolescents to confront their teachers and parents, root out "cow ghosts and snake spirits," and otherwise "make revolution." In practice, this meant closing China's schools. In the decades since, many have decried a generation's loss of education.

Liu Xiaobo, who won the 2010 Nobel Peace Prize a year after beginning an eleven-year prison sentence for "inciting subversion" of China's government, died of liver cancer on Thursday [July 13, 2017]. Born in 1955, he was eleven when his elementary school closed, but in high school, after his family had been sent to Inner Mongolia, he began to read voraciously in the books he was able to lay hands on. He loved the great modern Chinese writer Lu Xun. He also read Karl Marx—much more thoroughly, I am sure, than Mao Zedong ever did—and learned much about European history from doing so. Free of curricular guidance in what he was supposed to think about what he read, he began to think for himself—and he loved it. Mao had inadvertently taught him a lesson that ran directly counter to Mao's own goal of converting children into "little red soldiers."

But this experience only partly explains Liu's stout independence. It also seems to have been an inborn trait. If there is a gene for bluntness, Liu likely had it. In the 1980s, while still a graduate student in Chinese literature, he was already known as a "dark horse" for denouncing nearly every contemporary Chinese writer: the literary star Wang Meng was politically slippery; "roots-seeking" writers like Han Shaogong were excessively romantic about the value of China's traditions; even speak-for-the-people heroes like Liu Binyan were too ready to pin hopes on "liberal" Communist leaders like Hu Yaobang. No one was independent enough. "I can sum up what's wrong with Chinese writers in one sentence," Liu Xiaobo wrote in 1986. "They can't write creatively themselves—they simply don't have the ability—because their very lives don't belong to them."

He carried his candor with him when he went abroad. At a conference on Chinese film at the University of Oslo in 1988, he was surprised to learn that European Sinologists couldn't speak Chinese (they only read it) and were far too naïve in accepting Chinese government statements at face value. "Ninety-eight percent are useless," he observed. The conference itself was "agonizingly boring." From Oslo he went to Hawaii and then to New York, to Columbia University, where he found it irritating that postcolonial theorists were telling him how it felt to be the subaltern Other. Shouldn't he be telling *them* that?

In the spring of 1989, two experiences, the first in New York and the second in Beijing, profoundly altered the course of his thinking and his life. He was just finishing a book called *Chinese Politics and China's Modern Intellectuals* that explored several ways in which Western civilization can be "a tool to critique China." Now, though, visiting the West, he found that the model was not so clear. Issues like the energy crisis, environmental protection, nuclear weapons, and what he called "the addiction to pleasure and to commercialization" were human problems, not particularly Eastern or Western. Moreover, a visit to New York's Metropolitan Museum of Art had brought him an epiphany: no one had solved the spiritual question of "the incompleteness of the individual person." Even Lu Xun, whose fiction was so good at revealing moral callousness, hypocrisy, superstition, and cruelty, could not, in Liu Xiaobo's view, take the next step and "struggle with the dark." Lu Xun tried this, in his prose poems, but in the end backed off; he "could not cope with the solitary terror of the grave" and "failed to find any transcendental values to help him continue."

Chinese Politics had already been sent to its publisher, but Liu decided to add an "Epilogue" anyway, and, with characteristic honesty, used it to undermine his own book's main theme. To be "an authentic person," he wrote, he would now have to "carry out two critiques simultaneously": one of China, still using the West as a measuring rod, and another of the West itself, for which he would have to start over, from scratch, and rethink everything. He finished the essay in March 1989, ending it with the words "this epilogue has exhausted me."

The next month he boarded an airplane in New York and headed for Beijing, not from exhaustion but because he had read about the student demonstrations for democracy in Tiananmen Square and felt a duty to support them. "I hope," he wrote, "that I'm not the type of person who, standing at the doorway to hell, strikes a heroic pose and then starts frowning with indecision."

In Beijing, the students' idealism moved him even as (always critical!) he deplored some of their undemocratic methods and the physical mess they were making in Tiananmen Square. His political approach was non-confrontational, almost Gandhian. In a "June 2nd Hunger Strike Declaration" he wrote that "a democratic society is not built on hatred and enmity; it is built on consultation, debate, and voting...[and on] mutual respect, tolerance, and willingness to compromise." Less than two days later, Liu had an opportunity to put his words into practice. As tanks began rolling toward Tiananmen Square and it was already clear that people in their way were being killed, Liu and his friends Zhou Duo, Hou Dejian, and Gao Xin negotiated with the attacking military to allow students in Tiananmen Square to exit safely. It is impossible to say how many lives they saved by this compromise, but it was certainly dozens and maybe hundreds.

Afterward, though, Liu made what he later regarded as a "mistake" that he rued for the rest of his life. He sought temporary safety in the home of a foreign diplomat. He later heard that others—mostly ordinary citizens—had stayed in the streets to help people who were wounded or were still being shot at. They risked their own lives to offer help, and when the government set punishments for participants in the "counterrevolutionary riot," these ordinary people were treated more harshly than the student demonstrators. Many received prison sentences of eighteen to twenty years, and some were executed. Liu himself was sent to Qincheng Prison, an elite facility where the political opponents of top leaders are held, and stayed only nineteen months—"deathly bored, but that's about it."

Liu felt haunted by the "lost souls" of Tiananmen, the aggrieved ghosts of students and workers alike whose ages would forever be the same as on the night they died. He wrote that he could hear their plaintive cries—"weak, helpless, heart-rending"—rising from beneath the earth. Each year on the anniversary of the massacre he wrote a poem to honor them. His "final statement" at his trial in December 2009 opens: "June 1989 has been the major turning point in my life." In October 2010, when his wife Liu Xia brought him the news of his Nobel Peace Prize, she reports that he commented, "This is for the aggrieved ghosts."

After his release from Qincheng Prison in 1991, Liu was banned from publishing in China and fired from his teaching post at Beijing Normal University—even though students there had always loved his lectures. He began to support himself by writing for magazines in Hong Kong, Taiwan, and New York. Sent to a labor camp during 1996–1999 for advocating compromise with Taiwan, upon release he picked up where he left off. The emergence of the internet created much new space for commentary from him and other free-thinkers. He became a major figure in what became known as the "Rights Defense Movement," which included activists, journalists, and lawyers who went into society to find problems people were having and then used the internet to bring larger numbers together and to press for solutions and reforms. At the same time, the scope of Xiaobo's essays was reaching beyond Chinese literature and culture to include topics in history, politics, and society—ancient and modern, East and West—in startling variety and often with impressive erudition. He wrote about Confucius, Kant, St. Augustine, farmers in Jiangsu, Olympic athletes, humor in China and in Czechoslovakia, pornography and politics, the internet revolution, Obama's election, a murdered puppy, international relations, the Dalai Lama, China's "economic miracle," and much more.

In the spring of 2008, some of his friends conceived the idea of writing a citizens' manifesto calling for free elections and constitutional government in China. They called it "Charter 08," in conscious admiration of Václav Havel and Czechoslovakia's "Charter 77." Xiaobo did not join at first, but in the fall, feeling pressure from friends and teachers to pitch in, he worked on editing the Charter and on soliciting signatures—not only among known dissidents but from leaders of workers and farmers and even from state officials who were willing to gather under the broad tent of asking for a more open and liberal society. The language of the Charter is moderate, and much of it had already appeared in Chinese or United Nations documents. But some lines, like "we must abolish the special privilege of one party to monopolize power," went beyond what China's rulers could stomach. In December 2008, Xiaobo was detained—and, in the end, never went home. Several of Liu's colleagues were detained; all who had signed the Charter were summoned for police interrogation and warned; and Charter 08 was banned from the internet and from all state media.

Given the generally mild language of the Charter, the intensity of the regime's crackdown begs some explanation. The answer seems in part to be that the Charter movement was viewed as an unauthorized "organization." Liu Xiaobo was viewed as its head, even though he really was not. The men who rule China have shown in recent times that they can tolerate tongue-lashings from the populace so long as it comes from isolated individuals. An unauthorized organization, even if moderate, must be crushed. In 2005, Hu Jintao issued a classified report called "Fight a Smokeless Battle: Keep 'Color Revolutions' Out of China." It said people like Nelson Mandela, Lech Wałęsa, and Aung San Suu Kyi are dangerous. If similar movements appear in China, Hu instructed, "the big ones" should be arrested and "the little ones" left alone. In November 2008, when Chinese police learned that people were signing Charter 08, it was officially labeled an attempt to start a "color revolution." That made Liu Xiaobo a "big one" who needed to be brought down. There are signs that Liu himself understood the mechanism. When he joined the Charter effort he told his friends that, in addition to editing and gathering signatures, he would "take responsibility" for the Charter—in effect, risk being "the big one."

In any case, it is clear that Liu's work on Charter 08 led to his eleven-year prison sentence in 2009, which in turn led to his Nobel Prize in 2010. At the Nobel banquet in December 2010, a member of the selection committee told me that her group had for years been wanting to find a Chinese winner for their prize and that the previous year's events "made this finally seem the right time." Chinese President Hu Jintao and his Politburo were likely annoyed to realize (if ever they did) that their imprisonment of Liu paved the way to his honor.

It was hard to find people who disagreed with the Charter once they read it, and it was precisely this potential for contagion that worried regime leaders. That was their reason (not their stated reason but their real one) for suppressing the Charter, for imprisoning Liu Xiaobo, and for denouncing his Nobel Peace Prize. Their efforts have been effective: most young Chinese ten years later did not know who Liu Xiaobo was, and older ones who did were well aware of the costs of saying anything about him in public.

After the arrival of Xi Jinping at the helm of the Chinese state in 2012, controls on Chinese society tightened even more, and political life went pretty much in the opposite direction of what Charter 08 had called for. So was the Charter effort wasted? The question is difficult, but my answer would be no. The organization was crushed but its ideas have not been. The government's continuing efforts—assiduous, inveterate, nationwide, and costly—to repress anything that resembles the ideas of Charter 08 is evidence enough that the men who rule are aware of the potential of the ideas.

It would have been good to hear Liu Xiaobo himself answer the question. The world was not allowed to hear one sentence from him since his "Final Statement" at trial in 2009. In June of 2017, he was moved to a prison ward in a Shenyang hospital with late-stage liver cancer. He asked for safe passage for himself, his wife, and his brother-in-law to go to Germany or the U.S. to receive treatment. The Chinese government declined, saying Liu was already receiving first-rate medical care and was too weak to travel. He died on July 13.

Ever since he became well-known as a "dissident," Liu had rejected the idea of leaving China. Exile would distance him from his natural audience and the authorities might never allow him to return. It is unclear why, in the final weeks of his life, he agreed to change this policy and leave China. He may have wanted to allow his long-suffering wife Liu Xia and her brother Liu Hui to get out of the country. In any case, the authorities' reason for keeping him inside seems clear: it had nothing to do with medical care and everything to do with preventing Xiaobo from speaking his mind one last time. What were his thoughts during his eight years in prison? What did he foresee for a world in which China's Communist dictatorship continues to grow?

Liu Xiaobo has been compared to Nelson Mandela and Václav Havel, both of whom accepted prison as the price for pursuing more humane governance in their homelands. But Mandela and Havel lived to see release from the beastly regimes that repressed them, and Liu Xiaobo did not. Perhaps success of a movement is necessary in order for a leader to be viewed as heroic.

Still, it may be useful for a moment to compare Liu Xiaobo and Xi Jinping. The two were separated in age by only two years. During Mao's Cultural Revolution both missed school and were banished to remote places. Xi used the time to begin building a resume that would allow him, riding the coattails of his elite-Communist father, to one day vie for supreme power; Liu used the time to read on his own and learn to think for himself. One mastered the techniques of betrayal and sycophancy that a person needs to rise within a closed system; the other learned to challenge received wisdom of every kind, keeping for himself only the ideas that could pass the test of rigorous independent examination. For one of them, value was measured by power and position; for the other, by moral worth. In their final standoff, one "won," the other "lost." But two hundred years from now, who will recall the names of the tyrants who sent Mandela and Havel to jail? Will the glint of Liu Xiaobo's incisive intellect be remembered, or the cardboard mediocrity of Xi's?

Originally published in the *NYR Daily*,
July 13, 2017

Day Job Joys

Although much of my career, especially in its latter decades, has been spent on the problem of how the great civilization of China has been captured and twisted by a brutal, self-serving regime, I have also enjoyed teaching and writing about less "political" facets of Chinese language, literature, and popular culture. These, in my mind, are integrated aspects of the same lifelong calling, but to readers they may seem different enough to warrant including in this collection a few essays on my "day job."

The Joys of Teaching Beginning Chinese

꿰꿰

(1998)

B Y 1984, when I became a full professor, I had taught beginning Chinese twelve times, first as a Teaching Fellow at Harvard, then in the Chinese summer program at Middlebury College, then as a Lecturer and Assistant Professor at Princeton. It is not unusual that a scholar of Chinese literature also teaches language. It helps to pay the way through graduate school and to get started on the job market. The peculiarity in my case is that I continued with teaching beginning Chinese even after I didn't have to. At Princeton I taught it nearly every year until I retired in 2008.

People have asked me why. Didn't it soak up a lot of energy? Classes, quizzes, audiotapes, daily homework, staff meetings, charts—and shoulders for stressed students to cry on? It did. At Princeton, Chinese 101 met six hours a week, double the normal three, and was often the largest course in the East Asian Studies department. In 1995 the student newspaper *The Daily Princetonian* did a survey that ranked my course among the top ten best on campus but also noted that there were two courses that required a ridiculous amount of work and "they both begin with *ch*." They were Chinese 101 and Chemistry 301, Organic Chemistry. So what was I doing? Why didn't I settle for lecture courses on literature and graduate seminars on my research interests?

It is important to note that no one forced me. I taught beginning Chinese because I enjoyed it. But the question "why?" is still worth looking into.

For one, it is fun to teach a subject in which there are right answers. When I teach literature, which I also very much enjoy, I am not looking for "right answers." I want students to think independently. They get full marks if they can explain and defend their own views, however different from mine they might be; and I tell them it's quite all right to reach conclusions that are tentative or ambivalent, so long as the reasons that lead them into ambivalence are good reasons.

One problem with such teaching, though, is that the teacher has little sense of day-to-day progress. What *really* is in the minds of students when they walk out of the classroom at the end of an hour? One doesn't know. I am reminded of a *Peanuts* cartoon in which Charlie Brown reports his teacher's view that "teaching is like bowling—you just roll the ball down the middle and hope for the best." After that, what happens happens. I met someone recently who came up to me after a lecture and said, "Professor Link I want to thank you for something you told me at Princeton that changed my life." I asked her what it was and she went on to say a sentence that I could not remember ever having thought, let alone said. I am by no means the only professor who has had such an experience. They are common, and they cast those computerized end-of-semester teaching evaluations in an interesting light. Does a student know at the end of a semester what the value of the learning has been, or will be? In part, perhaps. But in whole?

Language courses are refreshingly different. Here there *are* right answers, and I the teacher know them and you the student don't and it is my job to get them into your head and onto your tongue and if you get something wrong I will tell you and persist with you (because I love you, not because I hate you) until you finally do get it right. There's no room or need for independent thought—at least not yet. But then, at the end of a language course, a teacher can point to a measurable result. When the bushy-tailed freshmen arrive in September and take beginning Chinese they can't say a word of it; by May they can sort of get along in the language and are on their way, if they like, to mastery of it. The teacher can point to them and say, "Look what I did!"

In this sense language teaching is something like gardening: you prepare the soil (get your teaching materials in order), plant some seeds (introduce some words and grammar patterns), add water and fertilizer (examples, homework, encouragement), pull weeds (correct mistakes), and in the end enjoy your harvest. Moreover, that harvest is unambiguously a good thing. This is pleasant because harvests elsewhere in academic life are "contested": people have different ideologies, politics, in-groups. But everyone agrees that knowing Chinese, and knowing it well, is better than not knowing it. The language teacher lifts all boats. That feels good.

Is my use of time and energy in language teaching a drain on my work in other fields? In one sense, yes. Language teaching is indeed time-consuming and enervating. But there is another sense in which both the learning and the teaching of Chinese language have been at the very core of my intellectual journey of understanding China. It has provided bene-fits, not just costs. Outsiders see only the costs side. The benefits are that language teaching keeps me in close touch with Chinese ways of think-ing about things. This holds for everything from daily-life language about tables and chairs to talk about power tiffs within the politburo of the Com-munist Party of China. To listen to Western China-experts talk in English about Chinese politics and to listen to Chinese people on the same topics in Chinese are very different experiences. The texture of thought is differ-ent, often very different, in the two cases.

I once wrote an essay on how, for me, Chinese language learning has been "the root of everything" in my study of China. When I submitted my Ph.D. dissertation in 1976, I dedicated it to my teacher of first-year Chi-nese, Rulan C. Pian. This surprised some of my graduate-level teachers, but in fact I was simply side-stepping protocol in order to say what is true. In a very real sense, beginning Chinese in 1963–64 at Harvard was the most intellectually seminal course I ever took.

Let me give an example of what I mean by "think differently," even at the elementary level. All Chinese nouns are abstract and unmeasured. *Zhuozi* 桌子is neither "a table" or "tables" but something like "tableness," and in order to say "a table" you say "one flat-item-of tableness"—except that this takes only four syllables, not eight, and does not sound at all awkward. Similarly, there are no words "the" or "a" to distinguish definite and indefi-nite reference; that distinction can be made by word order. Native speakers of Indo-European languages, inured in the habit that nouns like *table* have to be either singular or plural, and definite or definite, can have trouble understanding how Chinese conceives nouns differently. I remember once explaining to a beginning class that the sentence *shu zai zhuozishang* 书在桌子上 does not tell you whether it is "the book" or "the books" that is (or are) on the table (or tables). Then I tried to make the point that the ambi-guity is quite all right. I said something like, "you don't have to know every single detail in order to get along in the world. The Chinese language does have ways to make clear how many books you are talking about if that's what you want to do. But if the number of books doesn't matter, or if it is already obvious, then it's okay to leave that detail out of the sentence." After class, a student came up to me. He was a philosophy major and extremely bright. "But *in fact,*" he said, "I mean *in the real world*, it can't be 'bookness' that is on the table. It *has to be* one or another number of concrete books." He was afraid that Chinese was taking leave of the real world. Eventually he did catch on, though, and became very good at thinking in Chinese.

The subtleties of Chinese grammar and idiom, and of how they interface with the subtleties of English, seemed endless to me. This fact made it interesting to keep teaching beginning Chinese even after I had already done it fifteen or twenty times. New insights into language and thought kept popping up and shedding new light. This happened, in part, because of the recurring need to figure out how best to explain things to a beginner. It also came from colleagues on teaching teams. Courses like beginning Chinese at Princeton and Middlebury were team-taught by five or six people who shared the work of teaching classes, running drill sessions, correcting homework, creating and grading quizzes, and so on. We had weekly meetings not only to coordinate who would do what but to plan which grammar points to cover, and when. That, inevitably, led to seminar-like discussions on the grammar points themselves, and the discussions were often innovative and enlightening.

The benefits of team teaching were not only intellectual but personal. Some of my best friends in life began as colleagues on Chinese-language teaching teams. It is a deplorable fact that nearly all Chinese language programs in Western academe observe a de facto class system in which professors of history, literature, and other fields are the upper class and language teachers are the lower class. The professors are favored in rank, salary, prestige, and power. Administrators view the system as rational because they assume that professors can do what the language teachers do but not vice versa. And it is indeed true that most language teachers cannot handle the special fields of the professors as well as the professors do; but it is also true—although hardly anyone acknowledges this—that very few of the professors can do language teaching remotely as well as good language teachers do. The first reason they cannot is that they just don't know how subtle and complex good language teaching is. The second reason is that, even if they knew, the ability to walk into a classroom and do it would be beyond them. (Some don't even speak Chinese very well.)

I am annoyed when people refer to courses on Chinese culture taught in

English as "content courses" to distinguish them from "language courses." Setting aside the whole problem of the two-class structure of academic departments, to view language and culture as separate reveals a serious intellectual weakness. In fact, the two are a tightly integrated singularity.

Perhaps the most crucial aspect of getting started in Chinese is pronunciation, and in my teaching I drew special satisfaction from helping students to get this right. Chinese is a tonal language in which a syllable's meaning varies with voice pitch and contour. To train adult speakers of English in the habit of pronouncing tones properly requires patience and persistence. Yet the payoff for success is tremendous. There are hundreds of funny stories about Americans saying, for example, "horse" (low tone) when they mean "mother" (high tone). But this is not really the problem. Chinese people can figure out from context whether you are talking about your horse or your mother. The real cost of toneless Chinese is that the speaker always seems irretrievably alien—not a person one would want to trust, befriend, do business with, or the like.

When I began my Chinese-teaching career in the 1970s, very few Chinese programs in the Western world trained students in tonal pronunciation. They all introduced the concept of tones, but did not follow up with daily practice and made no objections as students formed wrong habits. One reason I enjoyed teaching beginning Chinese was that I used the foundational year to insist that students form correct habits. My inveterate badgering could be irritating to students, but when they went to China and understood for themselves the value of good tones, they were glad I had done it.

I must admit, in the end, that another reason I kept teaching beginning Chinese was simply that I love the language. I enjoy its sounds, and I find its grammatical puzzles interesting. Re-teaching the course never seemed like the same old road. Each time brought new insights.

Originally appeared in the spring 1998 newsletter of
the Consortium for Language Teaching and Learning

The Wonderfully Elusive Chinese Novel

(2015)

A book review of *The Plum in the Golden Vase* (*Jinpingmei*), translated from the Chinese by David Tod Roy

IN TEACHING Chinese-language courses to American students, perhaps the most anguishing question I get is "Professor Link, what is the Chinese word for _____?" I am always tempted to say the question makes no sense. Anyone who knows two languages moderately well knows that it is rare for words to match up perfectly, and for languages as far apart as Chinese and English, in which even grammatical categories are conceived differently, strict equivalence is not possible. *Book* is not *shu*, because *shu*, like all Chinese nouns, is conceived as an abstraction, more like "bookness," and to say "a book" you have to say, "one volume of bookness." Moreover *shu*, but not *book*, can mean "writing," "letter," or "calligraphy." On the other hand, you can "book a room" in English; you can't *shu* one in Chinese.

I tell my students that there are only two kinds of words they can safely regard as equivalents: words for numbers (excepting integers under five, the words for which have too many other uses) and words that are invented expressly for the purpose of serving as equivalents, like *xindiantu* (heart-electric-chart) for "electrocardiogram." I tell them their goal in Chinese class should be to set aside English and get started with thinking in Chinese.

This raises the question of what translation is. I'm afraid it is something quite different from what the person on the street takes it to be. It is not code-switching. Let's take a tiny example, chosen at random, from David Roy's translation of the immense sixteenth-century Chinese novel *Jinpingmei*, or *The Plum in the Golden Vase*, written during the Ming dynasty.

Here the doughty female protagonist, Golden Lotus, is waiting in a garden for her latest lover, who is also her son-in-law. To tease her, the son-in-law hides under a raspberry trellis, then jumps out as she passes by and throws his arms around her:

> "Phooey!" the woman exclaimed. "You little short-life! You gave me quite a start by jumping out that way."

Two other English translations of *Jinpingmei*, both published in London in 1939, put this line differently. Clement Egerton (assisted by the distinguished modern Chinese novelist Lao She) writes:

> "Oh," she cried, "you young villain, what do you mean by rushing out and frightening me like that?"

Bernard Miall, retranslating an earlier abridged German rendition by Franz Kuhn, has this:

> "You rascal, to startle me so!" she cried, scolding him and laughingly releasing herself.

A translation into French in 1985 by André Lévy reads:

> *Lotus-d'Or s'exclama: "Oh, le mauvais garnement! Qu'est-ce que c'est que ces façons de jaillir et vous causer pareille frayeur!"*

None of these translations can be called wrong, or even "more right" than any other. In each case the translator has grasped the original well, but then, in turning to the needs of second-language readers, handles dilemmas differently.

Is the mischievous lover a short-life, villain, rascal, or *garnement*? "Short-life" is a literal reflection of the Chinese *duanming*; "rascal" and "*garnement*" are attempts to find less literal cultural equivalents. How literal should one be? Egerton's "villain" trusts the reader to supply irony— fair enough, in this case, but how far should such trusting go? Miall's "laughingly releasing herself" is not stated in the original, but is certainly implied. Should the translator help out like this, if there is a danger that a reader from another culture might miss something? Lévy's "*Qu'est-ce que c'est que...*" captures the lady's surprise with precision, but it contributes to a sentence that is twice as long as the corresponding Chinese sentence and lacks its balanced rhythm of five-plus-five syllables. Where should the balance lie between matching form and matching sense?

In the end, none of the renditions feels exactly like the original. In that sense they all fail. But failure by that standard is inevitable, because my language students are incorrect to think that exact equivalence is possible. A translator chooses what to sacrifice in favor of what, and the choices are not "correct" or "incorrect," but value judgments.

The most fundamental dilemma is between how much to pull the reader into the original language, preserving its literal meanings and supplying footnotes to spell out complicated things, and how much to step back, be more "free," and try, as Kuhn and Miall in the examples above are most successful at doing, to offer the reader what might be called "comparable experience." Puns are an extreme and therefore clear example of the problem. Translators from Chinese usually ignore puns. Sometimes they dissect them in footnotes, and scholars appreciate the dissection because scholars are interested in innards. But a scalpel kills a pun, of course; a dead pun is no longer funny, and right there one aspect of "comparable experience" is lost. What is the alternative, though? To try to invent a parallel pun in the second language? Such efforts demand great ingenuity as well as a willingness to take considerable liberty with denotative meaning.

David Roy is aware of these dilemmas. He sometimes tries to give the modern American reader comparable experience—for example, in the above, "phooey!" for the Chinese *pei!*, which has a derisive flavor and might even have been "jerk!" or "get lost!"—in any case something a bit more colorful than the "oh" that Egerton and Lévy settle for. But on balance Roy comes down much more on the side of reflecting and explaining the word level in the original. He is the scholars' scholar. He writes more than 4,400 endnotes and advises in his introduction that they are necessary if the novel is to be "properly understood." Jonathan Spence, in a review of an earlier Roy translation, wrote that the meticulous notes make "even a veteran reader of monographs smile with a kind of quiet disbelief."

Today David Roy is eighty years old and has been working for at least forty-five on his translation of the stupendously lengthy *Jinpingmei*. He can point to a life's work of measurable heft: five volumes, 3,493 pages, 13.5

pounds. His is the world's only translation of "everything," as he puts it, in a huge and heterogeneous novel that has crucial importance in Chinese literary tradition. Roy was diagnosed with Lou Gehrig's disease just as he was finishing the last volume.

Jinpingmei is about the rise and fall of a corrupt merchant named Ximen Qing and others in his wealthy household, including his six wives, of whom Golden Lotus is one. Most of the characters accept that deception, bribery, blackmail, profligacy, flamboyant sex, and even murder are normal in life, although it is clear from the narrator's pervasive irony that the author disapproves of all such. A Buddhist frame for the story warns of consequences for karma—the effect on a person's destiny from bad and good deeds. Readers are invited also to see a political allegory on corruption at the imperial court. The story is set during the reign of Emperor Huizong of Song (1101–1126 CE), but the allegory points clearly to contemporary Ming rulers as well.

The story sprawls. There are more than eight hundred named characters, from high officials and military commanders to peddlers and prostitutes, with actors, tailors, monks and nuns, fortunetellers, acrobats, and many others, even cats and dogs, in between. Roy helps us keep track of everyone in a fifty-six-page "cast of characters." The narration is varied, too. In Spence's words, it includes "pretty much every imaginable mood and genre— from sadism to tenderness, from light humor to philosophical musings, from acute social commentary to outrageous satire." It is also full of puns and word games.

The author is unknown, and the question of who it might have been has generated extraordinary controversy, which remains unresolved. We do know it was a superbly erudite person because of the many insertions into the text of songs and set phrases drawn from the histories, drama, storytelling, and fiction available at that time. In the original woodblock printing of the text, Chinese characters follow one another, without punctuation, no matter their source. Modern printings provide punctuation, but Roy goes further by devising a system of indentation and differing type sizes to set off allusions, poems, and songs. With this editorial help, the translation is actually easier to read than the original.

During the four hundred years since it appeared, *Jinpingmei* has been known in China as an "obscene book." Governments have banned it and parents have hidden it from children. One widespread anecdote—a false story, but a true indication of the book's reputation—is that it originated as a murder weapon: the author applied poison to the corners of the pages and presented it to an enemy, knowing that his foe would need to wet his fingertips with saliva in order to keep turning the pages. The plan would not have worked, though, because the pornography is by no means so densely packed. Zhang Zhupo, the first significant critic of the novel, wrote in the late seventeenth century that "anyone who says that *Jinpingmei* is an obscene book has probably only taken the trouble to read the obscene passages."

Westerners, too, have sometimes become fixated on the pornography, and translators have handled it in different ways. In one passage Golden Lotus, after exhausting Ximen Qing's male member during a ferocious sexual encounter, reapplies her silky fingers but cannot get it to stand up. Ximen, in character, says, in Roy's translation, "It's all your fault." Lévy puts this as "*C'est par ton initiative.*" Egerton says, "*Tua culpa est.*" (Egerton puts all of the more pornographic passages into Latin—whether from prudery or to encourage British schoolboys in their studies, he does not say.) Kuhn and Miall omit the passage.

Serious scholars agree that it makes no sense to reject the wide-ranging novel as pornography but do not agree about how well-crafted it is. It contains odd turns of direction, abrupt shifts of mood, digressions that seem to lead nowhere, and discrepancies that result at least in part from the borrowing of much material from other sources. The controversial question is whether these are flaws or a different kind of careful writing.

Is the novel a haphazard pile, casually assembled and often tedious to read? Or, as Roy holds, as does Andrew Plaks in a remarkably learned commentary, is it a "finely wrought structure" in which "every thread is carefully plotted in advance," and which bears not only reading but careful rereading?

Plaks shows that apparently whimsical insertions actually can have significant parts in foreshadowing events or offering ironic comment. A knowledgeable Ming reader will know, he writes, that a song's reference to a faithless brother prefigures the way in which Ximen Qing's close friends will rob his widow blind right after his funeral. The huge novel also has an architecture that he and Roy explain. It consists of a hundred chapters, organized in ten groups of ten, called "decades." Each decade introduces a theme, then has a "twist," as Roy calls it, around the seventh chapter of the decade, and a culmination in the ninth. The first five decades of the novel show the rise of Ximen Qing and the last five his decline. The first two put the main characters on stage, the middle six say what they do there, and the last two take them off. Plaks notes many finer-grained mirrorings as well. It is in chapter 18, for example, that Golden Lotus and her son-in-law lover (mentioned above) first meet, and in chapter 82, eighteen from the end, that they make love.

It is hard to be sure that the author intended all of the finer patterns that these and other critics have identified. When an ocean of material is provided, there is plenty of room for readers to assemble their own patterns. Still, the evidence for Roy's claim that *Jinpingmei* is "the work of a single creative imagination" is very strong, not only because of structural features but because of the consistent moral point of view of the implied author.

Irony pervades the narration. It comes in part from the device of the "simulated storyteller," a voice that supplies the chapters with wry labels ("P'ing-an Absconds with Jewelry from the Pawnshop; Auntie Hsüeh Cleverly Proposes a Personal Appeal") and opens each with the phrase "The story goes that..." The cumulative effect is something like "let's watch, dear reader, as these clowns perform their next act." There is entertainment in the watching, to be sure, but Roy and Plaks are clearly right to point to an underlying moral seriousness as well.

The author is bemoaning a wholesale departure from the principles of Confucianism. The pleasures that the human beings in *Jinpingmei* enjoy are primarily sensual—food, drink, and sex; social pleasures are superficial, driven by ostentation and hypocrisy. Power inherent in social position gets people what they want, and they don't worry about any line between its proper and improper use; cleverness is important for its utility in manipulating one's way to a goal. Whether it is reached by wit or by might, a victory speaks for itself. Wealth and status—up to and including the imperial court—are no cure for the moral rot the author depicts; they only make it worse.

It is useful to reconsider the sex from this point of view. The author of *Jinpingmei* condemns promiscuity not because it is an affront to the divine, as it would be in much of the Abrahamic tradition, but because it is a form of abandon or excess, more like gluttony. When the rich and powerful are greedy, picking up concubines the way wealthy Americans pick up vacation homes, they need criticism. Ximen Qing says that his "Heaven-splashing wealth and distinction" qualify him even to rape goddesses if he likes. A good person, especially an official who has responsibilities in governance, should be spending his energies in better ways.

Yet the assumption that wealth and power do entitle men to multiple sex partners has lasted throughout Chinese history. The earliest records show kings having several consorts; in late imperial times the keeping of concubines in wealthy households was common; and even today the pattern of successful businessmen keeping "second women"—or third, or fourth— is widespread. Modern taboos now prevent the ladies from living under the same roof, but the assumption that keeping several women is a perk of wealth and power is not much different from earlier times.

If this seems discouraging, it should also be said for China that criticism of the practice, or at least of its excesses, has an equally long tradition. The earliest examples we have of pornography in China are descriptions of behavior in imperial harems. And on today's internet, where satire of the powerful is vigorous, sexual misbehavior is second only to illicit wealth as the favorite indictment. So *Jinpingmei* is in good company. I'm not sure whether David Roy should feel happy or sad that the novel had something of a resurgence on the internet in 2013, the year volume five of his translation was published. In February Lian Qingchuan, a prominent journalist, wrote an article called "We Live Today in the World of *Jinpingmei*." A flurry of enthusiastic reader comments said things like "I'm glad somebody told me this book was written five hundred years ago! I never would have known!" Others commented that Ximen Qing was a mere beginner in sexual aggression compared to his avatars today.

In using the novel as a mirror for society, these internet commentators recall another way that scholars have studied *Jinpingmei*. Because the novel was the first in China to describe daily life, as opposed to legends or ideals, social historians have mined it for data. If you study commerce, for example, the sizes of bribes, alms, and gifts are there, as well as prices for rolls of silk, peeled chestnuts, goose gizzards, new beds, old buildings, and much more, as well as the costs of the services of storytellers, go-betweens, carpenters, singing girls, and others. In the 1970s, F.W. Mote, the eminent Ming historian at Princeton, although he judged *Jinpingmei* "not a success" as a novel, taught a graduate seminar using it as a source for history. One problem with the approach was the distorting effect of the author's satire. For example, Ximen Qing bribes Grand Preceptor Cai Jing, arbiter of the dynasty, often and lavishly—once with a birthday present of two hundred

taels of gold, eight gold goblets, twenty pairs of cups made of jade and rhinoceros horn, and more. But when Ximen dies and a protégé of the Grand
Preceptor comes to offer respects, he brings only paltry gifts, including
woolen socks and four dried fish. This is not realism, as C.T. Hsia points
out, but satire to make a point.

Mote, to avoid this kind of problem in his seminar, devised a "principle
of inadvertency." Whenever a detail mattered to the story line, or to the
author's evaluation of something, the students were to set it aside. But the
thousands of details offered inadvertently were fair game.

Whether *Jinpingmei* is taken as broad social canvas, literary innovation, serious ethical criticism, or only spicy entertainment, a question that
has haunted its study over the last hundred years is whether it is—indeed
whether China has—a "great novel." I think China would be better off if the
question were not asked so much.

In the early twentieth century, when memories of humiliating defeats
by foreign powers had stimulated Chinese thinkers to go in search of the
secrets of wealth and power, Liang Qichao, a leading reformer, wrote a
powerful essay in which he argued that one reason Western countries are
strong is that the thinking of their people is unified and vigorous, and a
main reason their thinking has been vigorous is that they read vigorous
fiction. So, he concluded, China needs good novels. Beginning in the late
1910s, Hu Shi, Lu Xun, and other May Fourth thinkers began looking back
at China's past to see if some good novels might already have been written. A canon was born, listed often as *Romance of the Three Kingdoms*, *The
Water Margin*, *Journey to the West*, *Jinpingmei*, *The Scholars*, and *Dream
of the Red Chamber*, and these writings were compared to major works
of European fiction. In the latter twentieth century, sympathetic Western
Sinologists have supported China's quest to rediscover its great novels.

There has been progress in that direction. Advocating *Jinpingmei*, Roy
and Plaks, and before them Patrick Hanan, have established the novel's
importance as an innovation. Its unity of conception and elaborate design
epitomize "the Ming novel" and set an example for later long fiction in
China, most importantly *Dream of the Red Chamber*. This kind of argument for *Jinpingmei* resembles the way James Wood argues for Flaubert
when he writes that "there really is a time before Flaubert and a time after
him," and "novelists should thank Flaubert the way poets thank spring."

The particular strengths that Wood finds in Flaubert are very different from those that Roy and Plaks find in *Jinpingmei*, but the argument

about a historical watershed is similar—until, anyway, Roy and Plaks start acknowledging flaws in *Jinpingmei*. Wood credits Flaubert with immaculate planning and selection of detail, done as if by an invisible hand; Roy and Plaks see something like that in *Jinpingmei*, but also find "loose ends," "glaring internal discrepancies," and other infelicities.

When Roy defends *Jinpingmei* by calling it a "work in progress," he recalls for me G.K. Chesterton's insight that "if a thing is worth doing, it is worth doing badly." The first airplane didn't soar, either, but it's very good that someone got a prototype off the ground.

But why do I feel that China—and Sinologists—would be better off to relax about the idea that "we have great novels, too"? I feel this because I think that setting up literary civilizations as rivals (although I can understand the insecurities that led Liang Qichao and others to do it) only gets in the way of readers' enjoyment of imaginative works. What does it matter if the author of *Jinpingmei* might be less than Flaubert? Why should anyone have to feel defensive?

Let me put it the other way around. Novels were not the primary language art in imperial China. Measured by volume, *xi*, translatable as "drama" or "opera," would be in first place, and measured by beauty, calligraphy or poetry would be. Should we compare poetry across civilizations? If we do, classical Chinese poetry wins easily. The contest is almost unfair, because, as my students of Chinese language eventually come to see, the fundaments of language are different.

Indo-European languages, with their requirements that tense, number, gender, and part of speech be specified, and with the mandatory word inflections that the specifications entail, and with the extra syllables that the inflections add, just can't achieve the same purity—a sense of terseness and expanse at the same time—that tenseless, numberless, voiceless, uninflected, and uninflectible Chinese characters can achieve. In a contest, one person has a butterfly net and the other a window screen. Emily Dickinson might have come to be known as the greatest poet in world history if she had written in classical Chinese. Should Westerners feel defensive that this was not the case? Far better just to inherit what we all have done, and leave it there.

Originally published in *The New York Review of Books*
April 23, 2015

A Magician of Chinese Poetry

(2016)

A review of *19 Ways of Looking at Wang Wei (with More Ways)* and *The Ghosts of Birds* by Eliot Weinberger

SOME PEOPLE, and I am one, feel that Tang (618–907 CE) poetry is the finest literary art they have ever read. But does one need to learn Chinese in order to have such a view, or can classical Chinese poetry be adequately translated?

In 1987 Eliot Weinberger, who has written brilliant essays on topics as various as the mystical *Yijing* (Book of Change), Buddha as "impostor," Albanian Islam, and a connection between Michel Foucault and George W. Bush—and who has translated Chinese poetry, too—published a little book with Octavio Paz called *Nineteen Ways of Looking at Wang Wei*. There Weinberger and Paz choose a four-line poem by Wang Wei, one of the best Tang poets, and present it many ways: in Chinese characters, in a transliteration into modern Mandarin, in a character-by-character literal translation, and in seventeen different ways translators have tried to express its art in English, French, or Spanish.

They find that none of the translations is perfect (there is no such thing as "perfect" in such matters), but that some are very worthwhile as poems on their own. Weinberger writes that a good poem contains "living matter" that "functions somewhat like DNA, spinning out individual translations that are relatives, not clones, of the original." Now, in 2016, we have an updated version of the book, called *Nineteen Ways of Looking at Wang Wei (with More Ways)*, that offers sixteen additional offspring, three in German, for a total of thirty-four.

The title of the poem is "Deer Fence" (or Deer Park, Deer Enclosure,

Deer Forest Hermitage, and others). Weinberger's literal translation reflects the five-characters-per-line of the original:

> *Empty/mountain(s) [or] hill(s)/(negative)/to see/person [or] people*
> *But/to hear/person [or] people/words or conversation/sound [or]*
>   *to echo*
> *To return/bright(ness) [or] shadow(s)/to enter/deep/forest*
> *To return/to shine/green/moss/above*

Of the finished translations, this one by Burton Watson is among Weinberger's favorites:

> *Empty hills, no one in sight,*
> *only the sound of someone talking;*
> *late sunlight enters the deep wood,*
> *shining over the green moss again.*

How good are the good translations? How much of the original do we get?

Some of the art of classical Chinese poetry must simply be set aside as untranslatable. The internal structure of Chinese characters has a beauty of its own, and the calligraphy in which classical poems were written is another important but untranslatable dimension. Since Chinese characters do not vary in length, and because there are exactly five characters per line in a poem like this, another untranslatable feature is that the written result, hung on a wall, presents a rectangle. Translators into languages whose word lengths vary can reproduce such an effect only at the risk of fatal awkwardness. (Watson's translation, above, does about as well as one can do; instead of five characters per line it gives us six English words per line.)

Another imponderable is how to imitate the 1-2, 1-2-3 rhythm in which five-syllable lines in classical Chinese poems normally are read. Chinese characters are pronounced in one syllable apiece, so producing such rhythms in Chinese is not hard and the results are unobtrusive; but any imitation in a Western language is almost inevitably stilted and distracting. Even less translatable are the patterns of tone arrangement in classical Chinese poetry. Each syllable (character) belongs to one of two categories determined by the pitch contour in which it is read; in a classical Chinese poem the patterns of alternation of the two categories exhibit parallelism and mirroring.

Weinberger knows all of this and sensibly begins his inquiry at step two— after all the untranslatables have been set aside. Now the question becomes: How can one make another poem from the twenty bundles of meaning that the Chinese characters offer? Weinberger criticizes, astutely if sometimes unkindly, almost every translator he cites. He says the images in Wang Wei's poem are more "specific" than they are in a translation by Witter Bynner, and he has a point, but does he need to write that Bynner sees Wang Wei as "watching the world through a haze of opium"? Sometimes, too, Weinberger's standards seem not to apply uniformly. He scolds Chang Yin-nan and Lewis Walmsley for writing that the voices in the hills are "faint" and "drift on the air." These characterizations are not in the original, and for Weinberger are "a classic example of the translator attempting to 'improve' the original" and even show "a kind of unspoken contempt for the foreign poet."

But at the same time, Weinberger congratulates Kenneth Rexroth, whose translation inserts much more than Chang and Walmsley's does, for producing a "real poem" that is closest "to the spirit, if not the letter, of the original." Most translators will agree that we should not try to improve and also that loyalty to spirit must sometimes outweigh loyalty to letter. But to look at a specific addition to a poem and decide which of these things it is doing is very difficult.

Broadly speaking, the problems for a translator, especially of poetry, and especially between languages as different as Chinese and English, are two: What do I think the poetic line says? And then, once I think I understand it, how can I put it into English? Differences in translations sometimes arise from the first problem; most, though, come from the second, where the impossibility of perfect answers spawns endless debate. The letter-versus-spirit dilemma is almost always at the center.

At the literalist extreme, there is a school of Western Sinology that aims to ferret out and dissect every conceivable detail about the language of an original. The dissection, though, normally does to the art of a poem approximately what the scalpel of an anatomy instructor does to the life of a frog. Peter A. Boodberg, a distinguished Sinologist at Berkeley fifty years ago, translates Wang Wei's poem this way:

DEER WATTLE (HERMITAGE)

The empty mountain; to see no men,
Barely earminded of men talking—countertones
And antistrophic lights-and-shadows incoming deeper the deep-
*   treed grove*
Once more to glowlight the blue-green mosses—going up
(The empty mountain…)

Boodberg's is an extreme example, but it illustrates the principle in this school of Sinology that the further one goes with philology and literal translation, the closer one gets to the Chinese original. About a decade ago I heard a Sinologist at Princeton rise to express the view that *only* in translation can the deepest meaning of a Tang poem be brought to light. (The issue was dropped after someone else asked if the reverse were also true: Does Shakespeare's profundity emerge *only* in Chinese translation?)

Weinberger is contemptuous of the Boodberg approach ("sounds like Gerard Manley Hopkins on LSD") and is closer to, but not an extremist in, an approach that puts art at the center. He admires Ezra Pound's versions of classical Chinese poems in *Cathay*, published in 1915. Pound learned some Chinese characters later in his life but in 1915 could base *Cathay* only on translations that others had done. His genius for language apparently got him close enough to the spirit of Chinese originals that he could correct mistakes in other translations "intuitively," as Weinberger puts it. He stops short of calling Pound's work "translation"; he endorses a phrase by T.S. Eliot, who leavened the question with gentle ambiguity when he said that Pound was "the inventor of Chinese poetry in our time." Whether translations or inventions, though, Weinberger finds Pound's renditions "some of the most beautiful poems in the English language."

In the 1930s Pound became obsessed with the *Book of Odes*, China's most ancient collection of poetry and song (and, some say, guide to government). Convinced that the existing English translations of the *Odes* were "appalling" and "intolerable," and that there must be a great pearl inside the closed oyster if only he could get there, Pound, then over fifty years old, began to study Chinese characters. He could now "play the game of pretending to read Chinese," as Weinberger puts it, and unleashed his fecund imagination upon "pictographic" characters in ways that serious

Sinologists knew to be utterly groundless. Professors wrote articles exposing Pound's errors in both interpretation of characters and translations of
poems.

Weinberger's implicit riposte, which I support, is: *But do you do better?*
One can acknowledge a long list of Pound's technical errors and still point
out that phrases like Boodberg's "antistrophic lights-and-shadows" leave
a reader much further from a Wang Wei poem than Pound does. Wai-
lim Yip, a scholar of poetry who knows both English and Chinese well,
notes that, despite the literal errors, in Pound "the 'cuts and turns' of the
mind in the originals are largely preserved" and the "essential poems" are
"luminous." Could one say that of Boodberg? Options in the translation of
poetry are complexly interconnected, and gaining something in one place
almost inevitably means losing something in another. So here is a good
rule of thumb: anyone who criticizes a given translation should be ready to
offer an alternative that, all things considered, works better.

Pound's approach to Chinese poetry was deeply influenced by Ernest
Fenollosa, an American who in the late 1870s and 1880s taught Western
philosophy in Tokyo, where he developed a consuming interest in Chinese
and Japanese poetry and art. Fenollosa died of a heart attack in 1908, and in
1913 his widow, Mary, agreed to hand all his private papers and manuscripts
over to Pound. One of those papers, called "The Chinese Written Character
as a Medium for Poetry," was the progenitor of some of Pound's more dura-
ble views on the Chinese language. Fenollosa, and Pound following him,
grossly exaggerated the extent to which characters are "thought pictures."

More usefully, though, the Fenollosa essay showed Pound what it could
mean for poets that Chinese characters are free from the inflections for
number, tense, voice, and gender that are mandatory in Western languages.
It seemed to Fenollosa that in Chinese, bundles of meaning just came along
side by side. Grammar still had a place, in some simple rules of word order,
but it did not affect the characters themselves and left much more room for
poetic ambiguity. The meanings of Chinese characters, wrote Fenollosa,
could "be like the mingling of the fringes of feathered banners." Or:

> A word is like a sun, with its corona and chromosphere; words
> crowd upon words, and wrap each other in their luminous enve-
> lopes until sentences become clear, continuous light-bands.

For Pound, "luminous" became an important word, and later a Fenollosan understanding of Chinese poetry, through Pound, influenced the Anglo-American Imagist movement of Hilda Doolittle, Richard Aldington, and others. Later, it also had an effect on the American poets Gary Snyder and Allen Ginsberg.

The advantages of Chinese characters in avoiding grammatical specificity (advantages to poets, not necessarily to scientists or lawyers) can be analyzed primarily as absences of subject, number, and tense. Each of these three is worth a look.

Subjectlessness. It is the norm in classical Chinese poetry, and common even in modern Chinese prose, to omit subjects. The reader or listener infers a subject. In the first line of our Wang Wei poem ("empty mountain no see person"), only a perverse reader would say that "empty mountain" should be the subject because it is a noun and comes first. Common sense hears the phrase adverbially and infers the subject to be an unstated human viewer. But how can one put this effect into Western languages that ask by grammatical rule that subjects always be stated? Most of the translators in *Nineteen Ways* supply an "I." Weinberger points out, though, that when "I" is inserted a "controlling individual mind of the poet" enters and destroys the effect of the Chinese line. Without a subject, he writes, "the experience becomes both universal and immediate to the reader." This point is correct and very important.

Another way to handle the subjectlessness, which Wai-lim Yip chooses, is to use the passive voice in English: "no man is seen." But this, at least to my ear, again particularizes the experience too much. That marvelous sense of "both universal and immediate" remains lost. A third alternative is to leave the voice active and, following the Chinese, name no subject: "in empty mountains, see no person," or something like that. But this often sounds broken or childlike, which the Chinese line certainly does not. Burton Watson's "empty hills, no one in sight" is about as good as one can do.

Numberlessness. Nouns have no number in Chinese. Weinberger notes that "rose is a rose is all roses," but that formulation still leaves us too far inside Western-language number habits. "All roses" in English means the summation of individual roses, whereas in Chinese *meigui*, or "rose" is more like "roseness" or "rosehood." (If you want to talk in Chinese about one rose, you may, but then you use a "measure word" to say "one blossom-of roseness.") So, in the first line of Wang Wei's poem, it is not quite right to think of *shan* as either singular or plural, either *hill* or *hills*. The concept is more abstract. But what can a translator write? *Hillness* sounds odd and *hillhood* almost funny. Any attempt of this kind tends to exoticize, but the supple Chinese line is not at all exotic. (It is worth noting that Western views of Eastern expression as quaint have often originated not in Eastern languages themselves but in the awkwardness that results when rules of Western languages are applied.)

Tenselessness. There are several ways in Chinese to specify when something happened or will happen, but verb tense is not one of them. For poets, the great advantage of tenselessness is the ambiguity it opens up. Did I see no one in the hills? Or am I now seeing no one? Am I imagining what it would be like to see no one? All these, and others, are possible. Weinberger's insight about subjectlessness—that it produces an effect "both universal and immediate"—applies to timelessness as well.

But the effect isn't possible in a Western language, where grammar always forces a choice of one tense or another. For this reason I will quibble with Weinberger's choice of English infinitives as his glosses for Chinese verbs. He lists *ru* as "to enter," *zhao* as "to shine," and so on, but I am afraid that that little "to," which comes from English grammar, subtly reinforces the mistaken notion that Chinese verbs are, or should be, conjugatable things, when in fact they are not. Moreover, infinitives in Western languages can be nouns. On stage at the Met, *to enter* is *to shine*—one noun is another. I would prefer to say *ru* is "enter" and *zhao* "shine."

Although he is critical of nearly everyone's translation in *Nineteen Ways*, Weinberger wisely adopts the position that "quite a few possible readings" can all be "equally 'correct.'" Dilemmas about translation do not have definitive right answers (although there can be unambiguously wrong ones if misreadings of the original are involved). Any translation (except machine translation, a different case) must pass through the mind of a translator, and that mind inevitably contains its own store of perceptions, memories, and values.

Weinberger—rightly, in my view—pushes this insight further when he writes that "every reading of every poem, regardless of language, is an act of translation: translation into the reader's intellectual and emotional life." Then he goes still further: because a reader's mental life shifts over time, there is a sense in which "the same poem cannot be read twice." Here, too, I agree. But I feel Weinberger goes a bit too far when he writes that the possible word combinations in a translation are "infinite." Perhaps we can say that possible interpretations in receiving minds are infinite, since gradations of their differences can be infinitesimal. But "word combinations" in a translation cannot be infinite.

Weinberger's sensitivity to words and gift for clear thinking underlie nearly every page in *Nineteen Ways*, but in *The Ghosts of Birds* they spout like a geyser. The essays (some should be called poems) in this book have been published before or are continuations of a project begun before, but it is very good to have them in one place. The range of Weinberger's interests in human cultures might be summarized as "everything everywhere from the beginning until now," and he writes with erudition and charm. A horse in a painting from China's "horse-obsessed" Tang era is "almost ridiculously plump, like a candied apple on four sticks." His details often seem uncanny—perhaps fiction, a reader might wonder?—but they are not fiction. He does not footnote his sources, but when I checked his China stories I found good (not error-free, but good) bases for all of them.

A warm humanism pervades *The Ghosts of Birds*, and Weinberger has ways of making clear that it is universal. Sometimes, as in a gripping piece on Charles Reznikoff's book-length poem *Testimony*, a particular case glows so intensely that the reader feels the universality intuitively; it could not be otherwise. Elsewhere, the sense of commonality arises as Weinberger finds something the same across a wide range of cases. "A Calendar of Stones," for example, collects dozens of pieces of text that show how human beings from the ancient Greeks to the Jains to Buddhist monks to "the Orixás—Yoruba gods who are called 'saints' in Brazil," among others, have interacted with stones. No matter where he draws an example from, Weinberger's attitude is that human beings are amusing creatures.

Another piece, called "Changs Dreaming," recounts the dreams, collected from Chinese texts of different sorts and times over centuries, of eighteen unrelated people all surnamed Chang. There is self-satire in the conception of the piece. Surnames do not matter in the genesis of dreams, and to suggest even briefly that they do is sufficiently eccentric to remind us that the truth is the opposite: all of us humans dream. To find so many dreaming Changs is not, moreover, as odd as seems implied. The surname

Chang (now often spelled Zhang, but the same name) has always been extremely common in China; today only about fifteen countries in the world have more people than China has Changs.

In "The Story of Adam and Eve," Weinberger goes beyond the Bible to present a surprising variety of versions of the story from Armenian, Georgian, Greek, Slavonic, Latin, Ge'ez (Ethiopian), and other sources. Every account is vulnerable to his playful barbs. In the Garden of Eden, for example, when Yahweh (God) calls to Adam "Where are you?," Weinberger notes that He does this "although omniscient." The bite is terse, but elsewhere Weinberger's satire flows in cascades. He enjoys what Chinese comedians call "word fountains." Khubilai Khan (1215–1294 CE), for example, was cruel and efficient during his early years as emperor, but later

> became grotesquely fat, suffering from gout and other ailments, and detached from governing. He held huge and endless banquets of meat and koumiss, fermented mare's milk, and was in a near-continual state of inebriation. [At his hunting reserve] four elephants would carry him, lying on a couch, in a gold-plated palanquin decked with tiger skins, accompanied by five hundred falconers and leopards and lynxes trained to chase down bears and wild boars.

In his analytic observations, Weinberger likes to cut to a core in plain language. He writes:

> Confucianism taught that when the government is bad, one should head for the hills. (Taoism taught that, regardless of government, one should head for the hills.)

Professors might warn graduate students against such writing as too casual or "reductive," but I disagree. The points Weinberger makes here are essentially correct and are much clearer than they would be if dressed up in academic jargon. In addition to its clarity, plain language has the virtue of allowing ideas from ancient times and distant places to extend into our present, just as shared humanity itself extends. The alternative of studying ancient ideas as if they are pickled specimens in a jar cannot do that. Weinberger sees lines of Wang Wei's poems as "both universal and immediate," and he sees much else in human cultures in that same spirit, which I think is wonderful.

Originally published in The New York Review of Books,
November 24, 2016

Whose Assumptions Does the Artist
Xu Bing Upset, and Why?

꘏

(2006)

Xu Bing (1955-) is a famous Chinese installation artist.

MANY OF Xu Bing's works probe the mysteries of the Chinese written language. The shapes of characters, their balances, their relations to the things in the world that they refer to and to the sounds that accompany them through life, their central place in Chinese culture, their austerity, their borderline pomposity, their moral and spiritual seriousness—all this is food for his art. But Xu is always the artist, never the scientist, in that he won't tell us what to think about any of this. He stimulates us to explore thoughts and feelings on our own, but through questions, not answers. It is left to scholars and other plain-minded people to wade in and try to pin a few things down.

My first impression of Xu Bing's art was my most powerful. In fall of 1988 I entered upon his famous installation called *Tian Shu* "Book from the Sky" at an exhibition in Beijing. I say "entered upon" because it was not exactly a "viewing" experience. It was a feeling of being surrounded and consumed. From the ceiling, from the floor, and from the four walls, the work engulfed—and began to digest, it seemed—any person who walked inside it. I felt no fear, but do remember that my first sensation was more physical than intellectual.

The next impression, as I recall, was an overwhelming sense of the artist's labor. The books strewn all over the floor and the scrolls draped expansively from above were covered in Chinese characters that had been printed by hand using wood blocks that had been conceived, designed, and carved all by a single artist. Can this be?, I wondered. How many lifetimes must this have taken? Was the artist telling us something about the storied and stupendous patience of the Chinese people, using himself as Exhibit A? After someone in the gallery mentioned that the work took Xu Bing "a few years," I dropped the question from my mind—but more to escape it than to think I had answered it.

Next I looked more closely at the characters and saw that they were unreadable. I felt frustration, bordering even on anger. Other viewers, I could sense, felt similarly. Where did this response come from? Why should one care if meaningless bunches of lines on paper yield no meaning? Because, I think, there was so much else there that built an *expectation* of meaning: the characters were composed from recognizable character parts that suggested the possibility of meaning and then didn't, as it were, finish the job. The physical context of the work magnified this effect: there were books, scrolls, black ink on white paper in good calligraphy—everything that normally tells a viewer, "Here not only is meaning, but especially worthy meaning. You should try to figure it out."

It is acceptable in Chinese culture not to be able to read something immediately. On many occasions I have observed well-educated Chinese, including Chinese language teachers and eminent scholars, huddle around the calligraphy that I hang in my home, trying to figure out what it says. It is fine to spend time digging for treasure, but absurd and repugnant to suggest that there is no treasure to be dug. Xu Bing packs his bomb in elegant wrapping.

There are probably subtle differences in the ways native-speaking Chinese experience Xu Bing's art and the way it strikes a second-language learner like me. After the initial shock of not being able to read Xu's characters, I had a second—minor but intriguing—reaction that I wonder whether a native speaker would feel. This was an odd sense of relief. Why would I feel relief? I think the key to this response is that I had spent so much of my life studying China—this huge, immensely rich, always unfathomable language, history, and culture that gives to any student the impression that the more one learns the farther one falls behind. For decades people have asked me, "How did you learn Chinese?" and part of me always wants to say, "Some day I hope to." Any serious student of Chinese knows that the phrase "mastery of Chinese" is a gentle fraud; it makes sense only to people who have never begun. This big secret fact helps, I think, to explain why

Xu Bing's art can bring a twinge of relief to people like me. It seems to say: "Right, you can't read this. *And it's not your fault; nobody can read it.*"

In fall of 1988 the responses across Beijing society to *Tian Shu* were lively and varied. Intellectuals discussed it, rebellious youth cheered it, and Communist Party conservatives denounced it. It seemed to me that the cheering of the rebels and the denunciations by the Party had a common root. Both were based in Xu Bing's implicit claim to the autonomy of the mind. This point may need some explanation.

In the tradition of Chinese Communist Party control of literature and art, every articulate thought is supposed to be either "correct" or "incorrect." If a certain statement does not fall clearly into one of these categories, that is only because a proper determination about correctness has yet to be made. In theory such a judgment always *can* be made; there is no such thing as a statement beyond determination. Everything is either correct or refutable. But Xu Bing's *Tian Shu* suggested that there can be a third realm—the "neither correct nor incorrect." And in *Tian Shu* this subversive category did not just peek at you around a corner—it surrounded you.

To the political people, the implicit claim of life beyond correctness was about as comfortable as a body covered in ants. The problem was not just that Xu's quasi-characters might be harboring subversive meanings. The deeper challenge was to the undergirding of the whole control system. If decisions on "correctness" sometimes could not be made, then the people who make them could no longer claim absolute authority. But if the authorities aren't in control, who is? And if we don't know who is in control, will the whole system wobble?

To the young rebels, the same claim about an area beyond the reach of the arbiters of correctness had an opposite effect. It was exhilarating. Even if Xu's characters were meaningless, there were tens of thousands of them, and each trumpeted its own autonomy. Collectively they were like a meadow full of happy daisies, silently asserting that, "We are not incorrect! You cannot ban us!" And after their irrefutable claim had been made (here was the real point!), the meadow remained. An intellectual field had been opened. Others, albeit cautiously, could play in it.

This was *Tian Shu's* contribution to artistic freedom, but its challenge to Chinese culture was, and is, something more profound. It is something that transcends partisan politics and transcends an oppressive control system.

Chinese people everywhere, both inside and outside the PRC, have found something about Xu Bing's ersatz characters to be deeply unsettling. The characters are "wrong" technically, but that is only the beginning. The cultural affront of their wrongness runs much deeper than the matter of linguistic code. If we could, for example, somehow push a magic spell-check button and see all of Xu Bing's characters switch instantly into authentic ones, the "correction" would be only superficial. The memory of the phony characters would still be upsetting.

At a show of Xu Bing's work in Pittsburgh in 2001, a Chinese man, who I think represents many, shook his head and mumbled, "Xu Bing is not Chinese." This man interpreted Xu's art as claiming that "Chinese characters are a fraud" and that therefore, somehow, perhaps "Chineseness is a fraud." Why do Chinese characters mean so much to Chinese people? Why can distorting them be so upsetting? Weighty things like history, morality, and identity seem to be at stake.

First, history. One of the first facts anyone notices about Chinese history is the huge amount of it. The word "history," like its Chinese counterpart *lishi*, is commonly used to mean two very different things: "events that happened" or "written records of events." For China, there is an overwhelming amount of history no matter which of these senses one means, and this vastness is somehow conjured in the expansiveness of Xu Bing's *Tian Shu*. The work evokes ancient history especially. Its form of scrolls and string-bound books pulls one back toward imperial China, out of the twentieth century and into the historical immensity that anchors the civilization. The impact of the work would be greatly diminished if its focus were modern. Imagine, for a moment, that Xu Bing's characters had been based on modern simplified characters (*jiantizi*) and had been arranged horizontally on the page, reading left to right, instead of vertically reading top to bottom. What would be different? Some interesting questions about resistance of political control would remain, but the deep cultural questions would all but disappear.

In Chinese tradition the elision from history to morality happens easily. The written lines that Xu Bing's work imitates were not just records but morally relevant records—*exalted* records. They suggest propriety and respectability. In part this is because they appear in black and white: Chinese art and calligraphy in handsome black and white beats any color or technicolor, past or future, for elegance, purity, and dignity. But a stronger link to practical morality inheres in Chinese attitudes toward the characters themselves. The very earliest examples of Chinese characters, on ancient oracle bones, often had to do with advice about action: When should the king go to war, or perform rituals? When should farmers plant? and so on. This is not the place to address the huge questions of the ways in which classical learning in imperial China, from memorization of the *Three-Character Classic* through passing of the highest imperial exams, consisted in internalizing the sounds, forms, and meanings of properly arranged *written Chinese characters*. Such writing was the food that could nourish personal cultivation, lead to appropriate moral response to other human beings, qualify one to guide and govern others, first in the family and then in the larger society, and finally, at the pinnacle, to connect one to the highest authority on earth, the emperor, and even to the immanent power in the cosmos called *tian* (as in *Tian Shu*). To address all of this would take a full-year course and still not be adequate; hence I will leave the topic and move on, hoping that you're with me in feeling that Chinese characters are conceived as carrying moral as well as historical freight.

What happens, in this context, when Xu Bing calls his work a "Book from the Sky," a *tian shu*? The term *tian shu* itself has a long history in China. It can mean "word from the emperor," or sometimes "word from heaven's spirit." Peasant rebels, hoping for better times, often had their own *tian shu*, less as a practical guide than as a moral warrant for their rebellion. A written document could show that *tian* was on their side. At the emperor's court, official histories aimed less at recording what had happened than at exalting the proper view of what had happened. When Xu Bing suggests that austere writing might be a fraud, he subverts value as much as fact.

What about "identity," the third word I mentioned above in connection with written characters? Why would a Chinese man in Pittsburgh feel that Xu Bing is "not Chinese"? If this way of putting the question seems too narrow, let's start at the other end and put the question perhaps too broadly: if languages give rise to cultures, and if cultures are often important in forming nations, then why do Chinese people think they are one nation, not many? In terms of spoken languages and local cultures, China is about as varied as Europe. Some scholars have postulated that what holds China together is Han ethnicity, while others feel that a shared sense of history or a common writing system has been most important. Without trying to decide such a question, we can at least agree that written Chinese characters have played an important role in Chinese senses of "Chinese-ness." A speaker of Shanghainese and a speaker of Cantonese have no trouble identifying each other as Chinese even though they speak languages as different as French and Italian. Their written language holds them together, and, I think, is especially important to them *precisely because* it holds them together. There is, to be sure, a certain circularity here: the written language permits a sense of unity, and the sense of unity in turn leads people to treasure the written language. But no matter; to paraphrase C.I. Lewis, circular reasoning is fine as long as the circle is big enough. In Chinese tradition, it is big enough.

My argument that written Chinese carries Chinese identity assumes that spoken Chinese carries it less so. Is this true? If Xu Bing had done his word-play in oral Chinese instead of written Chinese, would the consequences have been so "deep"? Would people assume them to be as involved with things like history, morality and identity?

There is probably no quick answer to such a question, but I would like to propose a modest experiment to get us started with it. Just as Xu Bing dismantled characters into component parts and recombined them into nonsense characters, he could have done a similar thing with Chinese sounds. The syllables of standard Mandarin Chinese are composed of three parts—an "initial" sound that contains no vowel, a "final" sound that includes a vowel, and a "tone" that has to do with voice pitch. Every syllable has a final and a tone, and may or may not have an initial. By widely accepted consensus, there are twenty-one initial sounds, thirty-seven finals, and four tones. (The values of some of the tones and finals can change with phonetic context, but this does not change their "phonemic" status, i.e., their potential to distinguish one lexical item from another.) The Mandarin sound system is "closed" in the sense that no standard syllable falls outside of it. A teacher of beginning Chinese can train students in the twenty-one initials, thirty-seven finals, and four tones, and then promise that student that he or she can pronounce any syllable of Mandarin Chinese. A mathematically inclined student can calculate that twenty-two initials (adding a "zero" initial to account for initialless syllables) times thirty-seven finals times four tones yields a product of 3,256 possible syllables in Mandarin.

But it is an interesting fact—and fertile ground for a mischievous spirit like Xu Bing's—that only about 1,000 of these 3,256 possible syllables are actually used. Of the other 2,000 or so, some are passed over because they are hard or impossible to pronounce. None of the four "retroflex" initials, for example, can combine with any of the ten finals that begin with an "i" sound, because such combinations would demand that the tongue be in two places at once. In other cases, the reasons certain combinations do not occur are historical. Unaspirated bilabial initials, for example, tend not to accompany the second tone: Mandarin has several *bang1* words (here I use numbers to indicate tones), and also has *bang3* and *bang4*, but has no *bang2*. There are hundreds of other "proper" and pronounceable sounds that go unemployed. Mandarin has several *gua* and several *zhua*, but no *dua* or *tua*—in any tone.

In short, there is plenty of room to dismantle and recombine genuine sound components in Mandarin Chinese in a way exactly parallel to the way in which Xu Bing dismantles and recombines character parts. The question I want to ask is: would such a maneuver be as upsetting to "deep" notions of morality and identity as play with written characters can be? Would anyone find it disturbingly "un-Chinese" to do such a thing?

We can test the case by imagining what a classical-style poem would feel like using possible-but-bogus sounds. To set a base line, let's begin by reading a Tang poem, *Shan Xing* 山行 "Walking in the Mountains" by Du Mu (803–852 A.D.):

远上寒山石经斜
白云深处有人家
停车坐爱枫林晚
霜叶红于二月花

No one can say exactly what this sounded like in Du Mu's day, but in modern Mandarin the effect is exquisite and, to modern Chinese speakers, feels natural and "feels Chinese":

yuan3 shang4 han2 shan1 shi2 jing4 xie2
bai2 yun2 shen1 chu4 you3 ren2 jia1
ting2 ju1 zuo4 ai4 feng1 lin2 wan3
shuang1 ye4 hong2 yu2 er4 yue4 hua1

Now let's try a "poem" composed of nonsense syllables. I will not try to be Xu Bing and invent characters, but offer the following in *hanyu pinyin*:

dua1 pun1 chei3 tiang4 mong1 fi1 dui3
fai4 xin3 zua2 gang2 shueng3 ten4 kin1
puai2 biong2 zhuo4 chuei4 bia1 bia1 seng3
keng4 mua3 qiai2 tue1 cei3 reng4 lin1

Now our question: How upsetting is a "poem" like this to Chinese cultural assumptions? Utter gibberish would be easy to set aside. But when, as here, the sounds are plausible, and when rules of line length, rhythm, rhyme, and even *ping/ze* alternation are observed—as here they are—then the sounds seem to imitate something. It is precisely their half-authenticity, their impostorhood, that can be upsetting.

When I read this "poem" at the inaugural symposium for Princeton University's Tang Center for East Asian Art, I invited members of the audience, which included Chinese native speakers as well as seasoned Sinologists, to try to articulate their visceral responses to it. Was it puzzling? Upsetting? Disgusting? During the coffee break a number of people offered their responses, and I was interested to learn that there was a unanimity among them. The sounds had not been particularly upsetting. Several people said they just sounded like another dialect. "Of course," I told myself. Chinese includes hundreds of dialects, many of them mutually unintelligible, and Chinese people are accustomed to hearing weird sounds from the mouths of other people whom they have no problem identifying as Chinese. But not so for characters. These are—and are supposed to be—standard everywhere. So Xu Bing had hit a nail on the head: weird characters are upsetting in ways that weird sounds seem not to be.

To argue that Xu Bing's art disturbs ancient Chinese assumptions begs a question, however. *Tian Shu* appeared in 1988, so any claim that it *would have* upset people who lived a thousand years earlier can only be speculative. The people whom it actually upsets are limited to those who have lived since 1988. If we claim that "ancient traditions" help to explain why modern people are upset, then we need to argue that such traditions have remained strong despite all of the turmoil, revolution, Western influence, and modernization of the tumultuous twentieth century. Did anything survive all the erosion that accompanied this turmoil?

Yes, I believe. More has survived than first meets the eye. My teacher (and later colleague) Yü Ying-shih remembers, as a boy in Anhui in the 1930s, that scraps of paper bore the message *jing xi zi zhi* (respect and treasure the written word). Such practice has probably died out. But the deeper tradition has persisted, sometimes in altered form, often outside the conscious notice of participants, and sometimes even despite conscious efforts to stamp it out.

The best test of this claim might be Mao Zedong, who sought the eradication of tradition and commanded immense power to try to make it happen. In the late 1960s Mao called upon the Chinese people to *po si jiu*—"smash the four olds" (old habits, old customs, old culture, old ideas). Subsequently many visible and tangible things were indeed smashed, but much cultural undergirding remained—and thrived, even inside Mao's own projects. When, for example, Red Guards flocked to Tiananmen Square in the late 1960s, they chanted "*women yao jian Mao zhuxi!*" (we want to see Chairman Mao). The line had seven syllables, and fit a 1-2, 1-2, 1-2-3 rhythm that has deep roots in Chinese poetic and song tradition. Smash the four olds? I wonder if any Red Guard perceived the irony that the structure of the chant presented. I doubt that Mao himself realized it. To Mao and the Red Guards alike, the traditional rhythm "felt good," and that is what mattered.

The example is hardly an anomaly, either. Maoist language is full of seven-character and five-character lines whose rhythms are rooted in tradition. "*Linghun shenchu gan geming*" (make revolution in the depths of your souls), Mao commanded, his lilt wondrously contradicting his articulate message. His wife Jiang Qing fashioned "revolutionary model operas" with names like *Zhiqu weihushan* (Taking Tiger Mountain by Strategy) and *Hongse niangzijun* (Red Detachment of Women), which use the familiar five-character pattern and 1-2, 1-2-3 rhythm. Even Mao's mammoth economic experiments were described using classical rhythms: *nongye xue Dazhai* (in agriculture, learn from Dazhai, a model agricultural village) and *gongye xue Daqing* (in industry, learn from Daqing, a model oilfield).

Rhythm is primarily a matter of oral, not written, language, but the rhythms in the preceding examples are relevant to our point here because they are so closely associated with traditional written forms. Persistence of "the four olds" in other aspects of written culture—during the Mao years and afterwards as well—is not hard to spot. When Mao re-published his own classical-style poetry in 1973, he approved its appearance in a string-bound volume made to imitate imperial-period Chinese books. Why would Mao forbid all signs of tradition in the poetry of others and yet choose a traditional form to publish his own work? This odd fact seems to show that, *even in Mao's mind*, the assumption survived that when something really counts, when it is truly deep, it should be done in classical language and form. In April 1976, when citizens of Beijing gathered at Tiananmen to protest Mao-style political extremism, their favorite linguistic form, by a wide margin, was not banners or slogans but poetry—and not modern poetry, but classical poetry in classical rhythms. Some called these poems *xin shi*, or "heartfelt history": when you lay bare what you *really feel*, this is how you do it. Shortly after Mao died, when other top leaders were again allowed to publish, some of them also chose to reveal their moral character by publishing their poetry. The poetry of Chen Yi, a former mayor of Shanghai and Foreign Minister of the PRC, was published in two thick volumes in 1978.

In China calligraphy, like poetry, has maintained an implicit power despite the erosions of revolution and modernization. Even as he called for total revolution, Mao Zedong inadvertently underscored the traditional connection of written characters to core values such as morality and identity when he lent his own calligraphy to the masthead of *The People's Daily* (where it remains even today), to the Beijing Railway Station, and, as Richard Kraus has pointed out, to countless other places including the mosquito nets at the Fuzhou Normal School. Mao was so domineering that it might appear that this kind of political tinkling on fire hydrants was reserved to him alone. But not so. Many others have done it, especially after Mao passed away. In 1978, for example, literary commissar Zhou Yang donated his calligraphy for the front cover of the unofficial student magazine *Red Beans*, thereby instantly giving its young editors a certain political cover as they went to press. Around the same time, Marshal Ye Jianying donated his calligraphy for the front gate of Zhongshan University, an act that symbolized both his broad endorsement of the university and its general fealty to him.

The power of characters to symbolize propriety and identity in Chinese culture has many examples in the present day. In Princeton, New Jersey, as in countless other towns around the world that have Chinese communities, parents worry that their children will lose Chinese identity. They often send their children to "Chinese school" on weekends (usually over the complaints and foot-dragging of the children themselves), hoping that their offspring can learn how to remain Chinese. No one questions the basic method for pursuing this goal: it is language study. Learning Chinese bolsters Chineseness. Yet—and here is a key point—these weekend schools do not emphasize the speaking of Chinese. To learn Chinese, and to absorb Chineseness, is to *learn characters*. I once saw a Chinese father picking up his tiny daughter from the Chinese school at Princeton. Opening the door of his Nissan Infiniti, he asked her, "How many characters did you learn today?"

Chinese characters, and the identity they carry, can have political implications. Are you mainland Chinese or from Taiwan? Communist or anti-Communist? Ever since the PRC government announced its switch to simplified characters in the mid-1950s, the question of whether one learns and uses simplified or traditional characters has taken on a significance that runs much deeper than mere orthography. The question can turn red-hot when it comes to which version should be taught to the next generation. Parents at weekend Chinese schools can be moved to shouting over this question, and schools in many locations have split over it. Two schools, in parallel, teach two kinds of characters. China's rival governments have argued for decades even over the question of which kind of *romanization* to use for Chinese sounds. Again, please note: the argument is not over the sounds themselves. The initials, finals, and tones are not the point. All of the dialectical variations, which both sides recognize, are not the point. The point is *writing things down*. If you write them down my way, you are with me; if not, not. Something very important happens in Chinese culture when ink meets paper.

So Xu Bing has put his finger on something sensitive, something that has ancient roots as well as continuing power in the modern world, and something that Chinese culture cares mightily about, because it involves revered notions of propriety, morality, Chineseness, dignity, and identity. And Xu Bing "plays" with all this. Is he impudent? Is he, as his detractor in Pittsburgh felt, "not Chinese"? Or, as I would prefer to say, is he that unusual kind of person who can look deeply and critically at his or her own tradition, who can re-examine it in order to understand it, without necessarily either worshiping or rejecting it? Is he, in short, the best kind of patriot?

Originally published in Jerome Silbergeld and Dora Ching, eds.,
Persistence/Transformation: Text as Image in the Art of Xu Bing
(Princeton University Press, 2006) and reprinted by permission

The Crocodile Bird:
Xiangsheng in the Early 1950s

⊰≬⊱

(2007)

Xiangsheng are comedians' dialogues, a popular Chinese art that became one of my favorites. This essay was written for an academic conference on processes in the Communist takeover of China in the early 1950s.

INTRODUCTION

INDSIGHT CAN BE tricky. We often say that we "benefit" from it, and no doubt we do. But the benefits may be easier to see than the costs. To the serious historian, one cost of hindsight is that impressions of a past time are inevitably colored by what we know came later. We need to remind ourselves that people living at any past time did not know what would come later. If we really want to appreciate their position, to "get inside" their feelings and outlooks, we need to attempt a feat of imagination: we need to sweep from our memories certain obvious and important latter-day facts. Beyond that, we must try to weed from our minds all of the associations and implications, conscious and unconscious, that have grown up as a result of our knowing those facts. This is not easy. Indeed, I think we must acknowledge that perfection in the matter is impossible, and that the best we can do is to minimize the problem.

The matter is especially difficult when the later events were cataclysmic. What, for example, did the morning of August 6, 1945, feel like for a citizen of Hiroshima ten minutes before the Bomb? Ōe Kenzaburō, John Hersey, and others have tried to imagine that moment, have sought valiantly to re-capture its ordinariness, and have failed. How could one not fail? One can, yes, re-construct an image of morning toothbrushing: sink, mirror, brush, glass of water. We can "see" these things in our mind's eye. But we cannot, try as we might, get rid of another element in our re-constructed mental image of that Hiroshima morning—a horrible foreboding, that feverish sense that the imagined scene is about to explode. It seems to inhere in the very sink and mirror. Yet that foreboding was not there for people at the time. For us to sense it as inhering in the mirror is not historically accurate.

China's Anti-Rightist Campaign of 1957 and Cultural Revolution beginning in 1966 were not as abrupt as the Hiroshima bomb, and of course there are many other differences between these events and the bomb. But the challenge that the historian faces in trying to imagine a *status quo ante* is in principle similar. To understand Chinese writers and artists in the early 1950s, we need to try to imagine their outlook before anyone knew what was in store for them. Many of them (not all, to be sure) were enthusiastic about the Communist project. They saw and felt a new day for China; they wanted to help, and wanted to be part of figuring out the best ways to help; they had good intentions and assumed that others did, too; they were optimistic about the likely results; they had no idea they were about to get kicked in the teeth.

My case study looks at performers and writers of *xiangsheng* 相声, a popular art that translates literally as "face and voice," that is often mistranslated as "crosstalk,"[41] and that is perhaps best rendered as simply "comic dialogue." In a very rough sense *xiangsheng* resembles American vaudeville. Its stock-in-trade is humor, especially satire, but singing, imitation of sounds, and other kinds of oral antics are also involved. Its traditions in China are several hundred years old, but, because it is an oral art that has been passed from master to disciple largely without written records, its history before the Communist period is not very well known. In the 1930s and 1940s it was performed mostly in market places, where performers would pass a bowl among onlookers to collect donations; since the 1950s it has migrated to auditoriums and to radio and television broadcasts where the opportunity for live interaction with an audience has been sharply curtailed even as the size of the of the audience has grown immensely.

---

41. The mistake is to read 相 *xiang4* 'face, looks' as *xiang1* 'mutual'. This would be rather like translating "comedy" as *laixi* "come-plays" on grounds that the word "come" appears in the word "comedy."

Performances are normally done by two comedians, a *dougende* 逗哏的 or "funny man" and a *penggende* 捧哏的 or "straight man."[42] The essential relationship of these two is well captured in a sketch by the distinguished cartoonist Fang Cheng (figure 1).[43]

Here the *dougende*, on the left, is apparently presenting a crock of baloney to the *penggende*, whose role is to represent the common sense of the audience and whose combination of indulgence of the *dougende* and skepticism about his baloney is well captured by the straight lines of the eyes and mouth.

Traditionally, all *xiangsheng* routines were set, and performers memorized them by rote. Audiences did not look for creativity. As in listening to opera, they were attracted by the prospect of hearing the best possible renditions of well-known pieces. Only seasoned performers would dare to make ad lib revisions, and then only occasionally. In recent decades the emphasis has gradually shifted from rote performance to the creation of new works. Audiences now come to hear new satire more than to enjoy old favorites. I have written elsewhere[44] about the history and structure of *xiangsheng*, and will not address these questions in detail here.

The fate of *xiangsheng* artists in the 1950s—wanting to help the revolution and then being crushed—was perhaps even more poignant than it was for other writers and artists because of the sprightly nature of their

Figure 1

---

42. Pieces for a single performer—or for three, four, or five—also exist, but are not very common.

43. Reproduced from Xue Baokun 薛宝琨 *Zhongguo de xiangsheng* 中国的相声 (Beijing: Renmin chubanshe, 1985), p. 176.

44. "相声语言艺术杂谈" in 半洋随笔 (Taibei: Sanmin chubanshe, 1999) pp. 243–264; "The Genie and the Lamp: Revolutionary Xiangsheng" in Bonnie S. McDougall, ed., *Popular Chinese Literature and Performing Arts in the People's Republic of China 1949–79* (Berkeley and Los Angeles: University of California Press, 1984), pp. 83–111.

art. Writers of history, poetry, and fiction in China were accustomed to society's assumptions about the moral weight of their work. They inherited notions about "bearing responsibility for all under heaven" (以天下为己任) and "being first in the world to assume its worries" (先天下之忧而忧). More recently, Mao Zedong, borrowing a phrase from Stalin, had told them to be "engineers of the soul" (灵魂的工程师). But *xiangsheng* performers were newcomers to such ponderous phrases, and were generally as thrilled as they were stunned to see their whimsical art be given such a boost in status. They embraced the idea that their satiric vision could help to cleanse the new society by picking out its flaws. Why not?

In several ways their self-conception suggests the African plover known as the "crocodile bird" (*Pluvianus aegyptius*). This species feeds on parasites that infest the bodies of crocodiles. By legend, the bird sometimes even ventures inside a crocodile's open mouth to scavenge between the teeth. For their part, crocodiles (or so, at least, it is said) leave their jaws agape in respect for the symbiosis involved. How often have crocodile jaws come down on plovers? The question is beyond my scope here, but the perceptions and intentions of the plover at time "T minus one" provide a good metaphor for what I will try to do in the rest of this paper. I will try to set aside what we know happened in China after 1956 and to recreate the outlook of the *xiangsheng* world from 1950 to 1955.

THE LEGACY

Xiangsheng in the 1940s was performed in open areas of market towns or in urban entertainment quarters such as Tianqiao in Beijing. Tianjin and Shenyang were also major *xiangsheng* centers, but the art had not yet spread much in the rest of China. Performers wore long gowns (*dagua* 大褂) and used folding fans to fan themselves or—just as importantly—to slam shut and use as mini-clubs in mock attack on the other performer. They would begin by using a white powder to write on the ground a menu of their offerings. Then they used singing or a short comic piece (called a "cushion" *dianhua* 垫话) to try to attract a crowd, who, once captured, would be ethically obliged to address the question of how many coppers to put into their bowl after the performance. Disciples learned the *xiangsheng* art by living with their masters and serving them in daily life (presenting tea, washing feet, and so on) while memorizing and imitating the masters' performances in every detail. Master-disciple chains formed *pai* 派, which I will translate as "schools." Relations among the schools were competitive and sometimes bitterly adversarial.

The content of traditional *xiangsheng* pieces was not very "politically correct," if I may use this term anachronistically. Country bumpkins were a favorite object of satire: they stank of garlic, spoke in funny accents, and were hopelessly lost when they showed up in cities. Cripples, mutes, and idiots also made for good fun—as did the deranged logic of the *dougende* himself, whose nonsense, like Archie Bunker's, obeyed its own rules even if no one else's. (Caught in a blatant self-contradiction, a *dougende* can squirm out of it by saying, "You find that strange? ... Right! Even I find it strange!")[45]

Pornographic pieces were prominent. Such works were called *hun* 荤 "meat-eating" to distinguish them from the *su* 素 "vegetarian" pieces that steered clear of sex. Meat-eating pieces (or should we call them "non-vegetarian"?) were common, and women and children were not welcome at their performances. If a woman happened by during an open-air performance, according to one eye-witness,[46] the performers would stop, bow in her direction, fall silent, and wait for her to leave. But this ban on women had the interesting exception that non-vegetarian *xiangsheng* were sometimes played by female performers. (In most contexts, most of the time, only men performed.) But—probably because it sharpened the salacious edge—women often played one of the two roles in the meat-eating pieces.

By standards today, non-vegetarian *xiangsheng* are tame. The descriptions are indirect, subtle, and sometimes indeed very funny. A piece called "The Birdie Won't Chirp" (*Qiaor bujiao* 雀儿不叫)[47] relies on a double entendre in which "birdie" is code for "penis." The audience knows this, and so does the *dougende*, whose own penis is being discussed. But the *penggende*, played by a female, thinks that birdie only means birdie. She wants to know what the *dougende*'s birdie looks like.

---

45. Hou Baolin 侯宝林and Guo Qiru 郭启儒, "*Xiju zatan* 戏剧杂谈" ("Random talk on plays").

46. Wu Xiaoling 吴晓玲, Professor of Chinese in the Chinese Academy of Social Sciences.

47. Performed by Sun Yukui 孙玉奎and Hui Wanhua 回婉华and recorded in 1953 by Luo Changpei. See my essay "The Mum Sparrow: Non-Vegetarian Xiangsheng in Action" in *CHINOPERL Papers*, no. 16 (1992), pp. 1–27.

"Got feathers?" she asks.
"Nope, he's smooth and bare all the way to the tail, where there's a bunch of hair."
"You mean *feathers*, right?"
"No, hair."
"Hair? That's a new one! …What about the eyes? Pigeon eyes or phoenix eyes?"
"Mm…only one eye, up top."

And so on. In north China it was customary to take caged birds on walks (*liu niao* 遛鸟) and, arriving in a teahouse, to hook the cage up on a wall or rafter while having tea. The female *penggende* wants to know if the *dougende* does this service for his bird.

"Hang him up?," he answers. "No way!"
"Why not?"
"Get dizzy from the height."
"Nonsense. Birds don't get dizzy."
"No, *I* would get dizzy."
"What's it got to do with you?"
"It's *my bird*!"
"So? You hang him up, then sit down."
"Hang him up and I *can't* sit down."

This passage neatly illustrates a feature of *xiangsheng* humor that is common in non-pornographic pieces as well—the multiple cracking of a single joke to build an atmosphere. Having to hang one's penis from a teahouse rafter might seem funny enough the first time around, but in the art of *xiangsheng* essentially the same joke is cracked several times by unpacking further implications (it could make you dizzy, it would make it hard to sit back down, etc.). The re-cracking of the joke builds a cumulative effect—an atmosphere—that magnifies the enjoyment beyond what any of the punch lines taken singly could produce.

Published studies of *xiangsheng* as it was practiced before 1949 are generally dull.[48] Some offer speculative comments on cryptic references that

---

48. Wang Jue 王决, Wang Jingshou 汪景寿, and Teng Tianxiang 藤田香, *Zhongguo xiangsheng shi* 中国相声史 (Beijing: Yanshan chubanshe, 1995) is one of the best general

appear in texts as early as the ancient Confucian classic *Zuozhuan*. Others look at the oral tradition of the last two centuries or so, but are fairly dry accounts of schools and groupings. No one has tried in print to capture and describe the life of the art. It was also exactly that task—to capture the life of the art—that faced the *xiangsheng* world in 1950 when the new government turned to it for help. The "life" and "art" of *xiangsheng* had to be winnowed out from the politically incorrect dross in which they were embedded.

THE REFORM EFFORT

The distinguished writer Lao She (1899–1966), famous for *Camel Xiangzi* and other fiction, was a long-time aficionado of China's oral performing arts. He had already experimented in trying to "reform" them for modern uses during the war with Japan, when he himself wrote several *xiangsheng* pieces aimed at stimulating popular resistance to the Japanese invasion.[49] In 1946 he traveled to the United States on a program sponsored by the U.S. State Department, and was visiting the American west coast when the Communist victory arrived in 1949. He decided to return home to help.

A number of Beijing's *xiangsheng* performers—Hou Baolin, Hou Yichen, Yu Shide, and others—learned of Lao She's return to Beijing in December 1949 and went directly to "pay their respects" one evening. According to Yu Shide's memoirs,[50] Lao She was enthusiastic about the prospects for *xiangsheng*. "Let's reform it!" he is reported to have said, volunteering to get things started by personally re-writing some traditional pieces.

The next day a headline in *The People's Daily* read "*Xiangsheng* artists pay a visit to Lao She." This report in the Communist Party's central newspaper brought a major elevation in *xiangsheng* prestige. It also showed that the new government must have supported the idea of approaching Lao She, because such quick access to *The People's Daily* could not have happened

---

histories. Gu Yewen, *Xiangsheng jieshao* 相声介绍 (Shanghai: Wenyi chubanshe, 1952) was a precursor.

49. Wang, Wang and Teng, *Zhongguo xiangsheng shi*, p. 233.

50. 于世德, "Wo zhe ban beizi" 我这半辈子, from the internet, 马派相声网阅读775次, viewed April 25, 2003, 选自"黑龙江文史资料"第15辑, 黑龙江人民出版社 1984 年 12. See also Wang, Wang and Teng, *Zhongguo xiangsheng shi*, pp. 222ff.

otherwise. It seems likely, although I cannot prove it, that Mao Zedong himself was behind the initiative. Mao was a *xiangsheng* fan, and during the early 1950s regularly invited Hou Baolin to his residence in Zhongnan-hai for private performances. Hou recalls some of the details of these visits in a 1982 essay[51] in which he also notes that Mao was a moving force in the establishment of "The Small Group for the Improvement of Xiangsheng" (*xiangsheng gaijin xiaozu* 相声改进小组). This committee, which I will refer to as the "Small Group," played a big role.

It was formally founded on January 19, 1950 at Beijing's Qianmen, just north of the Tianqiao entertainment area. The group's members, in addition to Lao She and a few leading performers, included distinguished scholars such as the linguists Luo Changpei and Lü Shuxiang, and literary scholar Wu Xiaoling. Lao She and Wu Xiaoling, in different ways, played especially active roles. Yu Shide recalls that, for *xiangsheng* performers, the willingness of famous scholars and writers to descend to the level of the "xialibaren" (下里巴人) was deeply gratifying and motivating.[52] Until then, some performers apparently had feared that the revolution might choose to weed *xiangsheng* out, and were actually considering career shifts. But now the government had decided to honor them with the title "cultural workers" (文艺工作者).

Lao She notes that one drawback of lending his prestige to *xiangsheng* was that performers, apparently in awe of his reputation, were reluctant to criticize the *xiangsheng* pieces he wrote. On the other hand, an advantage of his prestige, as both he and others noted, was that he could draw performers together.[53] Factions and jealousies tended to soften under the warm, unifying gaze of great writers and scholars backed by the new government.

The Small Group formally existed for two years, after which two larger groups, the Beijing Work Group for Popular Performing Arts (北京市曲艺工作团) and a Great Assembly of Xiangsheng (相声大会)[54] inherited its mission. The work of reform began in 1950 with the drawing up of an

51. *Quyi* 曲艺, July 1982, pp. 11–12.
52. Yu Shide, *op cit.*
53. "Xiang xiangsheng xiaozu daoxi" 向相声小组道喜, "Jieshao Beijing xiangsheng gaijin xiaozu" 介绍北京相声改进小组", and "Tan xiangsheng de gaizao" 谈相声的改造" in Lao She, *Lao She quyi wenxuan* 老舍曲艺文选 (Beijing: Zhongguo quyi chubanshe, 1982), pp. 186, 188, 190–1. Wang, Wang and Teng, *Zhongguo xiangsheng shi*, p. 231.
54. Wang, Wang and Teng, *Zhongguo xiangsheng shi*, p. 228; Yu Shide, *op cit.*

ambitious list of tasks: *xiangsheng's* importance would be consecrated through a study of *xiangsheng* history; *xiangsheng* would be transformed from a regional art to a national one; this expansion of scope would benefit China not only by spreading new ideas of the revolution but by helping speakers of dialects to master northern Mandarin, which was now called *putonghua*. (In an interesting exception to the latter goal, the Small Group also favored creation of *xiangsheng* in non-Mandarin dialects and even in national minority languages such as Tibetan and Mongolian. This shows that the goal of spreading social and political ideas took precedence over the goal of promoting Mandarin.) The Small Group even took on the task of setting up "literacy classes." This may seem an odd activity for practitioners of what was, until then, a purely oral art, but it shows again how deeply the Small Group had embraced the broader social goals of the new government.

All of these tasks were secondary to the Small Group's main work, which was to produce *xiangsheng* whose content would be appropriate to the new society. This job in turn was divided into two: the overhaul of existing pieces and the creation of new ones. Lao She began the overhaul work by re-writing pieces called "Phony Dr. Jia" (*jia boshi* 贾博士) and "Vitamins" (*weishengsu* 维生素). These works relied heavily on "word-fountains" (*guankou* 贯口), a technique of sustained, rapid-fire speech that is reminiscent of auctioneers in the American Midwest a generation or two ago. Word fountains were relatively easy to "revise," because it did not much matter which syllables spewed forth, so long as there were a lot of them. In "Phony Dr. Jia," for example, Lao She strings together the names of sixty-six Party-approved literary works in one long sentence—and there it was: a piece that was politically correct, had "educational value," and was all set for delivery by the nimble tongue of a performer.

Lao She also began writing new pieces, but only reluctantly, because he felt that *xiangsheng* performers were better positioned than he to do this. Writers could have ideas, Lao She later wrote, but only performers produced the best work.[55] This was because they had closer contact with audiences. Traditionally, a *xiangsheng* piece evolved as it was passed around among performers, each of whom put it to the test in front of live

---

55. "Jieshao Beijing xiangsheng gaijin xiaozu" in *Lao She quyi wenxuan*, p. 188.

audiences.[56] By a sort of Darwinian logic, only works that adapted and improved could endure.

Understanding this principle, the Small Group set up a honing process for its creation of *xiangsheng*. After a writer produced a text, the Small Group reviewed it and suggested revisions. Then the piece was put before an audience while experienced performers watched the performance from backstage and took notes. The audience itself was invited to contribute opinions. There is anecdotal evidence that political correctness was not just something that the Party was pushing in the early 1950s; performers also sometimes felt pressure "from below" to make their content more socially healthful. Yu Shide tells of audience jeers when performers sometimes reverted to smut.[57] In any case, a piece was published only after revisions that followed live-audience testing. In its first ten months, the Small Group released thirty-two new or substantially revised pieces.[58]

These works were very uneven in length, artistic quality, and sophistication of message. But an enthusiastic idealism runs through all of them, as it does the clappertales, drum songs, and other "popular performing arts" *quyi* (曲艺) produced at the time. "Let's help make China a better place!" seems to leap forth from page after page of the early 1950s issues of the government's new *quyi* magazine "Telling and Singing" (说说唱唱).

Figure 2

When the official campaign to "Resist America and Aid Korea" got underway in fall 1950, the Small Group moved quickly to put *xiangsheng* to the task. In March, 1951, a delegation of *xiangsheng* performers traveled to Korea to cheer Chinese troops. I suspect, but cannot prove, that the trip was in part a response to the U.S. having sent comedian Bob Hope, a few months earlier, to cheer American troops in Korea. Figure 2 shows Bob Hope with U.S. troops in 1950;[59] figure 3 shows Chinese *xiangsheng*

56. "Tan xiangsheng de gaizao" in *Lao She quyi wenxuan*, pp. 190–191.
57. Wang, Wang and Teng, *Zhongguo xiangsheng shi*, p. 221, 223.
58. Wang, Wang and Teng, *Zhongguo xiangsheng shi*, p. 226.
59. CNN.com, July 29, 2003.

Figure 3

performer Chang Baokun with Chinese troops in 1951.[60] Chang, whose stage name was "Little Mushroom" (小蘑菇) and who was a favorite in the Tianjin school of *xiangsheng*, was killed during the visit. This horrible fact only fueled further dedication in the *xiangsheng* world to "resist America." In June, 1951, *xiangsheng* performers traveled the length and breadth of China spreading the message. This was the first issue that brought *xiangsheng* truly nationwide. Pieces were translated into dialects and minority languages, and performances were broadcast over the radio.

Three signature pieces of the campaign were produced very quickly in late summer of 1950 under the aegis of the Small Group. They were called "Paper Tiger" (纸老虎), about the cowardice of U.S. soldiers; "This is America" (如此美国), about the gap between rich and poor in the U.S.; and "Uphold Peace" (拥护和平), about the international struggle against U.S. hegemonism.[61] As experiments in the adaptation of *xiangsheng* they are almost disastrously bad, and certainly would have gone nowhere had it not been for the cause that animated them. They insert utterly humorless political jargon, as when "The Soviet Union long ago applied its atomic energy to industrial uses!" comes from the mouth of the ostensibly "funny" man.[62] A "word fountain" gives numbers for all the standing armies of the world.[63] As if to leaven the preachiness, some not-very-subtle smut is dropped in from time to time: U.S. soldiers in Korea write to their girlfriends asking them to send toilet paper, a high priority because "as soon as they hear the People's Army coming, they shit in their pants."[64] But the most interesting flaw in these pieces was that many of the images of

60. *Chang Baokun xiangsheng xuan* 常宝琨相声选 (Tianjin: Baihua wenyi chubanshe, 1981), before page 1.

61. Collected in Xi Xiangyuan 席香远and Sun Yukui孙玉奎, ed. *Zhi laohu* (Beijing: Sanlian shudian, 1950).

62. op cit, p. 7.

63. op cit, pp. 24–25.

64. op cit., p. 4.

America were ones that could cut both ways with Chinese listeners. How high are American skyscrapers? Somebody was in an elevator for three hours and still didn't reach the top! (Wow! Impressive!) But, we then learn, that was only because the elevator workers were on strike.[65] The joke works, but the impression lingers that U.S. skyscrapers are unimaginably tall. The same ambiguity attends the debunking-and-yet-underscoring of U.S. military power, technological capability, and opulent daily life. The two-edged nature of these messages does not seem to have been intentional. It seems, rather, that the writing was done in haste, before the creators had time to think very much about possible complexities in audience response.

The best of the "resist America" pieces were the work of Lao She, whose experience in the U.S. gave him first-hand impressions to work from. Lao She commented that *xiangsheng* was an especially good medium for satirizing America because of its "unreliable" (*bulaoshi* 不老实) nature: more than other art forms, *xiangsheng* could get away with turning things upside-down.[66] It is not clear whether this meant that *xiangsheng* a) can invert the Chinese people's positive impressions of America and still be believed, or b) display the U.S. government's tendency to turn things upside down. He may have meant both. Let us consider an example of each.

In a piece called "Matching Couplets" (*dui duilian* 对对联),[67] the *dougende*, who is a virtuoso of verbal parallelism and a feisty critic of capitalism, travels to America. As soon as he arrives he pastes up a couplet (A = *dougende*; B = *penggende*):

> A: And on it I wrote: "I speculate, I get rich, I live it up, my life is good; pleasure's all I seek."
> B: How come everything's "I…"?
> A: Because the matching line is all "You…"
> B: How does it go?
> A: "You're honest, you're poor, you're hungry, your life is shot; death serves you right!"
> B: (*pretending to misinterpret the "you" as referring to himself*)
> Death would serve *you* right!

65. op cit, p. 12.
66. "Jieshao Beijing xiangsheng gaijin xiaozu" in *Lao She quyi wenxuan,* p. 189.
67. Partially reprinted in Gu Yewen, *Xiangsheng jieshao,* pp. 88–89.

> A: I don't mean you! This is about the gap between rich and poor in America!

The funny man then goes in succession to a dance hall, a hospital, a draft board, the Supreme Court, the FBI, Hollywood, and a few other places. At each he writes his satiric parallelisms while cleverly avoiding capture by the police. The piece is much more successful than "Paper Tiger" and "This is America" in "turning around" positive impressions of the U.S.

A piece that shows the other use of *xiangsheng*'s "unreliability"—to reflect upside-down U.S. government rhetoric—is a "cushion" piece called "Interviewing Dulles" (*fangwen Dulesi* 访问杜勒斯):[68]

> A: Mr. Secretary of State, why do you think it is that the Soviet Union keeps reducing the size of its military?
> B: Because the more it cuts the bigger it gets—and the scarier!
> A: Is the U.S. also planning to reduce its military, Mr. Secretary?
> B: No, we are expanding the military!
> A: Why, may I ask?
> B: The more we grow the smaller we get—and the more peaceful!
> A: Pardon me, but I'm a bit confused: why do Soviet troop numbers go up the more they are cut and U.S. troop numbers go down the more they grow?
> B: Numbers sometimes go down as they grow and go up as they shrink.

The contrast here between smoothness of delivery and utter nonsense in content is a standard technique in traditional *xiangsheng*. The rhythm, parallelism, and confidence in Mr. Dulles' lines implicitly claim a "legitimacy" that is simultaneously undermined by his ridiculous logic—and the contrast is funny.

Despite Lao She's expectation that *xiangsheng* performers would be best positioned to create new pieces, the record shows that professional writers did better after all. The weakest of the new work, such as the "Resist Amer-

---

68. Zhongguo quyi yanjiuhui 中国曲艺研究会, *Xiangsheng dianhua xuanji*相声垫话选集 (Beijing: Zuojia chubanshe, 1958), pp. 1–3.

ica" pieces noted above, were the creations of performers. A few pieces by the performer Hou Baolin were strong on *xiangsheng* technique, but not very good at working in reformist content. A piece called "A Miracle Worker Brings Disaster" (*miaoshou chenghuan* 妙手成患), for example, tells of a surgeon who works in a hospital that has a department of *xiangsheng* because laughter helps in healing, but who keeps sewing up the bodies of his patients with operating tools left inside.[69]

The combination of art and thought was made most successfully by three writers who adored *xiangsheng* but did not perform. Lao She was one. He produced more than thirty new or reworked pieces in the early 1950s,[70] and in matters of rhythm, word choice, and authenticity of dialogue, no sensibility was finer than his. The only blemish in his work was a tendency to over-use political phrases such as "We all love the Soviet Union!" or "The greatness of Stalin blankets the landscape."[71] (The awkwardnesses are more signs of Lao She's sincere wish to help the Communist Party than flaws in his talent.) He Chi 何迟, another highly successful writer of *xiangsheng*, had a background very different from Lao She's. Lao She knew English, had gone to a Christian Sunday school as a boy, and had lived in both England and America. He needed to prove his loyalty to the Communists. He Chi, a Party member and veteran of guerilla struggles in both the Jin-cha-ji and Shaan-gan-ning border areas, had no such burden. He had been on the side of the revolution from the start. The new society was "his" as much as anyone else's, and hence was his to criticize as he saw fit.[72] Gifted with a marvelously dry sense of humor, He produced works like "Buying Monkeys" (买猴) and "Hooked on Meetings" (开会迷) that were among the most successful and controversial social and political satire of the early 1950s. A third notable writer was Wang Guoxiang (王国祥), a worker, apparently, and author of "The Flying Oilcan" (飞油壶) and a

69. Zhongguo quyi yanjiuhui 中国曲艺研究会, ed. *Xiangsheng chuangzuo xuan ji* 相声创作选集 (Beijing: Zuojia chubanshe, 1957), pp. 185–192.

70. According to Wang, Wang and Teng, *Zhongguo xiangsheng shi*, p. 233.

71. These examples are from "In Praise of the October Revolution" (*Shiyue geming songzan* 十月革命颂赞), Shuoshuo changchang no. 23 (November, 1951) and "The History of Sino-Soviet Relations" (*Zhong-Su guanxishi shuoben* 中苏关系史说本) no. 3 (1950)

72. These generalizations are clear from He's autobiography *He Chi zizhuan* (何迟自传) (Beijing: Zhongguo minjian wenyi chubanshe, 1989). See also Xue Baokun, *Zhongguo de xiangsheng*, pp. 135 ff.

few other *xiangsheng* pieces that display true artistic genius. Wu Xiaoling, the literary scholar and member of the Small Group, wrote an article in 1955 singling out Wang's work for possessing exactly the right combination of new thinking and authentic *xiangsheng* art.[73] We will return to He Chi's and Wang Guoxiang's work after a closer look at the problems that they and others confronted.

How Can Satire Praise?

Communist Party guidelines on *xiangsheng* reform appeared in the early 1950s from the new government's Ministry of Culture. Although perhaps good as moral support for writers and performers, they were not very helpful in practice. They said that new works should avoid all that is "brutal, terrorizing, obscene, enslaving, abominable...and unpatriotic" and substitute "healthy, progressive, and beautiful elements."[74] Writers had to imagine for themselves what actually to do.

The easiest changes had to do with oral mimicry, word fountains, and other verbal acrobatics in which the meanings of words did not much matter. One set of words could substitute for another. But these superficial switches did not get to the heart of *xiangsheng*. They were only peripheral aspects of the art. And even if successful, they did little to promote progressive thought. A string of syllables listing the names of fraternal countries in the socialist camp sounded funny, and was amusing, but did not bring listeners much closer to the principles of socialism.

For that goal, meaning mattered. *Xiangsheng* would somehow have to communicate new thinking. Party guidelines said that "praise" (*gesong* 歌颂) of the new society was the key. Writers and performers of *xiangsheng* were generally happy to embrace this guideline, but it led to an intractable dilemma that dominated the *xiangsheng* world for several years.

The problem was that the essence of *xiangsheng* is satire. The very conception of the *dougende* on stage is grounded in a premise of self-mockery. So how could a fundamentally satiric art begin to "praise" things? And

73. "Luetan xiangsheng de chuangzuo wenti" 略谈相声的创作问题 *Beijing wenyi* 北京文艺 no. 8, 1955, pp. 20–21.
74. Quoted in Marja Kaikkonen, *Laughable Propaganda: Modern Xiangsheng as Didactic Entertainment* (Stockholm East Asian Monographs, no. 1, 1990), p. 122.

how could "praise" cause an audience to laugh? It was a technical challenge *xiangsheng* performers had never faced before.

Certain early attempts to incorporate "praise" foundered when satire, like an unwanted guest, tended to seep back in. Lao She tells of a Korean-War piece (author unnamed) in which a man has donned a uniform, a helmet, and a gas mask, and holds a machine gun, a rifle, and a bayonet.[75] Someone asks him:

"What are you doing?"
"Helping the army to move!"
"Going to the front?"
"No."
"Why not?"
"I was so afraid that I forgot to wear my pants."

Ostensibly in "praise" of the Korean war effort, this joke (aside from its intrinsic weakness, which is a different question) feeds on satire of exactly what it is supposed to be praising. Another piece, Xi Xiangyuan's "Notes on Travel to the West" (*xixing manji* 西行漫记), tells about building a highway from Xikang to Tibet.[76] It is supposed to praise the building of ties between Han and Tibetan compatriots. But the finer texture of the joke-cracking belittles Tibetans. Their language sounds odd, and they wash cars for the Han Chinese while ignorantly referring to the cars as yaks.[77] Yet another piece, designed to discourage grain thievery, in the end generates considerable sympathy for the thief, whose clever methods the audience cannot but admire.[78] A piece ostensibly promoting equality of the sexes, on close reading, in fact depends on satire of pushy women:[79]

75. "Tan xiangsheng de gaizao" in *Lao She quyi wenxuan*, pp. 191–2.
76. Xi Xiangyuan 席香远, Liu Baorui 刘宝瑞, and Guo Quanbao 郭全宝, "Xixing manji" 西行漫记in Zhongguo quyi yanjiuhui 中国曲艺研究会, ed. *Xiangsheng chuangzuo xuan ji* 相声创作选集 (Beijing: Zuojia chubanshe, 1957), pp. 12–22.
77. Ibid, pp. 18–19.
78. Chen Yongquan陈涌泉 and Zhang Shanzeng 张善曾, "Daoyun liangshi de ren" 盗运粮食的人 *Beijing wenyi* no. 8, 1955, pp. 11–14.
79. Xia Yutian 下雨田, "Nü duizhang" 女队长 in (no author) *Xin Xiangsheng ji* 新乡省集 (Shanghai: Shanghai wenhua chubanshe, 1965), pp. 28–29.

A: In the old society women were oppressed, and in the new
society women control men.

B: Right... (*then realizing*) Hunh? No, men and women are
equal in the new society.

A: Equal? I don't think so.

B: What's your evidence?

A: Just come visit our production team: female team leader,
female deputy team leader, female work-point officer, female
director of the militia...

B: All *women*?

A: Only the accountant is a man, but he's a traitor to the cause.

B: What do you mean?

A: He's still married to a female!

A is meant to be ridiculous here. His whole point of view is "incorrect."
Yet it was all too possible for an audience to laugh with him, not at him.
Satire could support exactly the things it was designed to discredit. To ask
performers to deliver lines in such a way that only "correct" laughter could
result would be to ask too much.

If people might laugh at something that is supposed to be praised, so
might they be indirectly impressed by something that was supposed to be
discredited. For example, in response to Lao She's piece "Matching Couplets," one Party theorist wrote:

> The audience of *xiangsheng* is, for the most part, the broad
> masses, and one must not assume that all of them are clear about
> the basic nature of American imperialism and its internal con-
> flicts. There are bound to be misunderstandings if one uses the
> satiric mode exclusively. The ironic use of a string of phrases like
> "democracy," "freedom of speech," "due process," "scientific civ-
> ilization," "full supply of soldiers," and "a million crack troops"
> is bound to create a certain amount of confusion in the realm of
> thought.[80]

---

80. "Gei 'Dui duilian' ti de yijian" 给 '对对联' 提的意见in Gu Yewen, *Xiangsheng jieshao*,
p. 109.

In short, the problem of "how can *xiangsheng* praise?" resolved into "how can such a slippery art be controlled?"

Between 1951 and 1955 the *xiangsheng* world came up with a series of answers. Some performers reserved real satire for the "cushion" pieces that preceded formal dialogues. These cushions did not have to be pre-approved and thus were more flexible. In one of his cushions, a storyteller named Zhang Yiming warned listeners against buying state bonds. Zhang joked that the character *guo* 国 in *guozhai*, "state debt," looks like a crying face—and said that's just what you will look like if you buy state bonds. Probably not for this reason alone, Zhang was eventually sent to a labor camp.[81]

Another technique, called "flowers inserted from the outside" (*waichahua*, 外插花), was useful in several ways. It allowed one to insert jokes into what was essentially a political monologue, or, the other way around, to stick political points into something whose main theme lay elsewhere. An early example was a revision of the traditional piece called "Major Job Shift" (大改行). A charming piece that had broad popularity before 1949, it tells about opera singers in the Qing period who are obliged to stop performing for three years out of respect for the death of an emperor; in search of work, they convert their opera voices to hawkers' calls and ply the streets. In the early 1950s, someone thought of putting it on the radio with the occasional insertion of lines like "Just look at how disgusting feudal society was!"[82] The insertions were mechanical, and the political messages poorly integrated.

Better integration was achieved in a work called "New Lantern Riddles" (新灯谜) by Zhao Peiru and Chang Baokun. Here "new society" content is inserted into traditional word games. The performers play a game in which A tries to get B to say the word "good" (*hao*) and B tries to avoid it:

---

81. I am indebted to James Z. Gao for this example. For more on Zhang Yiming, see Gao's book *The Communist Takeover Of Hangzhou: The Transformation of City and Cadre, 1949–1954* (Honolulu: The University of Hawaii Press, 2004), pp. 232–233 and p. 305, note 58.

82. Chen Sitong 陈驷彤, "Dui xiangsheng gaige gongzuo de yijian" 对相声改革工作的意见 in Shanghai wenhua chubanshe 上海文化出版社, ed., *Xiangsheng luncong* 相声论丛 (Shanghai, 1957), p. 102.

A: How are you?
B: Not bad.
A: And your family?
B: Depends on whom you ask.

B remains clever. Then the theme shifts to politics:

A: To join the army these days is…
B: Glorious.
A: Discipline in the PLA is…
B: Strict.
A: When an army has strict discipline the people support it, and that's why this war is going so…
B: Courageously.
A: The ordinary people think the PLA is…
B: Adorable.[83]

The drawback of Zhao's and Chang's approach was that, although lively and natural-sounding, it provided only a superficial analysis of the new society. There remained a need to go deeper.

But early attempts to go deeper often resulted in preachiness. "Notes on Travel to the West," about a highway to Tibet, starts off briskly enough but then drops the following:[84]

A: Traffic on the Xikang-Lhasa Highway commenced on December 25, 1954, and this link has had a major effect on economic construction and solidarity among the nationalities in our motherland. It has also brought great development to the politics, economy, and culture of the Tibetan people. You and I are literary and art workers—if we do not come here in person, and experience life for ourselves, how can we bring this great engineering accomplishment to the broad masses of the entire country?
B: Right. What are some of the other good points?

83. Zhongguo quyi yanjiuhui zhubian, *Xiangsheng chuangzuo xuanji*, pp. 4–5.
84. Zhongguo quyi yanjiuhui zhubian, *Xiangsheng chuangzuo xuanji*, pp. 13–14.

A: There are too many! The highway was constructed on the Tibetan plateau, known as the rooftop of the world, and is a total of 2,255 kilometers in length. In the few years since 1950, our PLA road-construction troops, together with civilian workers, have brought into play the high level of their spirit of patriotism and of revolutionary heroism to engage with Mother Nature in stubborn stalwart struggle, day and night, and in bitter cold of 30 degrees below zero. They have vanquished glaciers and quicksand, snowy mountains and grassy plains, and primeval forests. They have built more than 230 bridges across towering cliffs and raging torrents, have drilled more than 2,860 culverts through rock, and have moved more than 29 million cubic meters of earth and stone. Taking a walk along the Xikang-Lhasa Highway is excellent political study!

Such detail could suffocate *xiangsheng*.

When the new government sought to suppress *Yiguandao* (一贯道)—a folk religion that it could not control, and hence feared—Hou Baolin and Sun Yukui in 1950 created a piece that told how *Yiguandao* "superstition" leads to many ills, including a daughter's carving off bits of her own flesh to feed to her ill mother, etc.[85] This was hardly *xiangsheng* material. In short, there were problems with "flowers inserted from without." If the flowers were too light, they seemed merely distracting; if too heavy, they were counterproductive.

Another approach to the dilemma of how to combine satire and reform held more hope. This was to release the spirit of satire in a friendly way toward people who are basically good but have flaws. *Xiangsheng* can help such people to overcome their flaws, and this helps the revolution. Good people who put too much stock in old-style thinking are satirized in Hou Baolin's 1949 piece "Marriage and Superstition" (婚姻与迷信).[86] A 1954 piece called "Traveling at Night" (夜行记) tells of a man who jaywalks, won't line up for buses, disobeys traffic rules on his bicycle, and so on.[87] He is flam-

---

85. (No editor), *Hou Baolin xiangsheng xuan* 侯宝林相声选 (Beijing: Renmin wenxue chubanshe, 1980), pp. 12–22.

86. *Hou Baolin xiangsheng xuan* 侯宝林相声选, pp. 1–11.

87. Lang Defeng 郎德沣, Chen Wenhai 陈文海, Jiang Qingkui 蒋清奎, Jia Hongbin 贾鸿彬,

boyantly miscreant, but not evil. From *xiangsheng* he receives "benevolent admonition" (*shanyi de guiquan* 善意的规劝), whose aim, in the words of *xiangsheng* historian Xue Baokun, was to "wash the face, not chop off the head."[88] Wu Xiaoling spelled out the rationale more explicitly:

> Satirical works are especially well suited to highlighting the struggle between progressive and backward forces in vivid and concrete ways. By contrast with the strong, indomitable new forces, the laughable, disgusting, and ultimately futile aspects of the decaying patterns stand out all the more clearly. That is why satire not only can hasten the demise of the backward, rotting things, but also can encourage the growth of new, progressive ones.[89]

But in practice, the strategy had mixed results. "Superstition and Marriage" is dull, and "Traveling at Night" descends into slapstick. Only a few pieces achieved true success with the new formula. Three such pieces were "Buying Monkeys" and "Hooked on Meetings" by He Chi, and "The Flying Oil-can" by Wang Guoxiang.

"Buying Monkeys" criticizes a department store copy clerk whose carelessness leads to big problems. His name is Ma Daha (马大哈), where Ma is from *mamahuhu*, Da means *dadalielie*, and ha is from *xixihaha*—to translate freely, "what the heck?," "this'll do," and "who cares?"[90] Ma Daha is supposed to put labels on canisters of sesame oil and tung oil, and does—except that, distracted by a phone call from his girlfriend, he reverses the labels. A few days later the bakeries in town are outraged that their cakes stink of tung oil, and the furniture shops complain that sesame oil has ruined their tables. But this is just a warm-up. Ma Daha's biggest gaffe is

Hou Bozhao 侯伯照, and Li Peiji 李培基, "Yexingji" 夜行记 in Zhongguo quyi yanjiuhui, *Xiangsheng chuangzuo xuan ji*, pp. 217–226.

88. Xue Baokun 薛宝琨 *Zhongguo de xiangsheng* 中国的相声, p. 139.

89. Wu Xiaoling 吴晓玲, "Luetan xiangsheng de chuangzuo wenti" 略谈相声的创作问题, in Shanghai wenhua chubanshe 上海文化出版社, ed., *Xiangsheng luncong* 相声论丛, p. 105.

90. He Chi tells us in his autobiography that soldiers were using these three phrases at the time to describe irresponsible work in their midst. *He Chi zizhuan*, p. 250. The text of "Buying Monkeys" appears in Zhongguo quyi yanjiuhui, *Xiangsheng chuangzuo xuanji*, pp. 88–105.

his copying of an instruction that reads, "Comrade So-and-so: Proceed immediately to the northeast quarter to purchase fifty crates of Monkey Brand soap." Again distracted, Ma Daha scrawls, "Proceed immediately to the Northeast to purchase fifty monkeys." The recipient of this order, Comrade So-and-So, also displays indifference to common sense by accepting it without question and immediately setting out for Manchuria (i.e., the Northeast) in quest of monkeys. The funniest passages occur when he arrives in Shenyang trying to explain himself:[91]

> "I am from the Tianjin Department Store. The leadership has
> sent me here to pick up some commodities. I hope you can
> help."
> "No problem. What's on your list?"
> "My company wants to buy fifty monkeys."
> "Buy what?"
> "Buy monkeys."
> "*What?*"
> "Monkeys."
> "What monkeys?"
> "You know, the kind that's covered with hair from top to
> bottom."

The Shenyang supply official, startled but obliging, refers Comrade So-and-So to Changbai Village in the foothills of the mountains, a place where monkeys are more accessible. The mayor of Changbai, equally bemused by the odd purchase order, suggests that they convene a general meeting of the local Hunters' Cooperative that evening so that Comrade So-and-So can explain his errand directly. Now finding himself up on stage and obliged to give a formal speech—but still with no idea of why he is buying monkeys—Comrade So-and-So does his best:

> "Countrymen!"
> (*Applause*)
> "Comrades!"
> (*Applause*)

91. Zhongguo quyi yanjiuhui, *Xiangsheng chuangzuo xuanji*, pp. 97–99.

(*Coughs*) "I..." (*coughs*) "I..." (*coughs*) [in an aside to the *peng-gende*] "What am I going to *say*?"

"Comrades! The leadership has sent me to your village. My mission is to buy monkeys. And what use are monkeys? Monkeys..." [to the *penggende*] "What do you think I should say?"

After further floundering So-and-So comes up with "monkeys make definite contributions to our country," which, upon further pressing, turns out to mean that monkeys can guard a house, can act in plays, and can provide hair for making thread. What's more, says So-and-So, humans evolved from them.

Author He Chi tells us that the piece was based on an actual reported incident in Tianjin in which "buy Monkey Brand soap" was inadvertently shortened to "buy monkey."[92] That single spark, falling upon the tinder of He's mischievous imagination, apparently led him to write out the whole piece during one night in 1953. It was adopted for performance by the famous master Ma Sanli and his partner Zhang Qingsen, and in November 1954 was published in the *Shenyang Daily*. Its popularity in society reached the point where the term "Ma Daha" came to be used in ordinary language. People said, "I pulled another Ma Daha" or "that guy's a complete Ma Daha."[93]

The success of the piece clearly sprang from its resonance with daily life. The idea of buying monkeys in Manchuria was utterly far-fetched, but the general problems reflected in the piece—indifference to sloppy work, unquestioning obedience of orders from above, and the stuffiness of official language—were all too familiar. The generality of the problems was also implied by the fact that Ma Daha was not the only character in the piece to exhibit the problems. Comrade So-and-So, the Shenyang officials, Ma Daha's girlfriend, and others are all imperfect. At the same time, none is an "enemy of the people." Ma Daha is irresponsible, but hardly ill-willed. He is human, funny, and in an odd sense even lovable.

92. *He Chi zizhuan*, p. 250–251; also He Chi, "*Cong 'mai hour' tan qi: dui biaoxian ren-min neibu maodun de xiangsheng chuangzuo de yixie kanfa*" 丛"买猴儿"谈起:对表现人民内部矛盾的相声创作的一些看法*Quyi* 曲艺1980, no. 3, p. 25.
93. Wang, Wang, and Teng, op.cit., pp. 238–239.

He Chi's "Hooked on Meetings" satirizes the long-winded, self-important official who thinks that the sound of his or her voice, droning interminably at meetings, is in itself worthwhile. On "the question of washbasins," the manager of an opera troupe says:[94]

> Comrades! The washbasins of our opera troupe are cracking. If they crack, of course, we should solder them. But now the cracking is so bad that soldering probably will not work. Accordingly we have decided to purchase two new washbasins. Now of course, these two washbasins will also, sooner or later, become cracked. But we will need to pass through a fairly extended period of time before the onset of cracking, and so, accordingly, we have determined to proceed with the purchase of the two basins. However, because our opera troupe includes male comrades and also includes female comrades, and because, under normal circumstances, male comrades favor the use of plain washbasins while female comrades, for a variety of reasons, tend to prefer washbasins bearing flowery designs, while, at the same time, a minority among the male comrades are willing to use flowery washbasins and a minority among female comrades are ready to use plain washbasins, we need, therefore, to unify our thinking. If we do not, and should we proceed with the purchase of plain washbasins only, then our female comrades will object; if, on the other hand, we buy only the patterned basins, then male comrades may be unhappy. Accordingly, we must look for unanimity to emerge from contradiction, and for unity to replace confrontation. In order to guarantee unanimity of action, we should first achieve unity in thought; otherwise the washbasin issue could lead to splits in our opera troupe.

The pomposity heads toward even higher levels of theory, but, as with Ma Daha, the satire is still fundamentally friendly. This official is self-absorbed and even a bit stupid (he wonders, for example, if workers should line up to go home or wander out individually); but he is not a villain. His concern

---

94. Zhongguo quyi yanjiuhui, *Xiangsheng chuangzuo xuan ji* pp. 202–203.

for the male and female comrades and their differing preferences in washbasins might be silly—but it is egalitarian, after all, and his faith that holding a meeting to talk things out does suggest a certain respect for group
opinion even if he dominates. He wears a constant smile, which can seem
phony, but at least it's a smile, not a scowl. He is always "positive" (*jiji* 积极).
He doesn't smoke or drink.

"The Flying Oilcan" by Wang Guoxiang is not as famous as He Chi's
works, but is even more successful at combining natural satire with support of reformist thinking. It is about a slothful and negligent worker who
shows up late, holds up the work of others, and neglects to oil a machine,
thereby causing a serious accident and sending himself—"gloriously,"
in his own view—to the hospital. The language of the piece is especially
lively, natural, and clean. It is no-nonsense worker idiom that shows little influence from political language, Westernized grammar, or the Sino-
Japanese compounds of modern Chinese. When the injured hero counts
himself "glorious," the *dougende* snaps at him, "别不嫌寒碜," roughly "Try
not to find yourself undisgraceful!"—thus packing two or three levels of
sarcasm into five pungent syllables. In *xiangsheng* pieces by Lao She and He
Chi, there is always at least some sense of the literatus writing "down" to a
worker audience; such a seam is not visible in Wang Guoxiang's work.

Wang also structures his work for excellent artistic effect. He makes the
troublesome worker utterly unaware of the bad impressions he is leaving
with others. When people criticize him he can't figure out why they would
do such a thing, and so indignantly repeats their criticisms ("They say I
come late to work!" "They think I'm not careful!"). Hence, deliciously,
we learn the details of his misbehavior directly from his own mouth. The
political lessons fit in naturally, with no sense of "flowers inserted from
without." For example, when the lax worker complains that "They're making me look bad!" the *dougende* snaps, "No, they're helping you!"—thus
making an up-to-date political point without any need for jargon about
"criticism and self-criticism."

These three *xiangsheng* pieces stand out for their quality, but not in their
general approach to reform. Many other pieces of the early 1950s showed
the same sincere, almost naïve, zest for the new experiment in *xiangsheng*.
They showed as well a generosity of spirit toward the objects of satire
whether they were workers, officials, clerks, or anyone else. The foreign
imperialists, to be sure, were enemies; but we Chinese people, flaws and

all, were pulling together to make the new society work. To compare these *xiangsheng* pieces with what had been standard only ten years earlier—i.e., ridicule of bumpkins and cripples, and "non-vegetarian" innuendo—a fair-minded person would have to say the changes had been remarkable. But not everyone in China saw it that way.

CROCODILE JAWS

Without intending to (or even knowing that they were doing it), the creators of the new *xiangsheng* began giving offense to Party ideologues who were watching from inside the Department of Propaganda and the Ministry of Culture. These people had no objection to satire of the old society, but when the problems of the new society began to appear in *xiangsheng*, they took notice.

"Buying Monkeys" had become a huge popular success by the end of 1954, but in 1955 the Party leadership instructed Central Broadcasting to cut back on broadcasts of the piece.[95] Then some "different opinions," including "negative views," began to appear in the controlled press. Editors of the journal *Plays* must have received specific instructions from above, because in 1955 they opened a "letters to the editor" forum in which, quite counter to public sentiment, they published more criticism than support for "Buying Monkeys." They followed this with a conference on "satirical plays" that took aim at "Buying Monkeys" and other pieces that had gone too far.[96]

If we put ourselves in the position of the authorities, it is possible to imagine why they had become leery. The humor in "Buying Monkeys" does rest heavily on the vulnerabilities of the new society—on problems either that did not exist in the old society or that did exist but now seemed to grow worse. Ma Daha seems alienated from public property; Comrade So-and-So seems a pawn in an authoritarian order; political meetings look a bit like charades. When the *dougende* turns in an aside to the audience and wails, "What am I going to *do*?" he strikes a chord that resonates with the daily life of the audience a bit too much.

---

95. Wang, Wang, and Teng, op.cit., p. 240.
96. Ibid., pp. 240–241.

Occasionally the implied criticisms are put into concrete words. (The published criticisms do not cite such lines, presumably because to cite them might only draw more attention to them and make things worse.) In a piece called "Unity-itis" (统一病), He Chi wonders why everybody in a certain family has to wear the same kind of clothing "just because the family head likes it."[97] In "Hooked on Meetings," one of the topics that appeals to the long-winded official, and on which he would like to hold a meeting, is "Workers' Welfare 100 Years from Now." This follows:

> B: A hundred years hence? Then why do we have to discuss it now?
> A: We need to lay out the beautiful destiny of Communism!
> B: Beautiful it may be, but we don't have to start the talk so soon!

I do not find it plausible, in context, to read these words as subversive. He Chi, who had grown up in the Communist movement, still meant them as friendly satire. But nervous bureaucrats may well have seen the passage as a poisonous weed.

And that, I believe, is the essential mistake that Party ideologues made during the *xiangsheng* reform. They were too suspicious and insecure. They should have trusted *xiangsheng* writers and performers to ply their trade, and to do it with basically good intentions; and they should have trusted the Chinese people to laugh in normal, healthy ways, without any need for their micro-management. They should have relaxed. The crocodile bird was there to help.

The error on the side of the *xiangsheng* artists was their naïveté. They might have noticed the crocodile jaw looming above them somewhat sooner than they did. Intermingled with their first efforts at new *xiangsheng* in magazines like *Shuoshuo changchang,* they might have noticed the confessions of "bourgeois thought" by a senior left-wing writer[98] and "self-criticisms" by magazine editors for "mistaken views" and insufficient attention to the "thought-character" of performance literature.[99] Political jargon like "Mao Zedong Thought" and "a tiny handful of trouble-makers" (*yixiaocuo*一小撮, used many times since, and featured even as late as the

97. *He Chi zizhuan*, p. 264
98. *Shuoshuo changchang,* no. 2, 1952, pp. 9–13 (article by Duanmu Hongliang端木蕻良).
99. *Shuoshuo changchang,* no. 19, 1951, p. 51 and no. 2, 1952, pp. 4–8.

June Fourth Massacre in 1989) were also popping up here and there.[100] In the larger cultural world, criticisms of "Between Husband and Wife" by Xiao Yemu and the film *The Story of Wu Xun* had been elevated to national object-lessons. But the *xiangsheng* world did not see these signs—or, if it did notice, assumed that they would not apply to *xiangsheng*.

It is clear from He Chi's autobiography that he had no idea he might be labeled a "rightist" in 1957. When he was paraded up on stage and taunted for "hating socialism," "organizing an anti-Party clique," and "pursuing fame and profit," he kept cooperating with his tormentors in an apparent confidence that, with the next turn, they would certainly perceive his innocence and leave him alone.[101] He agreed to come back for a second struggle session even after the first was a disaster. He "admitted" to pursuing fame and lucre even while he felt, inside, that "the question simply did not exist." He agreed to hand over his personal letters, confident that these would exonerate him, and then watched as the letters turned into "ironclad evidence" against him. In short, he was squeezed between two unmovable articles of faith: 1) that he was innocent of any ill will toward the Party, and 2) that the Party could not be incorrect, so there must have been something, somewhere that indeed was wrong with him. In any case, the "rightist" hat did fall on his head and stayed there as he moved in and out of labor camps for the next twenty-two years.

He emerged in 1979, was officially "exonerated," and the next year published a long self-exculpatory article in *Quyi*, the major national magazine for the popular performing arts. In it he continues to insist that "I wasn't anti-Party" and, borrowing a phrase that Mao Zedong had made famous in 1957, said that he was writing only about "contradictions among the people." But he also gives considerable ground to the attacks against him. He writes, for example, that Ma Daha's behavior "was not a product of socialism, but an individualist thing that had been left over from the old society."[102] In fact, the very opposite had clearly been the case in 1954: the popularity of Ma Daha had sprung largely, if not entirely, from its comment

---

100. "Mao Zedong sixiang" appears, for example, in Lao She 老舍, "Wenyi zuojia ye yao zengchan jieyue" 文艺作家也要增产节约in Shuoshuo changchang, vol. 4, no. 6 (1951), p. 9. "Yixiaocuo" appears in Xi Xiangyuan and Sun Yukui, *Zhi Laohu*, p. 26.
101. He Chi, *He Chi zizhuan*, pp. 283–288.
102. He Chi, "Cong 'mai hour' tanqi," *Quyi* 1980.3, p. 26

on the new society. Had He Chi forgotten this? Had twenty-two years of pressure permanently warped his views? Or was he just protecting himself, in case political storms should return? I do not know, but guess the third. Elsewhere in his 1980 article he writes that "to portray characters like Ma Daha in 1953 or 1954 was accurate realism. To write about this kind of character today would not be right."[103] This seems like patent self-protection. He Chi must have been aware that the Ma Daha phenomenon in Chinese society was, if anything, even more salient in 1980 than in 1954. The term "Ma Daha" was still alive in daily-life language, as it is even today.

Still, He Chi did survive the Cultural Revolution, while others in the *xiangsheng* world, most poignantly Lao She, did not. Lao She's suicide in 1966 was not over *xiangsheng* in particular, but his *xiangsheng* activities are as good an emblem as any for the unforeseen disaster that befell him. In 1949 he could have remained in the U.S., or could have gone to Taiwan, where he had been invited. Instead he returned to Beijing, wrote satire about America, supported Chinese troops in Korea, praised the Soviet Union, extolled Stalin, penned the phrase "Long Live Chairman Mao" as early as 1951[104] (before it became fashionable), and, when political troubles began to arise, simply could not, as He Chi could not, imagine that his good will and hard work would go unappreciated. Trapped, as He Chi had been, between wanting to help and trying to comprehend the attacks that came from precisely those whom he thought he was helping, Lao She gave up.

But let us try, one more time, to banish this latter-day bad news from our memories and re-imagine the situation and mood of the early 1950s. Programs of social reform were underway, and the *xiangsheng* world, recently elevated to a higher social status, was ready and willing to help. It got organized. It tried various things, some of which worked better than others. It learned from its mistakes and by 1954 was closing in on a pretty good answer to the question of how to make satire fit the goals of the revolution. The popular audience of *xiangsheng* was following along and expanding rapidly. Things looked fairly good. The question whose answer we will never know is: *could it have worked*? If no crackdown had come, if a more secure and tolerant political regime had been in charge, might the *xiang-*

103. Ibid., p. 24
104. *Shuoshuo changchang*, no. 10, 1951, p. 10.

sheng experiment have succeeded? The question is not as narrow as it may seem. It has, I believe, parallels in other aspects of the early 1950s.

Originally published in Jeremy Brown and Paul Pickowicz, ed.
Dilemmas of Victory: The Early Years of the People's Republic of China
(Harvard University Press, 2007)

The Mind: Less Puzzling in Chinese?

(2016)

PEOPLE WHO STUDY other cultures sometimes note that they benefit twice: first by learning about the other culture and second by realizing that certain assumptions of their own are arbitrary. In reading Colin McGinn's essay, "Groping Toward the Mind," in *The New York Review of Books*, I was reminded of a question I had pondered in my 2013 book *Anatomy of Chinese*: whether some of the struggles in Western philosophy over the concept of mind—especially over what kind of "thing" it is—might be rooted in Western language. The puzzles are less puzzling in Chinese.

Indo-European languages tend to prefer nouns, even when talking about things for which verbs might seem more appropriate. The English noun *inflation*, for example, refers to complex processes that were not a "thing" until language made them so. Things like inflation can even become animate, as when we say "we need to combat inflation" or "inflation is killing us at the check-out counter." Modern cognitive linguists like George Lakoff at Berkeley call *inflation* an "ontological metaphor." (The *inflation* example is Lakoff's.)

When I studied Chinese, though, I began to notice a preference for verbs. Modern Chinese does use ontological metaphors, such as *fāzhǎn* (literally "emit and unfold") to mean "development" or *xìnxīn* ("believe mind") for "confidence." But these are modern words that derive from Western languages (mostly via Japanese) and carry a Western flavor with them. "I firmly believe that…" is a natural phrase in Chinese; you can also say "I have a lot of confidence that…" but the use of a noun in such a phrase is a borrowing from the West.

Wanting to test my intuition that classical Chinese was more verb-heavy than its Indo-European counterparts, I opened Confucius's *Analects* and an English translation of Plato's *Apology of Socrates* and counted nouns and verbs. Confucius uses slightly more verbs than nouns. Plato uses about forty-five percent more nouns than verbs. In search of a more recent example (but still from before the major Western-language influence on Chinese), I chose at random a page from Cao Xueqin's eighteenth-century novel *Dream of the Red Chamber* and a page from Charles Dickens's *Oliver Twist*. The Cao page had 130 nouns and 166 verbs (a 0.8 to 1 ratio), while the Dickens page had 96 nouns and 38 verbs (a 2.5 to 1 ratio).

I wondered: in Western languages, especially in their modern versions, do we sometimes use nouns to conceive things when we don't really need to? For example, when electrical impulses are speeding along neurons in the brain, might not a verb be best? Why do we create the noun "neural connectivity" and then refer to it as an actor: "neural connectivity makes it natural for complex metaphorical mappings to be built"? This sentence is from Lakoff, but similar examples are everywhere. A medical researcher at the University of California at San Francisco in 2003 discussed mad cow disease in terms of its "high infectivity." Infectivity? Why not just say the disease spreads easily?

Next I wondered: does this question matter? Does unnecessary turning of verbs into nouns ever do any harm, or am I just fussing?

Where it can cause trouble, I think, is at the point where people begin to assume that a noun somehow says something more than a verb or adjective does. "The neurons connect well" and "the neural connectivity is good" say the same thing, but I fear that people begin to suppose that "neural connectivity" somehow *adds to* "neurons connect" and becomes a "thing" in itself, not just a label for an action. We can, I'm afraid, be led into thinking that a mere tautology is intellectually significant. If I were to say, for example, "Her neurons connect well because she has good neural connectivity," the emptiness of the explanation would be plain. Yet even an experienced writer like George Lakoff seems susceptible to the problem when he writes:

> What gives human beings the power of abstract reason? Our answer is that human beings have what we will call a *conceptualizing capacity* [emphasis in the original].

Lakoff goes on to explain what he means by "capacity," and his explanation, like the thing explained, is heavy with nouns. My point here is not to criticize Lakoff's idea; it is to note that his thought, as he has expressed it, would need to be fundamentally restructured before going into natural-sounding Chinese. In Lakoff's English sentence, people reason abstractly because they *have* something (an ability, a capacity, etc.); in Chinese it is more natural to say that people reason abstractly because they *do* something.

A deeper kind of worry about our fondness for nouns occurs to me: does it happen, perhaps, that speakers of English are drawn to believe that certain things exist because nouns that serve as their labels exist? Might it be only the labels that exist? I read the anthropologist Hoyt Alverson who, in a good book on how time is conceived in English, Chinese, Hindi, and Sesotho, writes that the "ontogeny" of time is indeterminate. He explains "ontogeny" as meaning the "character" of something's "being." We have, then, the proposition that the *character* of the *being* of *time* is indeterminate. Do the nouns in this proposition refer to things that exist? In addition to time, is there a "being" of time? And if there is, is that being the kind of thing that can possess something else, as here it is supposed to possess a "character"? These problems are by no means Alverson's alone; he writes in a way that is common in English. In Chinese, though, it is almost impossibly awkward to say "the character of the being of time." A literal translation is opaque and would signal to a Chinese speaker that "this phrase came out of a Western language and you might well go there to figure out what it is supposed to mean." Ancient Chinese philosophers did discuss "being," but to do it they used the words *you*, "there is," and *wu*, "there is not," both of which are fundamentally verbs. By contrast, ancient Greek thinkers often conceived their puzzles in terms of nouns: What is "justice"? "Beauty"? "The good"? And so on.

I wanted to see whether "assuming that things exist just because nouns that refer to them exist" might cause problems for serious Western philosophers. I read Colin McGinn's book *The Mysterious Flame: Conscious Minds in a Material World* about the "mind-body problem"—which, briefly put, is the problem of how "mental substance" and "physical substance" can affect each other. Although a major problem in Western philosophy since Descartes, the question has scarcely been noticed in the history of Chinese philosophy. I much admire McGinn's writing; I chose him purposefully as a powerful representative for the West.

At one point in his book, McGinn focuses on the curious fact that our perceptions of the world are often perceptions of things in space, and yet the perceptions themselves occupy no space. He writes:

> Consider the visual experience of seeing a red sphere two feet away with a six-inch diameter. The object of this experience is of course a spatial object with spatial properties, but the experience itself does not have these properties: it is not two feet away from you and six inches in diameter. …When we reflect on the experience itself, we can see that it lacks spatial properties altogether.

For me, the crucial phrase here is "the experience itself." Is there such a thing? The noun "experience" exists, but that is not the question. Does *the experience* exist? We might feel intuitively that it does. But does that intuition arise, in part, from the grammatical habit of using nouns like "experience" and assuming that they refer to things? Classical Chinese poets see, hear, and feel in all sorts of ways—they have no trouble "experiencing." But they find no need to talk about "experience" as a noun. The modern Chinese word *jīngyàn*, "experience," was invented to accommodate Western language.

Is there a way we can test whether our intuitions are shaped by noun-habits in our thinking? The English word *experience* is perhaps not the best example for doing such a test, simply because it has the same form as both noun ("experience") and verb ("experience"). "Feeling" might work better, because the noun ("feeling") and the verb ("feel") have different forms.

To the experiment: in most cases, two statements of the forms "I feel X" and "I have a feeling of X" will not differ much, if at all, in meaning. But if we ask about "spatial properties" for the two cases, we get very different results. If I say "I feel X," you cannot grammatically ask me in English "Does your feel have spatial properties?" You *could* ask, "Do you feel with (or in) length and color?" but this question, although grammatical, does not "make sense." No matter how you put them, questions about the spatiality of X are hard to phrase if you use the word "feel." But if, on the other hand, I say "I have a feeling of X," then the same question—"Does your feeling have spatial properties?"—does make sense. It not only makes grammatical sense but makes enough philosophical sense to get into the writing of an excellent philosopher like Colin McGinn. So we can see that from a starting point where there is no real difference in everyday usage (i.e., between "I feel X" and "I have a feeling of X"), the choice of whether to use "feel" or "feeling" can lead to (or perhaps create?) a philosophical puzzle if one goes one direction and no puzzlement if one goes the other.

McGinn goes on to point out that numbers, like the experience of red spots, do not occupy space. "We cannot sensibly ask how much space the number 2 takes up relative to the number 37," he writes. "It is hardly true that the bigger the number the more space it occupies." Then he writes:

> To attribute spatial properties to numbers is an instance of what philosophers call a category-mistake, trying to talk about something as if it belonged to a category it does not belong to. Only concrete things have spatial properties, not abstract things like numbers or mental things like experiences of red.

In my imagination an ancient Chinese philosopher might well accept McGinn's point, but then ask him: why do you talk about mental "things"? Is that not also a category-mistake? If I see a red spot, do I not simply see a red spot? The red spot, yes, is a thing, but "I see" is not a thing. I see is I see. If you change it into "my sight" or "my experience of seeing," you are performing a grammatical act, but that grammatical act has no power to change the way the world is. Your perplexity about how two "things" relate comes only from your grammar.

The first time I wrote down some of these thoughts, I showed them to a colleague in the philosophy department at Princeton (I was in the East Asian studies department). He said, "You haven't solved the mind-body problem, you know." I agreed with him; indeed, I was a bit surprised at his impression of what I had been aiming to do. Once one enters an Indo-European language, the mind-body problem indeed is hard, and I had not been trying to solve it on that turf. At most, I have discovered only a question: are people who think in Indo-European languages better off because their languages lead them to clear conceptualization of an important puzzle, or are thinkers in Chinese better off because their language gets them through life equally well without the puzzle?

Originally published in the *NYR Daily*,
June 30, 2016

Chinese Names in the Text
(dates are supplied for pre-modern figures)

———— ⤳||⤶ ————

Ai Xiaoming. Professor at Sun Yat-sen University, documentary film-maker, activist, feminist, and regime critic.

Ba Jin. Pen name of Li Yaotang, author of famous long novels in the 1930s and 1940s and appreciated after Mao's death for essays that were critical of both the regime and himself.

Bei Cun. Pen name of Kang Hong, avant garde fiction writer in the post-Mao years.

Chang Baokun. Famous performer of *xiangsheng* comic dialogue, died during the Korean War while cheering Chinese troops.

Chao Yuen-ren. Brilliant linguist, author of *Mandarin Primer*, Perry Link's first-year Chinese language textbook, and father of R.C. Pian, Link's first-year teacher.

Chen Rong. Author of "At Middle Age" and other fiction that was important during the years of post-Mao "scar literature."

Chen Ruoxi. A writer from Taiwan who published brilliant stories about her life on the mainland during the Cultural Revolution.

Chen Yi. A Chinese Communist military commander who later became Foreign Minister of the PRC and a mayor of Shanghai.

Chiang Kai-shek. Also Jiang Jieshi. Head of the Nationalist government that Mao Zedong's communist armies overthrew in 1949.

Chu Anping. A politically liberal journalist in the 1940s who stayed on the mainland after the communist takeover, trying still to be a liberal. Died during the Cultural Revolution.

Cong Weixi. Novelist famous in the post-Mao years for fiction describing labor-camp life under Mao.

Cui Weiping. Professor at the Beijing Film Academy, social and political critic, leader in the Citizens Movement of the mid-2000s.

Dai Qing. Pen name of Fu Xiaoqing, adopted daughter of Ye Jianying. Writer, critic, filmmaker, and activist in the post-Mao years.

Dai Sijie. Chinese writer living in France, author of the famous story (and later film) entitled "The Little Chinese Seamstress."

Deng Xiaoping. Colleague of Mao Zedong and paramount leader in China from 1978 to 1997.

Ding Ling. Pen name of Jiang Bingzhi, author of "The Diary of Miss Sophie" and other famous fiction. A communist official, persecuted under Mao.

Ding Zilin. Professor of philosophy at People's University, founded the Tiananmen Mothers after her son was killed in the June Fourth Massacre of 1989.

Du Mu (803–852 A.D.). A distinguished poet of the Tang dynasty.

Fang Cheng. Famous satiric cartoonist based in Beijing.

Fang Lizhi. Distinguished astrophysicist who became a leading political dissident in the 1980s.

Gao Xiaosheng. Writer of elegant short stories in the 1980s.

Gao Xin. A Communist Party member who wanted to play a conspicuous role in the 1989 democracy protests in order to show that at least some people inside the Party sympathized.

Gao Xingjian. Novelist, playwright, artist, émigré to France, and winner of the Nobel Prize in literature in 2000.

Gao Zhan. A sociologist at American University whom the PRC accused of being a spy for Taiwan in 2001.

Guo Feixiong. Sobriquet of Yang Maodong, a human-rights lawyer active in the Citizens Movement in the decade of the 2000s. Detained and imprisoned several times.

Guo Yushan. Human rights activist, played a key role in the escape of rights lawyer Chen Guangcheng from detention to the U.S. embassy in 2012.

Ha Jin. Pen name of Jin Xuefei, a distinguished professor at Boston University and author of much prize-winning fiction in English.

Han Shaogong. Distinguished author of stories in the post-Mao years and known as a founding figure in "root-seeking" fiction.

Han Suyin. Belgian-Chinese writer of fiction and travelogue during the Mao years, known for her glowing accounts of Maoland.

He Chi. One of the Mao era's best writers of *xiangsheng* comic dialogues.

He Qinglian. Economist and sharp critic of the Chinese Communist Party since the 1990s.

He Weifang. Distinguished professor of law, political critic, and defender of dissidents.

Hong Xiuquan (1814–1864). Charismatic but mentally challenged leader of the Taiping Rebellion in the mid-nineteenth century.

Hou Baolin. Arguably the all-time most skilled performer of *xiangsheng* comic dialogue.

Hou Dejian. Pop singer from Taiwan who played a key role defending student demonstrators in June, 1989.

Hsia, C.T. Hsia Chih-tsing, scholar of Chinese literature at Columbia University whose contributions to the field of modern Chinese literature were without peer.

Hu Jia. Civil rights activist in free speech, environmental protection, rights of AIDS victims, and other fields.

Hu Jintao. General Secretary of the Chinese Communist Party, 2002–2012.

Hu Ping. A leading Chinese overseas dissident, 1987 to the present. Editor of *Beijing Spring*.

Hu Qili. High-ranking Communist official in the 1980s who was punished after 1989 because of his sympathy for the pro-democracy demonstrations of that year.

Hu Shi. Also Hu Shih. A leading scholar, language reformer, and diplomat during the Nationalist era before the Communist takeover in 1949.

Hu Yaobang. General Secretary of the Chinese Communist from 1982 to 1987; purged in 1987 for sympathy with student demonstrators. His death sparked the pro-democracy demonstrations of spring, 1989.

Huang Jinping. One of three founders of the Tiananmen Mothers group in 1989.

Jia Pingwa. Author of *Ruined City* and other well-known fiction in the post-Mao era.

Jiang Jielian. Son of Ding Zilin and Jiang Peikun. Killed in the Tiananmen massacre of June 3–4, 1989.

Jiang Peikun. Professor of Linguistics at People's University. Husband of Ding Zilin, who founded the Tiananmen Mothers.

Jiang Qing. Wife of Mao Zedong and creator of the "Eight Model Operas" during the Cultural Revolution.

Jiang Zemin. General Secretary of the Communist Party of China, 1989–2002; known for allowing capitalism into CCP ideology.

Jin Yong. Pen name of Zha Liangyong, a Hong-Kong-based author of very popular martial arts (*wuxia*) novels.

Kang Zhengguo. Writer from Xi'an. Taught Chinese at Yale for many years.

Lao She. Pen name of Shu Qingchun. Author of several famous novels in the 1930s and 1940s and backer of socialist *xiangsheng* after 1949. Persecuted to death by Red Guards in 1966.

Li Boyuan (1867–1906). Poet, calligrapher, and author of famous muckraking fiction.

Li Hongzhi. Semi-mystical leader of the popular religion known as Falun Gong.

Li Peng. Adopted son of Zhou Enlai; Premier of the People's Republic, 1988–98; denounced in public opinion for advocating force in the repression of pro-democracy demonstrators in 1989.

Li Shaomin. Princeton Ph.D. in sociology who teaches business at Old Dominion University. Once arrested and imprisoned during a research trip to China.

Li Shenzhi. An idealistic communist in the 1940s, he joined CCP's academic establishment until, beginning in the 1990s, he began to write withering criticisms of how the revolution had turned out.

Li Shuxian. Professor of Physics at Peking University who later became a dissident. Wife of astrophysicist Fang Lizhi.

Li Zhisui. Mao Zedong's personal physician and author of *The Private Life of Chairman Mao*, which drew wide attention after its publication in 1994.

Liang Qichao (1873–1929). Polymath thinker, reformer, essayist, politician, and leading public intellectual.

Liu Binyan. A leading writer of "reportage literature," famous especially for his muckraking journalism in the 1980s. Expelled from the Communist Party in 1957, he rejoined after Mao died and was expelled again in 1987.

Liu Chün-jo. Professor of Chinese at the University of Minnesota, aficionado of popular performing arts in China.

Liu Di. Internet-based dissident in the Citizens Movement during 2002–08. Known as "The Stainless Steel Rat."

Liu Junning. Political philosopher known for his view that liberal democracy is a universal value, invented in the West but properly to be shared everywhere.

Liu Xia. Poet and artist. Wife of Liu Xiaobo, held under house arrest during much time when Liu was in prison.

Liu Xiaobo. Scholar, writer, dissident. Winner of the Nobel Peace Prize in 2010; died in 2017 in prison for "inciting subversion of the state."

Liu Xiaoyan. Daughter of Liu Binyan.

Liu Zaifu. Distinguished theoretician of literature. Head of the Literature Research Institute in the Chinese Academy of Social Sciences in the late 1980s, he lived in exile in the U.S. after 1989.

Lü Shuxiang. A pioneer in the field of modern linguistics research in China.

Lu Xinhua. Author of the short story "Scar" that he posted in 1978 on a wall at Fudan University and that became the catalyst for post-Mao "scar literature."

Lu Xun. Pen name of Zhou Shuren, master of short stories and prose poems and arguably modern China's finest writer.

Luo Changpei. Professor of Linguistics at Peking University and pioneer in the fields of Chinese historical phonology and Chinese dialects.

Ma Daha. A fictional character in He Chi's comic dialogue called "Buying Monkeys," the name became a synonym all across China for lazy, careless work.

Ma Sanli. A distinguished *xiangsheng* teacher and performer in the "Tianjin School."

Mao Zedong. Tyrant ruler of the Communist movement in China until his death in September, 1976.

Mo Yan. Pen name of Guan Moye, a famous writer of long and short fiction, winner of the Nobel Prize for Literature in 2012.

Pai Hsien-yung. Arguably the best writer of fiction to emerge from Taiwan in the twentieth century, author of a famous collection of stories called *Taibei People*.

Peng Dehuai. Minister of Defense in China from 1954 to 1959, then sacked for daring to tell Mao Zedong that his Great Leap Forward had led to a disastrous famine.

Pu Zhiqiang. A student leader in the 1989 pro-democracy demonstrations, later a rights lawyer famous for his eloquence in defending underdogs in court.

Sha Yexin. Dissident playwright and essayist based in Shanghai, creator of the post-Mao hit called "What If I Really Were?"

Shi Tiesheng. Novelist and short-story writer famous both for avant-garde works and for conscientious introspection about politics.

Su Xiaokang. Distinguished author of many works of literary reportage, has lived in exile in the U.S. since 1989.

Sun Yukui. Famous performer of *xiangsheng* comedians' dialogues in the 1940s.

Tan Sitong. A reformer and rebel against the Qing dynasty, who is famous for his intrepid claim, just before his execution, that beheading by a "bandit" regime is "a joy."

Teng Biao. A lecturer at the Chinese University of Political Science and Law, became an outstanding rights lawyer and now lives in exile in the U.S.

Tian Jiyun. A vice premier of the PRC's State Council from 1983 and 1993, known as liberal-leaning among his peers.

Tong Yi. A student leader at the pro-democracy demonstrations in 1989, sent to a labor camp for her aid to Wei Jingsheng, now lives in exile in the U.S.

Wang Anyi. Distinguished writer of short and long fiction, especially about Shanghai life. Vice-chair of the China Writers Association since 2006.

Wang Guoxiang. Successful writer of "socialist comedians' dialogues" in the early 1950s.

Wang Ruowang. Dissident writer based in Shanghai, expelled from the Communist Party in 1987 for "bourgeois" tendencies.

Wang Shuo. Satirical writer of short and long fiction, master of Beijing brogue.

Wang Wei (699–759). Tang dynasty poet, painter, and musician of immense reputation.

Wang Yangming (1472–1529). Sobriquet of Wang Shouren, a "Neo-Confucian" philosopher best known for "the unity of knowing and acting."

Wang Yi. A rights activist during the Citizens Movement of the mid-2000s and founding pastor of the Early Rain Covenant Church.

Wang Zengqi. A fiction artist known in the post-Mao years for his authentic language and lyrical style.

Wei Jingsheng. Advocate of democracy as early as 1978 who spent eighteen years as a political prisoner. Lived in exile in the U.S. after 1997.

Wei Junyi. Joined the CCP in her youth from idealism; rose in the PRC to head the People's Literature Publishing House, then wrote frank memoirs about disappointments in the revolution.

Wen Kejian. Businessman turned activist in the Citizens Movement of the mid-2000s, worked extensively on the democracy manifesto called "Charter 08."

Wu Jianmin. A student leader in Nanjing during the pro-democracy demonstrations in spring 1989; imprisoned for seven years afterward and exiled to the U.S. in 2015.

Wu Jingzi (1701–1754). Author of *Rulin Waishi*, translated as *The Scholars*, a compilation of satiric stories on the lives and corruption of scholar-officials during the Qing period.

Wu Woyao (1866–1910). Pen name of Wu Jianren, author of the late-Qing muckraking novel *Bizarre Happenings Eyewitnessed over Two Decades.*

Wu Xiaoling. Eminent scholar of traditional Chinese fiction at the Literature Research Institute of the Chinese Academy of Social Sciences. Friend of *xiangsheng* performer Hou Baolin.

Xi Jinping. Princeling son of Xi Zhongxun, a comrade of Mao Zedong; holder of top positions in the CCP, its government, and its army beginning in 2012.

Xiao Hong. Elegant writer of fiction and memoir.

Xiao Qiang. Studied physics with Fang Lizhi and later became a human rights activist. Founder of *China Digital Times.*

Ximen Qing. Fictional wealthy merchant of the Song Dynasty, protagonist of the great classic novel *Jinpingmei.*

Xu Bing. A leading installation artist in post-Mao China. Originally with dissident tendencies, in 2008 became a vice president of the Central Academy of Fine Arts in Beijing.

Xu Wenli. An activist at "Democracy Wall" in Beijing in 1978–79, founder of the China Democratic Party, spent sixteen years in political prison. Has lived in exile in the U.S. since 2002.

Xu Youyu. Intellectual historian known for his liberal views. A supporter of the student pro-democracy demonstrations in 1989, later moved to New York to live in exile.

Xu Zerong. An Oxford-educated historian from Hong Kong, sentenced in 2002 to thirteen years in prison for unspecified crimes of "leaking state secrets."

Xu Zhiyong. Human rights activist and founder of The New Citizens Movement. Sentenced in 2023 to fourteen years in prison for "inciting subversion of the state."

Xue Baokun. Arguably the leading academic authority on the history of *xiangsheng* comedians' dialogues.

Yan Lianke. A contemporary fiction writer, known for satire and for playing cat-and-mouse with censors.

Yang Jiang. Pen name of Yang Jikang, a playwright known for her brilliant stage plays in the 1940s and her account of life in a labor camp during the Cultural Revolution.

Yang Jiechi. A high-ranking diplomat of the PRC known for his skills in English and maneuverability with Western diplomats.

Ye Jianying. Born Ye Yiwei, joined the CCP in 1927 and became a top military leader, known in his later years as a partisan of Deng Xiaoping's reformism.

Yu Hua. Distinguished contemporary Chinese writer of short and long fiction; author of "To Live," which was made into a famous film.

Yu Jie. Prolific dissident writer whose books include a laudatory biography of Liu Xiaobo and a scathing exposé of Premier Wen Jiabao.

Yu Shide. A performer of *xiangsheng* comedians' dialogues in the 1940s.

Yü Ying-shih. Professor of Chinese history at Harvard, Yale, and Princeton, in that order; arguably the twentieth century's leading scholar of Chinese history.

Zha Jianying. Writer, in both Chinese and English, of fiction and commentary on contemporary China and topics in Chinese history.

Zhang Liang. Pen name of the compiler of *The Tiananmen Papers: The Chinese Leadership's Decision to Use Force Against Their Own People—in Their Own Words.*

Zhang Ping. A CCP official who once rose as high as vice governor of Shanxi Province but also writes novels, including ones that use fictional disguise to expose corruption.

Zhang Xianliang. Author in the post-Mao years of a spate of novels about his experiences in a labor camp. One of the best has been translated as *Grass Soup.*

Zhang Xianling. Mother of Wang Nan, who was killed in the June 4 massacre of 1989. A founder with Ding Zilin of the Tiananmen Mothers.

Zhang Zhupo (1670–1698). A scholar who failed China's civil service exams five times and died at age twenty-nine but gained fame for his commentaries on the great novel *Jinpingmei.*

Zhang Zuhua. Fired from his posts in the PRC government for supporting the pro-democracy protests of 1989, he later played a leading role in the democracy manifesto called "Charter 08."

Zhao Ziyang. General Secretary of the CCP, 1987–89; purged in June, 1989 for showing too much sympathy with student protesters; held under house arrest until his death in 2005.

Zheng Yi. Once an ardent Red Guard, became one of the Communist regime's most telling critics. Known for his exposé of politically-induced cannibalism in Guangxi in 1968.

Zhong Acheng. Fiction artist and essayist in the post-Mao era, known for his mold-breaking story "The Chessmaster."

Zhou Duo. An academic sociologist who later worked in business and, with Liu Xiaobo, Hou Dejian, and Gao Xin was one of the "Four Gentlemen" hunger-strikers at Tiananmen in 1989.

Zhou Yang. A Communist theorist who was a literary hatchet-man in the 1950s but by the 1980s was writing about "socialist alienation" and promoting "Marxist humanism."

Zhou Yong. A minor official in the Washington, D.C., embassy of the PRC.

Zhu Rongji. Premier of the PRC from 1998 to 2003, known for releasing controls on China's economy.

Zi Zhongyun. A distinguished "America expert" in the Chinese Academy of Social Sciences; wrote in her senior years about disappointments with the Communist revolution.

Acknowledgments

Most of the pieces in this book originally appeared elsewhere, and we would like to thank those publications for allowing them to appear here. Thank you to

The New York Review of Books for the use of:
"A Magician of Chinese Poetry" "Capitulate or Things Will Only Get Worse," "How to Deal with the Chinese Police," "Liu Binyan, 1925-2005," "On Fang Lizhi (1936-2012)," "Seeing the CCP Clearly," "The Anaconda in the Chandelier," "The Chinese Communist Party's Culture of Fear," and "The Wonderfully Elusive Chinese Novel"

The *NYR Daily* for the use of:
"Censoring the News Before it Happens," "Dawn in China," "The Passion of Liu Xiaobo," "The Mind: Less Puzzling in Chinese?" and "Why We Should Criticize Mo Yan"

Harvard University Press for the use of:
"My Teacher Ezra Vogel (1930-2020)." Reproduced by permission of the Harvard University Asia Center from Martin K. Whyte and Mary C. Brinton, eds., *Remembering Ezra Vogel*, pp. 311–313 (Cambridge, Mass.: Harvard University Asia Center, 2022) © The President and Fellows of Harvard College, 2022. Further reproduction or distribution of this material is prohibited.

"The Crocodile Bird: Xiangsheng in the Early 1950s" from DILEMMAS OF VICTORY: THE EARLY YEARS OF THE PEOPLE'S REPUBLIC OF CHINA, edited by Jeremy Brown and Paul G. Pickowicz, Cambridge,

About the Author

PERRY LINK has authored or co-authored ten books including *Evening Chats in Beijing* which was named a *New York Times* "Notable Book of the Year." He studied British analytical philosophy (B.A. 1966) and modern Chinese history (Ph.D. 1976) at Harvard University. His dissertation on popular fiction and his early brilliance in Chinese language teaching led to a career of teaching "language and literature" at Princeton University, with intervening stints at UCLA, Berkeley, and Middlebury College. Link was drawn to Chinese writers who dared to tell the truth in the face of fierce intimidation from their government, and for that reason moved, in his later years, increasingly toward the study of Chinese "dissidence" and human rights more generally. He has written dozens of pieces for the broader public in *The New York Review of Books, The Times Literary Supplement*, and elsewhere, and has served on the boards of Human Rights Watch/Asia, China Human Rights Defenders, the Committee for Freedom in Hong Kong Foundation, and elsewhere. One or more of these affronts to the Chinese government led them to deny him entry visas beginning in 1996. After Link's retirement from Princeton in 2008 he has taught at the University of California, Riverside, as Chancellorial Chair for Teaching Across Disciplines.